Mediations

Mediations
TEXT AND DISCOURSE IN MEDIA STUDIES

——

Andrew Tolson

ARNOLD

A member of the Hodder Headline Group
LONDON • NEW YORK • SYDNEY • AUCKLAND

First published in Great Britain 1996 by
Arnold, a member of the Hodder Headline Group,
338 Euston Road, London NW1 3BH
175 Fifth Avenue, New York, NY10010

Distributed exclusively in the USA by
St Martin's Press Inc.,
175 Fifth Avenue,
New York, NY10010

British Library Cataloguing in Publication Data
A catalogue record for this book is available from the British Library

Library of Congress Cataloging-in-Publication Data
A catalog record for this book is available from the Library of Congress

ISBN 0 340 57489 5

Typeset in 10/11 pt Sabon by
Scribe Design, Gillingham, Kent
Printed in Great Britain by
J. W. Arrowsmith, Bristol

Contents

Acknowledgements   vii
Introduction   ix
   1. Mediations   ix
   2. Text and discourse   xii
   3. About this book   xv

PART ONE TEXTS   **1**

Chapter 1: Sign and meanings   **3**
   1   Mythologies   3
   2   Preferred readings   7
   3   Intertextuality   10
   4   The 'arbitrary nature' of the sign   13
   5   Case study: TV news   17

Chapter 2: Structures   **28**
   1   Anchorage   28
   2   Argument   29
   3   Montage   33
   4   Narrative   38
   5   Case study: British documentary films   43

Chapter 3: Modes of address   **53**
   1   Interpellation   53
   2   Direct address in broadcasting   57
   3   The regime of broadcasting   62
   4   'Dominant specularity' in Hollywood cinema   65
   5   Case study: Modes of address in TV advertising (1956–90)   70

PART TWO   CONTEXTS   **81**

Chapter 4: Genre   **83**
  1 Reading the romance   83
  2 Theory of genre   91
  3 Genre and television: Reading the *Radio Times*   97
  4 'Genericity' in the new Hollywood cinema   105
  5 Case study: Genre and photography – from 'fashion'
     to 'glamour'   111

Chapter 5: Stars and personalities   **120**
  1 Dimensions of stardom   120
  2 Stars, personalities, celebrities   126
  3 Personality and television: Reading the *TVTimes*   134
  4 The face of Marilyn   141
  5 Case study: TV talk shows and the 'personality effect'   145

PART THREE   SUBTEXTS   **151**

Chapter 6: Ideology   **153**
  1 Femininity as ideology   153
  2 Theory of ideology   160
  3 A Scottish landscape   165
  4 The Queen at Christmas   170
  5 Case study: 'Black and white in colour'   175
     A speculative postscript   182

Chapter 7: Discourse   **185**
  1 On stereotypes   185
  2 Theory of discourse   191
  3 The male gaze   196
  4 Spectacular ethnography   201
  5 Case study: Looking at men . . . and boys   207
     An afterword   215

Notes   218
References   222
Index   229

Acknowledgements

This book is largely the outcome of a decade or so teaching media and cultural studies as part of the programme in Communication Studies at Queen Margaret College, Edinburgh. As such, it has been produced in a collective context, involving fellow lecturers, research students and undergraduates past and present. My thanks in particular go to my colleagues Jim Bee, Richard Butt and Shaun Moores, for many stimulating discussions and comments, and to Nicola Fleming for her help with the illustrations. Michael Stewart, Shiona Wood and Helen Wood have also made helpful suggestions, and the students who have put me right on so many occasions are too numerous to list. Lesley Riddle at Edward Arnold has been patient and supportive in seeing this project through from start to finish.

For permission to reproduce the illustrations I would like to thank the following individuals and organisations: Frances Angela, BBC Television News, The British Library, Chefaro Proprietaries Ltd, Condé Nast Publications Ltd, Cover Shots International Ltd, Billy Graham, Granada Television, Hitachi Sales (UK) Ltd, Kimberly-Clark Europe, Lever Brothers Ltd, Roberto Matassa, Metro-Golwyn-Mayer, Pretty Polly Ltd, The Post Office Film Library, *Radio Times*, the *Sun*, *TVTimes*, United Distillers PLC, Verso Publications and Turner Entertainment Co.

For assistance in obtaining prints for publication I would like to thank the British Film Institute and the British Library (Newspaper Library).

Introduction

1 MEDIATIONS

The title of this book is intended to suggest something of the influence, and the cultural power, of the mass media in the modern world. It is a truism to say that we live in a world that is saturated with mass media, consumed on a daily basis. But this is not just a matter of recognising that the average time spent viewing television is four hours each day, and the average time spent listening to the radio a further ten hours each week, and that in addition, many of us purchase a daily newspaper and a weekly or monthly magazine (1). These are all forms of media consumption in which we have some choice. What about the fact that, as we travel to work, we cannot avoid the billboards which line the route? Or that, even as we sit at home, our mail regularly includes forms of advertising and publicity? In short, the truism about media saturation must also recognise that we all consume various media, most of us in massive amounts, whether we like it or not. We live in a mass-mediated world – what are the consequences of this way of living?

This book is concerned with the way media structure our experience. Let me try to clarify the background to this statement. Over the past twenty years or so, media studies has developed, in various contexts, as a theoretical and analytical field. It can be argued that this development is one way of coming to terms with the phenomenon of media saturation. Many readers of this book will be students of the media, or engaged in courses with titles such as Communication or Cultural Studies where media studies plays a significant part. But it is possible to study the media from different angles. At one end of the spectrum, we might be interested in the economic development of the media industries, and in policies for media growth and regulation. Alternatively we might be interested in what goes on in people's houses, or elsewhere, as they actively consume media products. This book is positioned somewhere between these two possibilities. It looks at the product of the industries, that is media texts; and it examines the different ways in which these texts offer potential experiences to consumers. Not all consumers will necessarily accept the experiences that are on offer, but the point about media saturation is that everyone, in modern society, is obliged to respond, in one way or another, to what mass media are doing.

To this extent, everyone's social and cultural experience today is 'mediated'. Let us now explore briefly some of the key implications of this point. In a recent introduction to media studies (designed primarily for students in further education, but nevertheless a very useful background to this book) the point about mediation is related to an argument about 'situated culture'. Here it is suggested that we all inhabit particular situations, in homes, neighbourhoods and places of work, where our experience is developed through face-to-face relationships, and meanings are transmitted by word of mouth. Into this world, since the mid-nineteenth century, has entered the media, so that, according to these authors:

> . . . we have increasingly learned to live not only in our situated culture, but also in a *culture of mediation*, whereby specialised social agencies – the press, film and cinema, radio and television broadcasting – developed to supply and cultivate larger-scale forms of communication; mediating news and other forms of culture into the situation. 'Our' immediate world co-exists with the mediated 'world out there'.
>
> (O'Sullivan *et al.* 1994b, p.13)

Certainly it is important to observe that one thing achieved by mediation is a vastly increased access to information, now transmitted instantaneously around the globe. In this respect, mediation offers the possibility of living in at least two communities – that is, both an immediate social network and an infinitely expanding mediated community of people with whom we share forms of communication, but are never likely to meet. But mediation achieves much more than simply expanding our horizons. What happens, I would argue, through this phenomenon, is that the 'situated' and the 'mediated' worlds gradually, but inexorably, interpenetrate. Ultimately, these two worlds become indistinguishable: the world 'out there' is now 'our world', and 'our world' is experienced with reference to the world 'out there'. The authors of *Studying The Media* suggest that Marshall McLuhan had this insight in the 1960s when he wrote about the 'global village' (McLuhan 1964).

Some of the dynamics of this mediated culture have been discussed in media studies. For instance, Shaun Moores (1995) has analysed the development of a peculiar kind of 'mediated interaction' in the medium of broadcasting. Moores refers to Anthony Giddens' (1990) discussion of the 'consequences of modernity', and specifically to the point Giddens makes about 'time-space distanciation'. The modern world, argues Giddens, brings us into all kinds of relationships with anonymous or absent others, across increased distances of time and space. We are thus faced with the problem of sustaining these relationships and perhaps even of developing certain forms of mediated intimacy and trust. How is this possible? Moores suggests that one effect of broadcasting has been the development of an illusion of 'co-presence' with distant others; both with the others who talk to us, in friendly ways, through the medium itself, and with all the imagined others who might be simultaneously part of the audience. This effect allows for a sense of community to be maintained across the airwaves – a 'mediated community' which absorbs the 'situated communities' of which we are already members.

There are other ways in which the culture of the mediated community enters into our personal experience. It may be that we discuss the goings-on in the news or in our favourite soap operas, with our immediate friends and colleagues. Several writers on soap opera have suggested that this kind of audience participation is central to their appeal (2). It may also be that in the mediated world we develop a particular fascination for a film star, or a liking (or, equally possible, an antipathy) for a television personality. These are mediated forms of individuality which engage with our individuality – they transform us, for instance, into 'fans'. But what about the further possibility that, as we develop our most intimate relationships with our most significant others, we are, at some level, re-enacting the scenarios which we have seen previously on TV or at the movies? Who can truthfully say that they have never been influenced by mediated notions of romance or glamour?

Recently, and perhaps through the phenomenal success of a particular board game, we have all grown familiar with the concept of 'trivia'. One definition of this concept might be to say that it refers to mass-mediated knowledge. It is true that we can answer some Trivial Pursuit questions on the basis of knowledge which we might have picked up from school, or from travel. But, in my experience at least, the overwhelming majority of the questions in this type of quiz refer to knowledge about, or derived from, the media. Trivia game machines used to be ubiquitous in the pubs of central Scotland, and trivia quiz evenings are still held regularly. Here again, the culture of the 'situated community', of friends and neighbours is, at one and the same time, the mediated culture. The world of the 'local' is bound up with the global, through a ritual invented, like so many others, in America.

The concept of trivia is, however, particularly interesting and it points to one of the central themes of this book. Let us be careful, at this point, to distinguish between 'trivia' and 'triviality'. In using this concept to define a certain kind of mediated knowledge I am not thereby suggesting that the mediated culture is 'trivial' or that it inevitably 'trivialises'. For one thing, as will become clear, I want to avoid such negative value judgements in this book. And in any case the mediated culture can of course be serious, as when it reports significant political events, or disasters. Who can forget that poignant moment in 1990 when the world's media transmitted those live pictures of Nelson Mandela's release from prison? As I write this sentence, the world's media is being equally serious in its reports of a major earthquake in Japan. Nevertheless 'trivia', as a name for mediated knowledge, does imply that we have a certain kind relationship to the mediated culture which sometimes puts seriousness in its place.

As modern media have developed and expanded into every area of our experience, so they have become, in several respects, increasingly playful. It is not just that there are lots of sports and games; this point is more to do with our increasingly sophisticated way of relating to the media as consumers. As I illustrate in several ways during this course of this book, we have, during the second half of this century – but particularly since the 1980s – become 'knowing' consumers. We have lost our innocence, we now possess 'knowingness', and it is this that the concept of trivia suggests. This is not just knowledge *per se*, this is knowledge plus knowingness, which is an increasing awareness of, and sensitivity to, the forms of mediation. To adopt a marketing metaphor (which might be particularly appropriate), we now know that media information is packaged, and we also know a lot about the forms and techniques of packaging. We know this as ordinary viewers and listeners; we have learned to be sceptical and to treat much of what we see and hear, as fun.

In this book, I have tried to present an opportunity for us to all think again about the phenomenon of mediation. It is about the ways media shape our experiences, not simply through an increased access to the world 'out there', and not only in terms of our own personal involvement with the figures which inhabit this world. In addition, there is a question for which I can only find a somewhat old-fashioned word: the question of our modern 'sensibility'. I am not, however, going to pronounce on, or dismiss this sensibility, as some writers on media culture might have done in the past. As I have just indicated, I think the modern mediated sensibility is sophisticated and complex, it is responsive to form as well as content and it is, to an increasing extent, self-aware. All these points raise further questions about the ways we now understand ourselves, with our mediated cultural identities. What I hope this book provides, by suggestion as much as by definition, is some stimulus to thinking about these questions – about what it means to live in a mediated world.

2 TEXT AND DISCOURSE

The way the mediated world impinges on our experience is through our consumption of media texts. If we are to begin to answer any of the questions raised above, we not only need to appreciate the range of what is on offer, we must also develop some understanding of how media texts work. So this is a book which aims to introduce the reader to the analysis of a variety of media texts, within the wider context of the study of media culture. It will be useful in this introduction, to outline the particular approach to text analysis which is taken here, to avoid at least two possible sources of confusion.

There is a problem for many people who are beginning media text analysis, which is that they have already encountered other approaches to text analysis at school. In particular, many people's previous acquaintance with text analysis has been associated with the study of literature. This is not necessarily unhelpful, for there are some technical terms relating to literature which can be applied to the media, and it will be useful if the reader of this book has some previous knowledge of terms like 'metaphor', for instance, or 'narrative'. But there are also certain barriers arising from the study of literature as far as media text analysis is concerned. One barrier is the fairly obvious point that many media texts have a visual as well as a verbal dimension, so terms and concepts derived from the study of written texts can only take us so far. It has been necessary, therefore for media studies to develop its own specialised vocabulary to analyse visual imagery – a necessity which is unfortunately sometimes dismissed as 'jargon' by uncomprehending outsiders.

That is not the main difficulty however. The great problem for media studies, as regards the analysis of media texts, has to do with the approach that is often taken. This approach claims to be critical, but from a media studies perspective it is not usually critical enough. Particularly at school, students of English are still encouraged to form personal relationships with the works of literary authors. The texts are seen to be making important statements abut 'life' which, ideally, can be related to the reader's personal experience. As such it is possible for the reader, or student, to engage with the text in a dialogue of self discovery and moral education. From literature, students learn lessons about 'life' – for instance, what counts as authentic feeling, or good and bad behaviour. The value of the lessons is guaranteed by the fact that the books selected for students to read are the works of great authors. In the words of Matthew Arnold's famous phrase, they are 'the best that has been thought and said in the world'.

The current consensus in media studies is that this kind of approach is largely inappropriate. It is true that there has been some attempt to elevate classic films in this way, where some Hollywood directors, such as Ford or Hitchcock, have been granted the status of 'authors'. But this auteurism, as an approach to the study of cinema, is now largely discredited, or confined to a different kind of (non-academic) writing about film (3). Essentially, this is because media studies, in its approach to texts, wants to ask different sorts of questions. Perhaps the basic point here is that, whereas it is assumed that most students are unfamiliar with the literary classics (which is why English teachers sometimes display a sort of missionary zeal), it can equally be assumed that everyone is already an avid consumer of the media. Indeed, as the previous argument has implied, students often come to media studies with a highly sophisticated knowledge – which is in many respects superior to that of their teachers! So the task then becomes a collective enterprise which examines the way media texts are operating to reproduce the common, mediated culture. That is to say, it is no longer a question of learning *from* the text, but rather *how* the text actually works.

In this enterprise, we are initially interested in the way media texts offer meanings to their 'readers'. These readers may make their own interpretations, but we will also see that meanings are derived from meaning systems, to which everyone (more or less) in our culture has access. The text itself works to structure these meanings, so that our experience of them is organised; and the text also 'speaks' to its potential reader in a certain way. At the same time however, as we have insisted, the reader is neither naive nor innocent, but rather comes to the text with all sorts of prior knowledge and expectations. The reader will already know a lot about the text even before s/he opens its pages and, as s/he reads, will be able to relate the text not simply to personal experience of 'life', but more precisely to a knowledge of other texts. The modern consumer of the media is a reader of many different kinds of text, which inter-relate and feed off each other. For example, in Chapter 6, I refer to the fact that, in 1994, most readers of press reports about certain members of the British royal family will also have seen the photographs, and the TV documentaries, and will possibly have read the books (themselves written by media personalities) to which the press reports refer.

Now, I think, we encounter a second possible area of confusion. Implicit throughout this book, and increasingly explicit towards the end, is a question about what is involved in 'reading' a media text. Let us again begin with the obvious point, that although the term 'reading' can be used literally (for there are some words on some pages of some media texts); nevertheless it is, to a much larger extent, being used here as a metaphor. Again, it is a metaphor which is derived from the study of literature, and again, in this context, it might be misleading. For the consumption of media texts cannot be reduced to the notion of 'reading', and this is not only because there are other senses, such as hearing, involved. Reading is usually a solitary and largely cerebral activity; but the consumption of many media texts is both a more collective and a more sensuous experience.

In thinking about the consumption of many media texts, we are drawn towards the use of words like 'event', 'ritual' and 'practice'. To consume the media may be to attend a special event, such as a film show; or it may be part and parcel of our daily routine. Turning on the radio, reading the morning paper, collapsing in front of the telly, are ways we punctuate our daily lives – and so (despite what is sometimes said about 'couch potatoes') media consumption is inescapably a *social* activity. This basic point begins to change our understanding of the 'text', for it is no longer just a discrete object which we activate through 'reading'. It is rather a series of inter-related experiences forming a whole culture in which we actively participate. We have already discussed the way the mediated world constructs an imagined community. Now we need to examine the ways we interact with this community, through social practices in which we are actively involved.

In this book, many of these points will come together towards the end, when (in Chapter 7) we examine the concept of discourse. In essence, this concept insists that what a text *does* is just as significant as what it *says* – and what it does is to invite our participation in organised (and institutionalised) cultural practices. But this perspective on media texts also raises a further fundamental question. For if what a text is doing has as much (if not more) importance as what it is saying, this is to question the relevance of a critical approach which would focus on the question of 'representation'. In this approach, the critical interest is in what a text is saying (or not saying) about the so-called 'real world'. It is of course possible to ask this kind of question. But implicit in this book is my view that such questions basically miss the point about the more important function of media texts, which is their construction of a mass-mediated culture. Accordingly I would suggest that we concentrate our attention on the practices through which this culture is constructed, and suspend any temptation to judge it as 'true' or 'false', 'real' or 'unreal', as compared to any other preferred perception of the world.

3   ABOUT THIS BOOK

This book is in three parts, entitled *Texts*, *Contexts* and *Subtexts*. It is intended that there should be a progression through these parts, in terms of their degree of difficulty and the kinds of critical questions they are asking. Thus, Part One provides an introduction to the basic tools for media text analysis. These are derived from an approach which is now well established in media studies, namely semiology, the study of signs and meanings. From that starting point, we then proceed to examine the elementary structures of media texts, and to consider the ways in which media texts interact with their potential consumers, in terms of their modes of address. Up to this point, the first three chapters are entirely concerned with our immediate experience of the text – how we might interpret or 'read' it, in systematic and conventional ways.

In Part Two, the term 'contexts' is used to introduce the point that our interpretations of texts are always, to some extent, predetermined. That is to say, they are influenced by our general knowledge of media texts, from which is derived the expectations that we bring to any particular reading. Of crucial importance here is our knowledge of media genres, and our familiarity with regular performers and participants in the mediated culture – the stars and personalities. This general knowledge is exploited by the producers of media texts, and it is systematically recycled through such activities as scheduling, publicity and review. Such contexts constitute a wider frame of reference in which to locate the particular text under consideration.

My use of the term 'subtext', in Part Three, points to the possibility that our mediated experiences might, on some level, be problematic. This word suggests that there might be more going on in a media text than is apparent on the surface, and that we might have to critically examine its implicit, as well as explicit, operations. Another way of making this point is to say that, as well as reading or interpreting a text, and comparing it to others of which we have some prior knowledge, we are sometimes also able to identify where it is 'coming from'. Here I do not mean simply its institutional source, like Hollywood or the BBC; rather I am using this phrase in the American sense, to refer to an underlying perspective. In media studies, such perspectives are frequently defined as ideologies or as discourses – and we can say that, at the same time as the text is offering its immediate meanings, it is also reproducing a more general ideology or discourse, a 'sub-text' in other words.

Perhaps it is inevitable that an introduction to anything is bound to repeat some details which those interested in the subject will already know. In this book, my strategy has been to introduce key concepts through a detailed analysis and discussion of examples. These examples are quite varied, ranging from broadcasting and cinema, to advertising, still photography and some areas of print media. Each chapter has five sections, where a new concept or category or angle of discussion is introduced with reference to an example. Each chapter also concludes with a case study, which is either an attempt to apply relevant concepts to an extended example and/or to introduce new, and possibily unfamiliar material into the discussion. Hopefully then, even for those who are familiar with some of these topics, I have managed to achieve a fresh and stimulating approach – but that, of course, is for the reader to judge.

The original idea for this book was the product of discussions with colleagues in which we agreed that a comprehensive introduction to media text analysis was sorely needed. I have been teaching this subject for several years and there is still no textbook that I can recommend to students. There are some introductions to media studies, usually designed for teachers or students in further education (such as the excellent example to which I have referred). There are some useful collections of essays (see below) which are stimulating but not systematic. There are comprehensive and detailed introductions to particular media, especially advertising and cinema. But when new students ask me what I would recommend, I still find myself suggesting a book which is now almost a quarter of a century old: John Berger's excellent and provocative *Ways of Seeing* (1972). What's great about that book is its clear engagement with examples, in the context of a general critical perspective on mass-mediated culture. If I have captured something of that approach in this book, I shall be very pleased indeed.

FURTHER INTRODUCTORY READING

In addition to Berger (1972), I would also recommend two books which look at different aspects of modern media culture from a feminist critical perspective. These are Coward (1984), and Williamson (1986). Many of the key concepts which are introduced and illustrated in the course of this book are also discussed in O'Sullivan *et al.* (1994a), which will prove to be a useful text for general consultation.

1

TEXTS

Signs and meanings

MYTHOLOGIES

The first thing that any media text, indeed any act of communication, must do is to produce or reproduce meanings. Literary critics and philosophers have long debated the elusive nature of meaning, and the seemingly endless regress in the search for the 'meaning of meaning'. On one level it is true that meanings are ultimately located in people's heads, that we are all individuals with different life experiences, that we all make our own interpretations, and therefore that a final statement about the meaning of anything is impossible. It is remarkable however, how many approximate statements can be made; and any student of the mass media would have to conclude that what happens in our heads is, if not entirely predictable, at least to a large extent common and conventional.

Consider, for example, an advertisement for Kleenex® Boutique® tissues (see figure 1.1). It is apparent that, like the vast majority, this ad is following a very conventional communicative strategy. The strategy is to give meaning to a product by developing associations in the mind of the reader. These associations are cultural, in the sense that any member of the culture for which the advert is produced will find them easy to recognise. Of course, different individuals might come to different conclusions regarding the advert and the possibility of purchasing the product; but such differences do not alter the fact that, for a moment, a set of common cultural meanings has been reproduced as the desired effect of the strategy.

It will come as no surprise to learn that this advert for Kleenex® tissues appeared in several British women's magazines in 1991. This is not surprising, because somehow we already know that the meanings invoked by this advert have something to do with femininity or, to be more precise, what our culture conventionally understands as 'feminine'. But this is not simply that we associate the use of facial tissues with the application of cosmetics, which is defined in our culture as a feminine activity (and we shall encounter

Fig. 1.1. Advert for Kleenex® Boutique® tissues (1991). By permission of Kimberly-Clark Europe

later, in Chapter 7, a culture where this is not so defined). Our reading of this advert as 'feminine' has much to do with the way the tissues appear here as flowers (pink in the original), which quite possibly will remind us of a bouquet of roses. So these are 'flowery tissues', where a manufactured commodity now seems to be produced organically, and perhaps even with a hint of magic, from an apparently 'natural' source.

To a large extent, we might say, this advert is following a formula. It is a formula which is repeated over and over again in similar ads for cosmetic products, on television as well as in magazine advertising. Here, cosmetics are frequently associated with nature, or things natural, such as the purity of water and the freshness of flowers. Bouquets are ubiquitous in such advertising and, if the flowers are roses, then a further set of romantic associations is produced. If, in addition, the name of the product is French (even when the manufacturers are, as here, American) then other impressions of fashionable sophistication will be added to the mix. Indeed, what we are describing here could be defined as a recipe for cosmetics advertising, except that the trick is to make it turn out slightly differently each time.

Femininity/Nature/Romance – these are examples of what Roland Barthes (1957/1973) defined as mythologies. By this term he meant, not that the meanings contained in these texts are false ('myth' as opposed to 'truth'), but that they are part of a common cultural currency, a cultural heritage, into which we are all (formally and informally) socialised. Indeed these common cultural meanings are not simply false, they are also not simply confined to texts – they are reproduced by texts, but they also help to define real life situations. It is presumably not unknown for consumers to be influenced by the mythologies of 'femininity' in these ads and the association of roses with romance, for example, helps to keep Interflora busy on St Valentine's day.

Barthes would have said that the image of the flowery tissues in this advert is acting as a sign. The advert is actually a combination of signs (flowery tissues, boxes, captions and slogans) and its meaning is a product of this combination. Each individual sign (such as the tissues) is comprised by two elements: the signifier, which is the material or physical aspect of the sign which engages with our senses (in this case a composite photographic image); and the signified which is the meaning we conventionally associate with this image. In the first instance, the signified is simply a literal interpretation of the signifier – we recognise that this is a box of tissues which looks like a bouquet of roses. Barthes referred to this literal interpretation of the signifier as its denotation. However, as we have just seen, the meaning of this image cannot be restricted to its literal interpretation. It's not just that we recognise the flowery tissues, all sorts of other associations are brought into play.

It is most appropriate to think spatially and to imagine that what is going on in our heads as we look at this image is a passage through different levels of meaning. At the first level, before we can proceed to any other, we have to be able to supply a literal meaning: to observe, for instance, that these are indeed tissues which look like roses and not any other species of flower. On that basis, we may then introduce other levels of meaning which are not literal, but symbolic. These are the wider cultural associations which we bring to the literal meaning, and which Barthes called connotations. One of the connotations of roses is romance and one of the connotations of 'Boutique' (or, more generally, 'Frenchness') is cultural sophistication. The advert, in using these signs, is plugging into these cultural connotations in order to promote this product.

Of course, the written text cannot be ignored in our analysis of the advert. It makes its own important contributions which add further levels of complexity to our interpretation. In the first place, we should note that there is a difference between the ways we interpret visual and verbal signs: for if the visual signs invite, in the first instance, our recognition, the verbal signs inevitably involve a more complex process of decoding. This is because, whereas the visual sign can be said to resemble its denotation (this photograph looks like 'flowery tissues'), for the verbal sign there is no such resemblance, and the reader will need to have access to the language codes from which the words have been chosen (we will return to some of the implications of this point). More generally, the language codes are themselves potentially complex, which is why copy-writers can have such fun manipulating them. Here for instance, the metaphorical use of the word 'bloom' emphasises the fact that the whole advert is a metaphor ('flowery tissues'). The company slogan is a verbal paradox which offers a witty afterword. Such uses of language remind us that advertising is a form of rhetoric, dedicated to the arts of persuasion, and that even the most conventional ads can be pleasurable and amusing.

So, to recap: signs, which may be verbal or visual (or aural or tactile) are comprised by signifiers (their material aspect) and signifieds (their meaning, which is a mental construct). The signifieds are, on one level, literal denotations (what the sign says, what it depicts) and, on another level, cultural connotations (what the sign symbolises). These are the elementary concepts of semiology, the study of signs and sign systems (from the Greek word *seme*) which has influenced media studies through the work of Roland Barthes, though Barthes himself was influenced by the Swiss linguist, Ferdinand de Saussure, who first promoted the idea of semiology in his book *Course in General Linguistics* (1916/1974).

It is possible, on the basis of our analysis of this relatively straightforward ad, and with these basic concepts of semiology, to begin to explore more complex permutations of signs and meanings in contemporary advertising. There is, however one potential loose end which should be tied up before we proceed. We have spoken of romance as a connotation of roses, and of cultural sophistication as a connotation of 'Frenchness', but we (and Barthes) have also used the term 'mythology' to describe the process whereby objects are invested with cultural meanings. What is the precise relationship between these two concepts, connotation and mythology?

In fact there are two possible definitions, or understandings, of the term 'mythology'. One, which is current in media studies, is to suggest that the mythologies circulating in our culture provide individuals with the specific connotations they read into texts. Conversely, advertising agencies are mobilising these mythologies when they fashion particular images for adverts. Some common mythologies used in advertising, in addition to nature and romance, are: 'the good old days' (used particularly to sell food products); 'the happy family' (domestic consumer goods); and 'fun-loving youth' (soft drinks and so on). In this environmentally conscious age the 'naturalness of nature' sells everything from cosmetics to cars. In short, in this interpretation, mythologies are like common stores of meaning which can be raided by advertisers and consumers alike. Clearly it is useful to be able to identify the reproduction of such meaning systems in media texts.

For Barthes, however, 'mythology' also has an additional dimension. It is not just that media texts make use of particular meaning systems; it is more that these meaning systems become the taken-for-granted 'common sense' of the age. A meaning system, like romance, becomes a mythology when it becomes the 'natural' thing to do to purchase a bouquet of roses on St Valentine's day. The important point here is naturalisation: it seems 'obvious' that tradition means quality, or that the 'happy family' is an ideal to which everyone aspires. Mythology is then, in this definition, the translation of particular meaning systems into lived experiences; and advertisements, with their perpetual promise of the good life, play a major part in this process. By fostering a greater critical awareness of the meanings that media texts encourage us to take for granted, media studies is engaged in a process of 'de-naturalising' our familiar worlds.

2 PREFERRED READINGS

Some products are, however, easier to advertise than others. In a sense, cosmetics advertising comes with its mythologies ready made. For other products the available mythologies are restricted, either by official regulation and codes of practice (which apply for example to cigarette advertising in Britain) or because the product itself presents intrinsic difficulties. For instance, the critique of advertisers' approaches to AIDS awareness, where early campaigns included inappropriate metaphors (like icebergs) and horror film symbolism, was only one particularly clear example of a general problem. Health promotion generally runs the risk of offending some, while

Fig. 1.2. Advert for Predictor Colourtip (1991). By permission of Chefaro Proprietaries Ltd

appearing patronising to others. It may be that the mythological approach, perfected in consumer advertising, is simply inappropriate to this kind of serious social issue.

Other examples are intriguing, even unintentionally amusing. Consider the advertisement for the Predictor home pregnancy test kit, which appeared, in 1990, in a variety of women's magazines across the spectrum from *Elle* to *Bella* (see figure 1.2). It features a black and white photograph of a couple kissing in what appears to be a bistro-type restaurant at closing time. Some chairs have already been stacked on the tables and the waiters appear to be clearing up. Accentuated in the monochrome image is the whiteness of the table-cloth and the vase of flowers, close to the couple, by the right-hand wall. Superimposed is a caption, and a colour (pink) image of the product. Some verbal text, which we will consider later, underpins the main photograph and is set alongside the image of the product.

Again, if we now begin to look for connotations and mythology, this advert would seem to point towards romance (hardly surprising in *Bella*, where romance is a major preoccupation throughout). The signs are these: the kiss, the flowers, the wine glass, the white table-cloth, the bistro (equalling French style) location. In this example, however, not only the signified (ie. what we can recognise in the picture), but also the *signifier* (the fact that a monochrome photograph is used) point to these conclusions. In this age of glossy colour photography, the black and white image is anachronistic, perhaps nostalgic – this could be a still from a French film of the 1950s. The generally romantic image is reinforced by the caption, which is an example of hyperbole (rhetorical exaggeration): 'For the most fantastic news ever in the history of the world'. Presumably they're in love, she's pregnant, she's just told him, and they're both overjoyed. Presumably. Except that (and I am indebted to my students for this interpretation) it is equally possible that the good news is that she is not pregnant. And this possibility becomes just a little plausible when we consider who, and for what reason, would be more inclined to place her trust in Predictor rather than her GP.

Of course, this second interpretation is perverse: it isn't at all what the ad is supposed to mean. In the Predictor ad, a lot of work has gone into the equation of this product with romance, as the conventional mythology which surrounds sex and sexuality. A lot of work is necessary perhaps because, unlike the consumption of perfume or wine, home pregnancy testing is open to other, less than romantic, possibilities. Indeed, perhaps the accompanying text contains just a hint of the possibility of worry and anxiety. But the photograph, with its mythology, is in dominance. Predictor is associated with the positive rather than the negative consequences of romance.

What this advert illustrates, very clearly, is that the meanings constructed in media texts are generally open to more than one interpretation. The text is, as the semiologist would say, polysemic. Equally clearly however, the text is also constructed to make one interpretation seem more obvious, more natural. There is then a preferred reading of this particular text and, through this reading, there is a preferred association with the product. The preferred reading is the reading you might make which is preferred by the text (and presumably by the advertiser, though we are just inferring this from the text analysis) even though other readings are possible. Sometimes, however, texts contain hints and suggestions of other readings, rather like the guilty secrets which they are trying, desperately, to repress.

The Predictor ad is, I think, a good example of what Barthes really meant when he wrote about mythology in popular culture. It is, as I have said, partly about the identification of meaning systems, like romance, which are reproduced not only in adverts in women's magazines, but also in the stories and the problem pages. In the latter context, however, we learn, if we didn't already know, that romance has its limitations, its contradictions and its unintended consequences. In short, these meaning systems are always open to question, to debate, to critique and to rejection. There is a feminist reading of many of the adverts which appear in this book which is very different from that which the adverts themselves prefer. In making their preferences for some meaning systems rather than others, these adverts are acting as a form of cultural indoctrination, in the nicest possible way. Which is, again, what Barthes meant by mythology.

3   INTERTEXUALITY

The Lux advert is interesting because it too contains multiple meanings, but it organises them in a way which is very different from the previous example. There, as we saw, the Predictor ad did its best to repress alternative readings; here Lux positively welcomes a reader who can see that there is more than one thing going on (see figure 1.3). It is a clever and particularly modern type of advertisement which makes its appeal to the 'knowing' consumer. Ideally (in terms of the advert's preferred reading), this knowing consumer not only consumes mythology, but also knows, quite self-consciously, that this is indeed what she is doing – and moreover she may derive a certain pleasure from this knowledge. The knowing consumer is in fact an amateur semiologist.

Again the Lux advert presents us with a monochrome image and a hyperbolic caption. It is surely unnecessary to elaborate on the extremely conventional construction of this image, for it relies entirely on a familiar formula for advertising cosmetics: narcissistic self-indulgence. The model is alone, in her bathroom/boudoir, revelling in the soapy suds/creams/gels etc, and, in televised versions, to the accompaniment of light classical music. So this is a mythology of luxury: 'star treatment for your skin'.

Fig. 1.3. Advert for Lux Toilet Soap (1991). By permission of Lever Brothers Limited/J Walter Thompson

The fun, however, comes with the caption and this transforms the meaning of the ad – in fact it takes it to a higher level. The caption is, of course, not just hyperbole, it is a quote, (in fact it is a misquotation, but adverts are not constrained to follow academic standards of referencing). It reminds the 'knowing consumer' of Humphrey Bogart, in his cups, in *Casablanca* (1942), in which the 'bar' he refers to is the night–club of which he is the owner. The caption therefore also makes a pun on the word 'bar', and the slogan 'star treatment for your skin' takes on an additional meaning.

Moreover, once we recognise the reference to *Casablanca*, the image too, begins to look different. This may be a formulaic boudoir, but it also has some tropical foliage, vaguely visible cane furniture, slatted blinds and, in its lighting effect, a hint of 1940s *film noir*. The fact that the image is black and white begins to make more sense. And what of the model? This is not Ingrid Bergman herself (though her image has been used in contemporary cosmetic ads) but it is, on closer inspection, a 1940s hairstyle and what might pass, in the pose and the make-up, for a certain classical form of glamour. To sum up, the general mythology of luxury has been relocated, by the caption, and by certain signifieds within the image, in a reference to classi-cal Hollywood cinema. The fact that this is achieved through a pun might seem to be rather clever.

Of course, to achieve its full effect, the Lux advert relies on the reader's ability to perceive this cleverness. If the reader did not recognise the quote, the advert would still work, but only in one dimension, and only on the most conventional level. In this sense, it is much more important to be able to decode this caption than it is, for example 'Predictor – Right First Time'. For it is through this caption that the reader then has access to a further, second, level of meaning: the *Casablanca* connotations, and ultimately the mythol-ogy of Hollywood stardom. As a semiologist would say, this caption (reinforced by some aspects of the photo) constructs for this advert a certain intertextuality. It is on one level a conventional advert, and on another level it is (like) a scene from *Casablanca*. And the crucial thing is that the inter-textual reference transforms the meaning of the advert as a whole.

There are, however, not one, but two levels to this transformation. Certainly the intertextual references make a conventional advert more inter-esting. But they also, and this is the important point, fundamentally trans-form the relationship between the reader/viewer and the text. We are back once more to the 'knowing consumer', the amateur semiologist; and the key effect is this: in understanding the intertextuality and the cleverness of this ad, the 'knowing' reader/viewer is made aware, precisely, of the ad as a fabrication. Its artificiality is foregrounded; its mythology is, clearly and transparently, a mass-mediated construction (after all, it comes from Hollywood). So unlike the potential consumer of Kleenex® Boutique®, the consumer of Lux can have no illusions. Glamour is now a kind of game we might play (like the game of spot the quotation), imagining perhaps that a touch of Hollywood stardom might rub off in the privacy of our own bathrooms!

I have already suggested that this shift from a straight, to a more playful consumption of mass-media texts and their mythologies is a significant feature of contemporary mediated culture. It is certainly a widespread practice in contemporary advertising and it makes these ads more fun to decode. Quite what it implies in a wider context is, however, difficult to assess. Does it, for instance, imply that ads have lost some of their power to mystify and that the 'naturalisation' which Barthes thought was so essential to the work of mythology is no longer such a force? If we get the jokes in ads like that for Lux, does this help to de-naturalise the act of consumption (actually buying and using this bar of soap)? Or are we perhaps, in our cleverness, congratulating ourselves on our 'knowingness', reinforcing our credentials as members of the mass-mediated world culture? In short, does Lux undermine the myth of Hollywood glamour, or does it make it for us, as knowing consumers, that much more accessible?

4   THE 'ARBITRARY NATURE' OF THE SIGN

The intertextual references in the advert for Gordon's gin are to other ads in the same series (see figure 1.4). It is part of a protracted campaign which follows a formula first developed in cigarette advertising, where the association of this potentially harmful product with a healthy or glamorous lifestyle is prevented by the Advertising Standards Authority. This formula, pioneered in advertising for Benson & Hedges cigarettes, takes one aspect of the packaging for the product, its colour, and makes this symbolic of the product as a whole. In rhetoric, this strategy is called metonymy: one aspect of the signifier is taken to represent the entire signified. In advertising for Gordon's, the colour green represents this particular brand of gin. An amusing advert in the series uses an entire page of a magazine, coloured in slightly paler green than usual, with the caption: 'A weak Gordon's & Tonic. (Please do not adjust your magazine)'.

Again then, the appeal is to the knowing reader, and this is another instance of the tendency noted in the previous section. I have included this example here, however, in order to introduce some further general points which are fundamental for media text analysis. One thing which can be said about all the adverts considered previously is that they are, in a general sense, 'realistic' in so far as they present us with photographic signifiers which we are invited, in the first instance, to recognise. 'A man in his birthday suit hiding his modesty' is, however, abstract: the signifier does not resemble the signified, and perhaps the mythology of the advert is less explicit.

Fig. 1.4. Advert for Gordon's gin (1991). By permission of United Distillers plc

Actually, there is some connection here between signifier and signified. The advert presents us with a small green rectangle (green = Gordon's) on a flesh coloured page. But there the resemblance ends for, of course, the flesh-coloured page looks nothing like 'a man in his birthday suit . . .' Where the signifier is as abstract as this, it requires a lot of effort to work out what the signified could possibly be and, if we didn't have the caption, together with our knowledge of other Gordon's adverts, we would be lost. A similar situation arises when we are at a loss to understand a foreign language. Where there is little or no resemblance between the signifier and the signified, it becomes particularly important that we have knowledge of the codes which are being used. The Gordon's ad presents a kind of challenge to our decoding abilities, whereas it is a lot easier to make sense out of the Lux advert – even if you've never seen *Casablanca*.

One important point for media text analysis is that the advertisement for Gordon's gin illustrates what Ferdinand de Saussure termed the 'arbitrary nature' of the sign. Basing his pioneering theories on the study of language, de Saussure noted that, in most linguistic signs, the signifier shows no resemblance whatsoever to the signified, and this is true not only of abstract words like 'meaning' or 'analysis', it is also the case for concrete nouns like 'horse' and 'tree'. The four letters I have just written could, in principle, signify anything; that we take them to refer to a general category of plant life is entirely a matter of cultural convention. In this linguistic sign the signifier does not look like the signified, nor are these two aspects of the sign physically or materially connected. The linguistic sign is essentially symbolic – and if we were operating within a different set of codes and conventions the five-letter signifier *'arbre'* would do just as well.

In this respect, photographic visual signs are something of an exception to the general rule, precisely because they are so realistic. They are what de Saussure and Barthes termed 'motivated', as opposed to 'arbitrary signs'; and in photographs we do assume a physical connection between signifier and signified in so far as light, emanating from objects in the real world, must have entered the camera for the signifier to have been produced. But this is not the case for other types of sign, including other types of visual sign, such as paintings and drawings. Even realistic representational paintings are more arbitrary than photographs, and the arbitrariness increases the more abstract they become. Again, entirely abstract visual signs could mean anything – that they have identifiable meanings is either due to an agreed set of codes and conventions (such as the abstract, arbitrary, road signs in the *Highway Code*), or, in the case of some abstract paintings, a title or caption provided by the artist. Which brings us back to the Gordon's gin advert once again.

The important thing about signs like this is that they remind us that communication is always a creative process. Even with a camera there is (of course) some creativity, but with abstract visual signs, or with language, the point becomes inescapable. Constructing signs, and communicating through signs, is not about copying reality; on the contrary it is about signification (a key concept), producing meanings (signifieds) using more or less arbitrary symbols (signifiers). We are, however, discussing a conventional and collective process of creativity, because the arbitrary symbols which we have chosen to signify our experience must, at least potentially, be available for decoding by somebody else. It makes sense therefore, to say that we have inherited collectively, within our common culture, a variety of more or less arbitrary systems of signification (codes), and that it is by making choices and combining elements within these systems that we are able to communicate meanings.

De Saussure makes two further points about the practice of signification, which follow from this discussion of the arbitrary nature of the sign. The first point is concerned with the general characteristics of sign systems (and we must remember, again, that human language systems are taken as the model). The second point is an argument about the meanings which these sign systems construct. Firstly then, if sign systems are more or less arbitrary, so that their meanings can only be defined by cultural codes and conventions, de Saussure suggests that these codes must be founded on a principle of distinguishing one sign from another. Language, he suggests, is a 'system of differences', where the meaning of each element is defined, not by its natural or intrinsic properties, but by its relation to other elements in the system. What is being sugested here is that the signified of tree/*arbre* is a relative concept – 'tree-ness'– which we can only define if we can distinguish trees from bushes, hedgerows and so on. Semiology is then, as a matter of principle, relativistic in its theory of the construction of meaning.

It follows, furthermore, that different sign systems may, in so far as they make these distinctions in different ways, construct different versions of 'reality'. That is to say, if signs do not have intrinsic meanings, but on the contrary signify our experiences; and if these signs, in so far as they are arbitrary, rely on culturally specific codes and conventions, then it follows that the codes and conventions used by one culture to make sense of its experiences may differ from those used by another. It then becomes possible to suggest that in their use of different sign systems, different cultures will construct different 'life-worlds'. We've all heard about the Eskimos with their eighteen words for different shades of white. More relevant to our present purposes is Judith Williamson's (1986) essay in which she shows that advertising for Hoover vacuum cleaners now allows us to distinguish between three different types of dirt! (1) In representing our experience of the world, in culturally specific forms, sign systems are also shaping and defining those experiences. Developments in sign systems allow for the construction of new experiences – for instance certain developments in advertising have constructed the experience of the knowing consumer.

Ultimately, this argument raises fundamental philosophical questions about the construction of our experience and what we take to be 'reality'. As de Saussure points out, the idea that signs are used, as they were first used by Adam, simply to give fixed names to God's creatures, is (in the general sense of the word) a myth. On the contrary, sign systems produce new signifiers and signifieds, and they permit the combination and re-combination of signs to construct new experiences. This brief discussion of advertising supports de Saussure's general point. For even where the photographic sign is highly motivated and thereby instantly recognisable, it is of course, at a second level, an entirely arbitrary convention which associates cosmetics with romance and cultural sophistication. And to the extent that the formula for cosmetics advertising may develop and change – perhaps through external pressure (such as legislation), or in search of new ways of appealing to the consumer, all sorts of new meanings are possible. In short, though our mythologies may at first appear obvious and natural, they are in fact arbitrary and conventional – as arbitrary as the proposition about that little green rectangle in the ad for Gordon's gin.

5   CASE STUDY: TV NEWS

The principles of text analysis introduced in this chapter are basic principles which can be applied to any kind of media text. That is to say, all texts consist of signs, in which the reader/viewer is invited to associate certain physical or material forms (signifiers) with certain mental processes (signifieds). The signifiers do not necessarily look like the signifieds so, in making these associations, it is necessary to learn culturally specific codes and conventions. On the one hand, these are codes which may be shared by every member of a culture (for example, everyone who speaks the same language); but on the other, they may be very specific indeed (such as targeting that relatively small section of the population who can remember bits of dialogue from *Casablanca*). We have seen that the signified may be a simple and literal denotation, but also that this may give rise to secondary processes of connotation, in which general cultural mythologies are mobilised. Typically, where there is more than one possible interpretation, a text will attempt to place one meaning, its 'preferred reading' in dominance.

All the above points can, for instance, be applied to a media text which is apparently not in the business of selling commodities to consumers – that is, to the text of television news. In fact, to suggest that television news is reproducing cultural mythologies may seem to be controversial (it is almost certainly not what the broadcasters themselves would say!); but it is, nevertheless, a useful way of understanding how the news works as a media text, and, in particular, what people might mean when they accuse TV news of 'bias'. Let us remind ourselves then, initially, of two key features of this particular media text. First, it is constrained (legally) to tell the truth as best it can, and this not only means not making things up (dealing in fact as opposed to fiction), it also means aiming for objectivity and balance. Second, the news is a continuous text: there is no conclusion to the news – it is constantly updated and it punctuates many people's daily lives on a repeated, regular, scheduled basis.

However, like all media texts, TV news is also a combination of signs which are chosen to convey particular meanings. The signs are mainly visual and verbal, but there are other auditory signs, such as sounds emanating from locations and, of course, the sounds chosen to accompany opening and closing graphics (the connotation of signature tunes is perhaps a topic for analysis in itself). The visual and verbal signs which form the major part of news bulletins are carefully edited and synchronised. There is a particular kind of relationship, which may be defined as 'illustrative', between the use of visual imagery and the verbal narration spoken by the newscaster. This illustrative use of the image is one way in which the news gives the impression of 'fact' – that is to say, factuality is a produced consequence of this text's particular structure, and I shall return to such questions of structure in my next chapter.

Nevertheless, we have no reason to doubt the accuracy of the information provided, spoken as it is by a familiar and authoritative newscaster, and illustrated by visual evidence. We assume also, that the journalists have checked their stories, and that people really did say what they are quoted as having said. Some critics, such as the Glasgow University Media Group, have shown that the news has occasionally been 'economical' with the truth, and even misleading, particularly in times of war or national crisis (2). There are still those who allege that certain truths about the Falklands War have yet to be reported. But to make this kind of criticism we need to have access to privileged information, beyond that which the text actually contains. If we simply concern ourselves with the news as a media text, then we have to conclude that it does all it can, within its formula, to give the appearance of factual accuracy.

However, as we have seen, signs have connotations as well as denotations, and these connotations are open to different interpretations. As an illustration of where these interpretations can lead I will now consider three extracts from the *Nine O'Clock News* on BBC1, 20 March 1984. This was the first month of a year-long dispute in the British coal industry which, in addition to its major economic and political consequences, gave rise to many debates about TV news coverage, with the miners' union (the NUM) and its president (Arthur Scargill) claiming bias against the miners' side of the story. On 20 March, the main news story concerned picketing, and in particular the legality of police action in preventing miners from one area joining pickets in another area. Here's how the day's news was introduced by John Humphreys, for the BBC:

> The police in Kent have been told they are allowed to stop miners who are on their way to join picket lines in other areas. The High Court in London refused to grant an injunction against the Chief Constable after a number of pickets were prevented from leaving the county on Sunday. The Kent miners say they'll press for damages, and they'll continue to send pickets to other coalfields.
>
> The police operations have been attacked by miners' leader Arthur Scargill. He said they were turning the Midlands into a paramilitary state.
>
> The number of pits closed by the strike continues to grow. Tonight there are 38 pits open, four fewer than yesterday, and another 13 are only partly manned. Leicestershire has voted against by almost 9 to 1, but there are still no signs of an end to the picketing.
>
> Reporting first, from the High Court, John Fryer . . .

Now it might be possible to comment on various different aspects of this extract, depending on our particular analytical approach. For instance, a student of the media might be interested in the news values which have selected picketing as the most newsworthy and therefore the most highlighted aspect of the dispute. A critic of journalistic practice might also make something of the fact that Mr Scargill has been slightly misquoted in Humphreys' introduction (in a moment, we will consider a second extract from the same news bulletin, which contains the full text of the interview from which this quotation is taken). However, one immediate point to make is to recognise again that this inclusion of the interview within the bulletin reinforces its 'factuality' insofar as it provides direct evidence of Mr Scargill's opinion. And the fact that this is, according to the conventions of the sound-bite, a fairly lengthy interview, shows again that the BBC is presenting both sides of the story and allowing Mr Scargill to have his say.

I want to suggest that the most interesting questions to ask about this report are not so much concerned with what has been possibly omitted or censored, nor are they concerned with any overt lack of balance. Rather, it is more appropriate to focus on the way in which the news uses particular combinations of signs to present and package its (presumably accurate) information for consumption by the viewer. For instance, the reference to Mr Scargill in Humphreys' introduction is accompanied by a graphic which contains a photograph and the text '. . . a paramilitary state', on a red background (see figure 1.5). Now, Mr Scargill did use this phrase, though not quite in the way attributed to him by the newscaster; but from a semiological point of view, the main point concerns the fairly obvious connotations produced by this photograph, on this background (red equals danger, violence, communism) combined with this part of the quote, which actually

Fig. 1.5. (1–3) 'Policing the Pickets', BBCTV Nine O'Clock News, 10 March 1984. Stills by permission of BBCTV News

Fig. 1.6. Interview with Arthur Scargill, BBCTV Nine O'Clock News, *10 March 1984. Still by permission of BBCTV News*

zooms onto the TV screen, as the newscaster begins his (fifth) sentence. The *Nine O'Clock News* is therefore balanced and objective, in so far as it introduces both sides of the story; but by exploiting the semiological potential of its use of graphics, it is possible for the news to construct a form of negative visibility for an individual participant like Mr Scargill.

What can be said about the graphic which accompanies the statement about pit closures? A somewhat abstract but still recognisable sign of the mining industry (in black and red) is accompanied by a table. It may seem to be a peculiar kind of table which places by far the largest figure at the bottom, but this is consistent with the verbal report which mentions the number of pits open and partly manned, but not the much larger number of pits which are closed. Again then we can have no reason to doubt the accuracy of the figures themselves, and again the 'factuality' of the report is not at stake; but clearly a decision has been taken (consciously or otherwise) to present the figures in a particular way, and we can see where the emphasis lies.

Is this evidence of bias, as the striking miners claimed? Perhaps; but (to make the point again) it is not necessarily evidence of misreporting, or a lack of factual accuracy. Rather I think we should say, given the approach we are taking, that this TV news bulletin gives us evidence of a preferred reading. The denotations may well be factual and correct, but the connotations, suggested by the language of the report, its selection of graphics and its presentation of information, on one level reinforce its 'factuality', but on another level construct a preferred position for the viewer. In this bulletin, it is the strikers, encouraged by a leader whose politics are questionable, who are threatening the status quo, and in particular those who wish to work 'normally'.

After John Fryer has reported from the High Court, Mr Scargill is given his opportunity to comment. He is surrounded by a group of interviewers in a car park outside Broadcasting House in Leeds (see figure 1.6). What then follows is a very interesting interview, which includes the reference to a 'paramilitary state', but in a context where, arguably, the interviewee is placed under a certain amount of pressure. And in this context (his opponents would say this is typical) Mr Scargill proves himself to be something of an expert at avoiding the point of the question:

[*V/O. Film of Scargill entering BBC building*]

REPORTER: Mr Scargill began his day at the BBC's radio studios in Leeds where he took part in a phone-in programme after which he had something to say about the police operation in the coalfields.

[*Cut to Scargill surrounded by interviewers in car park*]

SCARGILL: I'm saying that the police presence in north and south Nottinghamshire and Derbyshire at the present time is unwarranted and unprecedented and it's almost tantamount to a paramilitary state. It's absolutely disgraceful when people have got to prove who they are in order to move around either that or other counties.

FIRST INTERVIEWER: Is it possible that some of your members in Nottinghamshire might appreciate the presence of police at colliery gates?

SCARGILL: I don't think anybody appreciates the imposition of police in these numbers which in fact intimidates, in my view, in an almost incredible fashion the whole situation and certainly leads to an exacerbation.

SECOND INTERVIEWER: But since the high level of police numbers there haven't been the scuffles and the violence that we've seen before.

SCARGILL: I don't believe that there were scuffles and violence to which you refer anyway. It's always possible during an industrial dispute to highlight an incident and I've no doubt that you are past masters at that. The fact that ninety-eight per cent of all the picketing that took place was, according to the information I've received from Nottinghamshire, peaceful, seems to have escaped your attention. I'm satisfied with the reports that I got both from the Yorkshire NUM and the Nottinghamshire NUM that things were not as bad as you're painting them and in fact were in line with normal picketing activities. The Nottinghamshire NUM of course take their own decisions and so do the NUM in the Yorkshire area. The National Executive Committee unanimously agreed that any area that wished to take strike action would do so, and that remains the position.

THIRD
INTERVIEWER: Any violence, small though it is, must worry you though.
SCARGILL: Oh violence from the BBC and ITV certainly worries me, yes.

Opinions may be divided on the impact of an interview like this. I have not carried out a survey, but I know from discussions with students that this can be seen as yet another example of a politician using the media to score points, rather than answering the questions in an honest and truthful fashion. On the other hand there are those, including some teachers of media studies, who find such interviews clever and entertaining and who regard Mr Scargill as a master of the art of the political interview (3). In the last line he subverts the point of the question by turning it back on his interviewers, in a way which some may see as witty and amusing – and, interestingly enough, the interview is cut at this point. Is there some sort of strategy operating in the presentation of this extended interview on the Nine O'Clock News? Is the BBC itself in the business of constructing an open, polysemic text which can be interpreted in different ways by its viewers?

In fact, I think we might see Mr Scargill's position, and his tactics, as further evidence of a 'preferred reading' in the news. To be precise, this news bulletin is working to construct a preferred reading of the situation in the coalfields where three basic propositions are implicit: proposition one is that all violence is wrong; proposition two is that picketing causes violence; and proposition three is that the police, by controlling picketing, have prevented violence and restored order to the situation. It is from this perspective, rather than any simple 'neutral' position that the questions put by the interviewers are coming; and in the heat of the moment, the second interviewer even neglects to cloak this perspective in the form of a question – rather he puts a direct proposition to Mr Scargill. For his part, Mr Scargill appears to be aware of this preferred reading, in that he resolutely refutes any suggestion of propositions two and three, and only accepts proposition one on his own

Fig. 1.7. Michael Sullivan reports, BBCTV Nine O'Clock News, 10 March 1984. Still by permission of BBCTV News

(somewhat contentious) terms. As an interviewee, he employs a variety of tactics: recycling the interviewers' questions (so, for example, the 'presence of police' becomes an 'imposition'); attacking their claims to objectivity (so they become 'past masters' at highlighting incidents); but also, crucially, exploiting all possible connotations of the word 'violence'.

This is an example that illustrates the important point about preferred readings, and indeed about signification generally – which has already been made in passing, but can now be restated more precisely. The existence of preferred readings only really becomes apparent insofar as they are contested, either by their intended audience (for example, perverse readings of the Predictor advert) or by participants in the text itself (for example, perverse interviewees like Mr Scargill). Such contestation is a precondition for the implicit meaning to be seen as 'preferred' – otherwise it would simply be taken as 'natural', which as we have seen is the situation mythology prefers. In fact, the concept of preferred reading was first applied empirically in David Morley's audience research (1978) which looked at the different interpretations made by audience groupings of the now defunct BBC news magazine programme *Nationwide*. It was found that some audience groupings produced 'negotiated' and 'oppositional' interpretations of this programme, thus refusing the full force of its preferred, or 'dominant' reading. The more general point again, is that all signification, operating through essentially arbitrary meaning systems, is open to dispute and contestation (and this connects with the concept of ideology discussed in Chapter 6). The preferred reading will strive for dominance, but the polysemic possibilities of the text are unlikely to be completely closed.

To return to our news bulletin, here is how Michael Sullivan, the BBC's reporter from Yorkshire, sums up the situation (see figure 1.7).

[*Piece to camera. Office building in background*]

MS: With the news today that the Leicestershire coalminers have also voted against the strike, Mr Scargill must now be considering the growing pressure from the rank and file inside his union, and from some of the members of the National Executive itself, for an emergency meeting of that executive – something that must happen if there's to be the strike ballot that many miners want. But tonight, here in Sheffield, there's no sign of Mr Scargill relaxing his resistance to that idea.

[*Zoom up to lighted office window*]

Thus, Mr Scargill's comments on the police action, and his gibes at the media are contextualised by a commentary which is not of his own choosing. In Chapter 3, I will return to the structural significance of commentary like this, which is a basic part of the regime through which TV covers newsworthy events. Here, I will simply observe that this commentary is built round a speculative scenario (an emergency meeting of the National Executive) which is itself driven by a (more or less explicitly stated) political agenda (the need for a strike ballot). In fact such a ballot never occurred – but arguably the function of the commentary is less to do with predicting a likely outcome to the dispute, and more to do with constructing a grid of expectations through which it can be interpreted. Here, the preferred reading, which has been temporarily contested by Mr Scargill, is once again reinforced, and in a way which ties together all the threads of the bulletin as a whole. For if Mr Scargill's position is problematic, it is because he is undemocratic, preferring to operate in a way which we know to be characteristic of 'paramilitary states', through the blinkered mentality of his own bureaucratic power.

Is it possible then, to suggest that there may be a mythology at work in TV news – a mythology which is perhaps most apparent in times of crisis? Following Krishnan Kumar (1977) it can be argued that, since the 1950s, broadcast news has adopted a particular interpretation of its statutory obligations. In this interpretation, objectivity is defined as taking neither side in matters of controversy but, on the contrary, acting as a public referee – 'holding the middle ground'. This middle ground, however, is not an empty space; on the contrary it contains certain values and attitudes, for example that people would in general prefer to be 'working normally'. The middle ground consists of peaceful law-abiding citizens, as opposed to violent lawbreakers, and it believes in democracy as opposed to 'paramilitary states'. The middle ground is protected by the police, who are 'only doing their job' in times of social unrest. In short, the middle ground is the space inhabited by the imagined audience for TV news, who from the privacy of their sitting rooms, on a daily basis, tune in to observe the controversy and disruption caused by 'extremists' like Mr Scargill.

In this context then, the word 'bias' is actually a rather misleading metaphor. In literal terms, it is not really possible to talk about a bias towards the centre. Much more appropriate, I would suggest, is the use of Barthes' concept of mythology to define the meaning systems which are naturalised in media texts, to which the connotations of these texts are directly related, and which are consumed by readers/viewers, insofar as they function mythologically, in a largely uncritical, taken-for-granted manner. To be sure, the text I have analysed here is somewhat unusual in that it does dramatise differences and conflicts which (briefly) call the dominant mythology into question. However, as the third extract shows, the mythology of the 'middle ground' is re-established. For the most part, it simply 'goes without saying'; it is implied, rather than directly stated, as in the connotations produced by the graphics in the first extract.

In this chapter I have tried to show how a few very basic semiological concepts can be used to analyse the ways in which meanings are constructed in media texts. It is important to recognise that there are different levels of meaning (denotation, connotation) and that texts operate in an intertextual environment where meanings are transferred from one context to another. It is helpful if we can begin to define and categorise the meaning systems which we discover. Semiology provides a starting point for this enterprise, but certainly not the last word – and so we will return to consider further critical approaches to the question of meaning in later chapters. Meanwhile, it is also necessary to recognise that the construction of meaning is only one element, and possibly even a minor element, in any media text. Whatever their meanings (stated or implied) texts also provide for a variety of different kinds of experience, which we can now begin to investigate by turning our attention to textual structures.

FURTHER READING

Perhaps the most accessible essay by Barthes, which demonstrates his use of semiology, is 'The Rhetoric of the Image', Barthes R. (1977) edited by Stephen Heath. The reader might also like to tackle Barthes' pioneering essay

'Myth Today', in Barthes R. (1973), though not without the useful clarification provided by John Storey (1993, p. 77-85). The semiological approach to media studies is also introduced in Fiske J. (1982), and applied to advertising in Williamson J. (1978) and in Dyer G. (1982).

The theory of preferred reading (or preferred meaning) is outlined in Stuart Hall's essay 'Encoding/decoding', in Hall S. *et al.* (eds) (1980). This theory is applied to TV news in Hartley J. (1982); and in the light of the argument presented here, a debatable analysis of TV news coverage of the 1984 coal dispute is offered by Len Masterman in 'The Battle of Orgreave', in Masterman L. (ed) (1984).

2

Structures

In media texts, signs never appear in isolation or even, like road signs, one at a time. Rather, as we have already seen, signs appear in combinations of various kinds, such as: flowery tissues, box, verbal captions etc. Clearly therefore, the meaning of any particular sign is conditioned, or qualified, by its appearance alongside others. In other contexts, roses might signify 'Englishness', while the use of the term 'boutique' might refer to a fashionable form of shopping. The specific way in which the different signs contained in a text have been combined together is known in semiology as the text's syntagmatic structure. In this chapter we will investigate different kinds of syntagmatic structure commonly found in media texts, and we will proceed, in Chapter 3, to consider some potential consequences of these structures for the experience of the reader/viewer.

In the work of de Saussure and Barthes, a distinction is made between the syntagmatic and the paradigmatic dimensions of texts. The syntagmatic dimension is the way in which the signs which appear in a text are combined in a particular structure. The paradigmatic dimension suggests that, at least in theory, these signs will have been chosen from a range of options, and therefore that their meaning is conditioned, not only by their combination with other signs in the text, but also, to some extent, by our awareness of other possibilities which have not been used. In the Kleenex® ad, roses are featured (not daffodils or daisies, which have symbolic connotations in other contexts). A paradigm is therefore a class of potential signs from which a selection is made. The chosen signs will then be combined, in more or less predictable ways, to form a syntagmatic structure.

A brief glance at all the adverts we have previously considered will suggest that, in fact, there is a fairly standard syntagmatic structure in this type of magazine advert. In each case, the page is dominated by a visual sign. A verbal sign may or may not be superimposed on this visual sign, but what always seems to happen is that a further verbal sign (or in the Predictor example, a quite complex verbal text) appears at the foot of the page. As a structure of meanings, it seems that the visual sign presents a number of polysemic signifiers and that these may be reinforced by an equally polysemic verbal sign, which typically contains some form of double meaning – an ambiguity or a pun. It is the function of the text at the bottom of the page to resolve these polysemic possibilities and to relate them to the product. In its abstraction, the advert for Gordon's gin is a very clear example of this strategy: the green rectangle on the flesh-coloured background means anything or nothing until the caption provides the answer.

This use of the verbal sign to provide a title or caption for a polysemic visual sign was defined, by Roland Barthes, as anchorage. Anchorage is perhaps the most simple form of textual structure, where images are combined with words. Anchorage places a verbal sign in a position of authority with respect to the other signs which appear in the text, insofar as it provides the 'last word'. There is then, a kind of hierarchy among the various signs combined in texts of this type: some signs carry more weight than others. Some verbal signs make authoritative statements ('Lux. Star treatment for your skin'), whereas others make suggestions or function as quotations.

It is not necessary or inevitable, however, that media texts will be structured in this hierarchical fashion; nor is it the case that the verbal will always have priority over the visual. Some texts make authoritative statements, but there are others, structured differently, which give the reader/viewer more space to speculate on what the meaning of the text might be. There is also a category of text where the phrase 'making a statement' is perhaps inappropriate, since these texts are concerned with telling stories, and stories may of course be fictional. In this chapter, we will consider three general types of syntagmatic structure, which I will classify as argument, montage and narrative. Adverts which are anchored by propositions relating to products (this is most clearly the case with the Predictor ad) are functioning, in this analysis, as arguments and, since this is perhaps the most basic form of persuasive communication, we will consider it first.

2 ARGUMENT

In essence, an argument makes a proposition, or series of propositions about something, and attempts to persuade or convince the reader/viewer that the propositions are true. It has to be said that, in some of the adverts we have considered, the strategy of persuasion is unorthodox, either because the proposition is frivolous ('A man in his birthday suit'), or because, as in the advert for Kleenex® tissues, it is highly metaphorical. Furthermore, as complex texts, many adverts which contain arguments also contain other elements which have a different function – for instance the image in the Predictor ad which tells a story. In the end, however, this advert is operating as an argument because it is anchored by verbal signs which make propositions: 'You can rely on Predictor'; 'You can trust Predictor'; Predictor is 'right first time'.

In a moment, we look in greater detail at the way this particular argument is structured. Before we attempt this analysis however, it should be acknowledged that, unlike montage and narrative, the study of forms of argumentation has not been taken very far in the development of media studies. This may be because the analysis of textual structures has been pioneered through the study of feature films which do not function as arguments – though documentary films, as we shall see, sometimes do. Thus, in developing an initial approach to the structure of argumentation it has been necessary to adapt a more general approach to the study of persuasive communication. In the USA, in particular, schools of communication have traditionally placed the study of rhetoric at the centre of the curriculum. One aspect of this study is practical, in that it contains advice on how to improve powers of persuasion, both spoken and written. Another aspect, however, is analytical and this will serve as a basis from which to investigate argument as a type of syntagmatic structure.

A useful model is, for example, provided by James McCroskey (1978), incorporating both the classical rhetoric of Aristotle and other contemporary research. According to this model, an argument can be seen to present a proposition or series of propositions (which McCroskey calls 'claims'), each of which is potentially supported by two other elements, namely: evidence (or 'data') and a form of justification (or 'warrant'). The syntagmatic structure of an argument is therefore serial, in that one proposition follows another; but it is also hierarchical, in that each proposition usually relies on supporting statements. There is an important distinction to be made between the two kinds of supporting statement. To be successful, the supporting statement must be believed – but there are two levels of belief. One level is empirical belief regarding matters of fact, and what counts is that the evidence is believed, whether or not the facts are true. The second level is conceptual, relating to what is generally believable, likely or plausible. Whatever the evidence, if a proposition offends our general level of belief, we are likely to conclude that it is 'unwarranted' or unjustified.

This model can be illustrated with reference to the argument for Predictor. This argument contains two propositions, each of which is backed up by evidence on one hand, and some general justification on the other. We should note, however, that general justifications ('warrants'), as matters of common belief, need not necessarily appear explicitly in the text – they can be implied or assumed. Indeed their status as common belief is probably enhanced by the extent to which they can 'go without saying'. Thus for Predictor:

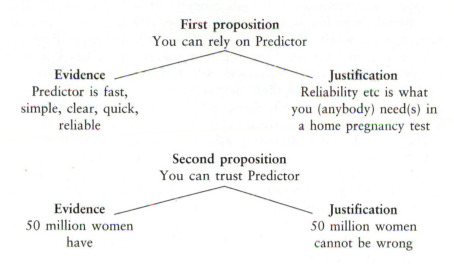

First proposition
You can rely on Predictor

Evidence
Predictor is fast,
simple, clear, quick,
reliable

Justification
Reliability etc is what
you (anybody) need(s) in
a home pregnancy test

Second proposition
You can trust Predictor

Evidence
50 million women
have

Justification
50 million women
cannot be wrong

McCroskey usefully identifies the major types of proposition, evidence and justification which are commonly found in arguments (I have slightly modified his terminology). Thus, there are four main types of proposition. The first is factual, for example it claims that an event took place, or that something does or does not exist. The second type of proposition is definitive, concerned with how an event or object etc. might be defined or what it might be called. The third type of proposition is evaluative, concerned with what is to be considered good or bad, positive or negative, desirable or undesirable. The fourth type of proposition is advocative, that is, it makes a case for what should be done about something. In these terms, it seems to me that the propositions in the Predictor ad are quite clearly evaluative, in that they are not concerned with the product's existence or definition, nor are they advocating a course of action; rather they are concerned with establishing the product's desirability on the basis of its reliability and trustworthiness.

Evidence in arguments comes in three main forms or, rather, functions at three different levels. The lowest level is simply what is commonly held to be matter of fact, or what we might call 'common knowledge'. The second level is what is asserted to be matter of fact, and relies for its credibility on the authority of the text. The third level is properly constituted evidence or data, which may not be common knowledge, and which thus requires the appearance of objectivity – for instance, it appears to result from an acceptable method of fact-finding such as experimentation, social survey, interview or quotation from bibliographical research. In the Predictor ad, the evidence for the first proposition is mere assertion (that is second level evidence) in that we are simply told about the qualities the product allegedly possesses. However the evidence for the second proposition appears as objective data, and interestingly, given the force of this data ('over 50 million women worldwide'), no further justification is necessary.

Justifications, which McCroskey calls 'warrants', are again classified under three main headings. There are motivational justifications (closely associated with evaluative propositions) which implicate what is generally considered positive or negative, desirable or undesirable. There are, secondly, authoritative justifications, which support a proposition by appealing to the authority of the proposer – this is the case 'because I say so'. There are, thirdly, substantive justifications, which are the main focus for traditional approaches to rhetoric. Here we are concerned with generally acceptable principles of causality (or deductive reasoning), generalisation and classification (or inductive reasoning). Substantive justifications can also be produced by indicators (where the evidence indicates that a proposition is true) and, more problematically, by analogies or comparisons. McCroskey gives detailed examples of each type of substantive justification. Returning to the Predictor ad, it would seem that the first evaluative proposition, with its asserted evidence, is supported by a motivational justification; whereas the second proposition relies on an (unstated) substantive generalisation – a form of inductive reasoning from the 50 million women worldwide to what is the case for all women, who might (therefore) put their trust in Predictor.

It is interesting that, by comparison with the other ads we have considered, Predictor should include this explicit and fairly lengthy form of argument. As was suggested above, this might be because it is a difficult product to advertise, and not only because it relates to intimate biological matters. The first part of the argument, with its asserted evidence and motivational justification is practically tautological – that is to say, it is almost completely circular: 'You can rely on Predictor . . . because Predictor is reliable'. Circular arguments are generally a sign of anxiety – as are explicitly authoritative justifications, and they are most likely to be produced when the preferred reading of a text is debatable. Other adverts, however, do not require such elaborate argumentation, indeed they present no evidence or justification at all. In the examples of Lux and Gordon's, the anchorage takes the form of a witty proposition; and in some cases, where a product is particularly well known, its brand name can simply 'speak for itself'.

Let me now then, summarise the model for argumentation which I have taken (with some terminological modifications) from McCroskey:

Model for argumentation

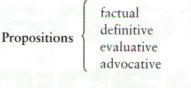

Propositions
{
factual
definitive
evaluative
advocative
}

Evidence
{
common knowledge
assertion
data:
   experiment
   survey
   interview
   quotation
   bibliography
}

Justifications
{
motivational
authoritative
substantive:
   causation
   generalisation
   classification
   indication
   analogy
}

This model will serve as an initial approximation towards the constituent elements of the argument, as employed as a syntagmatic structure in many media texts. It will also, I hope, prove useful to students in developing their understanding of the academic essay, which is (or should be) precisely a series of connected propositions, related to a particular topic or question, supported by specific evidence and general forms of justification. Are the connections between propositions in academic arguments always necessarily logical? In the strictest philosophical sense, the answer is probably no; but the point is that the reader will always be looking for logical links in a series of academic propositions, which is why essays are enhanced by the use of connecting words – however, moreover, furthermore, therefore and so on. Also, in academic essays the evidence should always take the form of properly constituted data, and the justifications will be substantive.

3   MONTAGE

The Billy Graham crusade to Scotland in 1991 announced itself in the form of a challenging proposition: 'Life Has Meaning' (see figure 2.1). This advert appeared on billboards throughout the country and was also contained within a leaflet which was distributed door to door. The leaflet contains a little essay about 'Life', and about Billy Graham's contribution to its meaning. Here, there are a series of propositions which link the questions many people are likely to ask with the answers Billy Graham has found. There is, condensed into a couple of paragraphs, considerable evidence of Billy Graham's track record. Finally, in addition to the motivational justification which is implicit

Fig. 2.1. 'Life Has Meaning'. Billboard/leaflet publicity for Billy Graham (Scotland, 1991). By permission of the Billy Graham Organization

in the proposition that many people are asking these questions, there is again (as in the Predictor ad) the substantive generalisation that the message has 'made sense to millions'. The leaflet, in short, presents us with a clearly argumentative form of advertising.

However, there is something very interesting about the context for this argument, within the strategy of the campaign as a whole. The leaflet which elaborated on the theme of the crusade, and issued the personal invitation to attend, followed, as I have mentioned, an extensive billboard campaign. This is how the people of Scotland first became aware of Billy Graham's impending visit. But the billboard campaign was itself in two parts. Part two announced (in black and white) that 'Life Has Meaning', and identified the various dates and venues. Part one, which appeared a week or two earlier, presented a riot of colourful imagery, together with the question to which the second poster, and Billy Graham's message, provided the answer. I, for one, was intrigued by the first poster when it appeared – which was presumably the intended effect.

The riot of colourful imagery in the 'Does Life Have Meaning?' poster is, of course, a collection of visual and verbal signs (see figure 2.2). Some signs are instantly recognisable, familiar faces – others are anonymous and obscure. Many signs are international, but some specifically relate to Scotland. The majority of the visual signs are highly motivated, but some are more abstract and arbitrary. Some signs appear to be clustered together (the politicians, slightly left of centre) but the connections between others seem tenuous and debatable. What kind of message is this?

It is clearly not an argument. The poster is not making propositions and its images are not functioning as evidence. Furthermore, its signs are not structured into any kind of recognisable series, certainly not a series in which we can detect a logical or rational order. On the contrary, we might almost conclude that the structure of these images is random, as if they have been thrown in the air and allowed to fall anywhere. Closer inspection, however, shows that the poster is not quite as random as it first appears, and anyway if the syntagmatic dimension is somewhat obscure, the paradigmatic dimension (news and current affairs) is more familiar.

I shall call this type of syntagmatic structure a montage. I am using this word in a way which is more general than its more specific uses in film theory. There 'montage' refers either to the general process of film editing, or to a more specific style of editing pioneered by several Soviet directors in the 1920s (Pudovkin, Eisenstein, Vertov and others) (1). This film theory, as we shall see, is relevant to this discussion, but we are now, I believe, familiar with a more general use of montage, as exemplified by the poster 'Does Life Have Meaning?'. In *Ways of Seeing*, John Berger describes the common domestic practice of assembling visual images (postcards, photographs, magazine images, children's drawings) on pinboards. Berger points out that it is because images are mechanically reproducible that they are frequently used in this way. A related concept, sometimes used in the study of subcultures (Hebdige, 1979), is 'bricolage' – the art of piecing together diverse items so as to construct a new fashion or style (classically in Punk: the bin-liner, the safety pin, the leopard skin, the chains and so on). Where this kind of assemblage, or piecing together, occurs in media texts let us, for want of a better word, call it 'montage'.

In many ways, montage is the antithesis of argument. As the Billy Graham Organisation recognised, it is the function of montage to raise questions, whereas an argument might try to provide the answers. But the difference between montage and argument goes deeper than this. It is partly to do with the fact that, in an argument, the connections between signs (propositions) is, or should be, explicit; whereas the structure of montage is less clear (and so needs working out). However, the difference is also to do with the type of information the two different structures can contain. As we have seen, it is possible for an argument to contain new information, such as properly

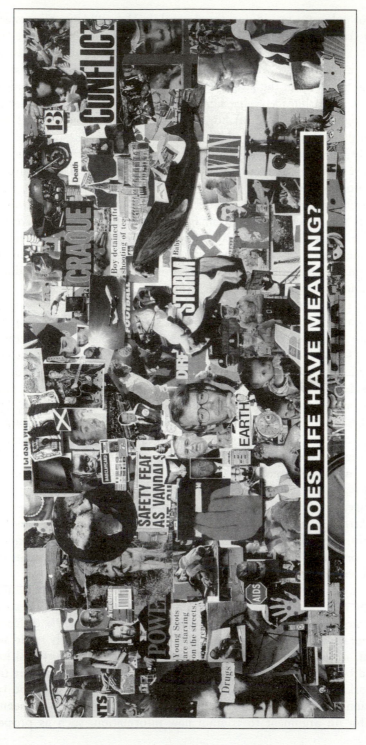

Fig. 2.2. 'Does Life Have Meaning?' Billboard/leaflet publicity for Billy Graham (Scotland, 1991). By permission of the Billy Graham Organization

constituted evidence (data) which the reader is encountering for the first time. Typically, however, montage deals in old information, instantly recognisable and reproducible images, which it recycles. Working out the meaning of montage is made easier by the fact that many of its signs are already familiar. We can then, perhaps, make the following observation: an argument constructs the (potentially) unfamiliar; whereas montage deconstructs the familiar – it makes the familiar strange.

Of course most uses of montage are certainly not random, though they might first appear to be so. In media texts there is usually a logic of some kind within this type of syntagmatic structure, but the point is that it is at first obscure and so must be discovered. As we have seen, there is a cluster of politicians at the centre of 'Does Life Have Meaning?' and it is probably no accident that the current British Prime Minister is given prominence. There is then a certain associative similarity within this cluster of signs. On the other hand, towards the top of the poster, left of centre, there is an image of a black boy adjacent to a Barclaycard. Is there a logic which connects these two, very dissimilar images? If so, it is a logic which is constructed out of their juxtaposition, rather than any apparent association, and it involves the reader/viewer in a conceptual process.

These various possibilities of montage were explored in theory as well as in practice by the Soviet film makers of the 1920s. In films like Eisenstein's *Strike* (1924) and *Battleship Potemkin* (1925) we encounter a range of different effects and principles of editing. These are narrative films, but the story is constantly interrupted, so to speak, by editing which draws our attention to conceptual comparisons and contrasts. In *Strike*, for example, the police spies are caricatured as animals (fox, monkey, bulldog) and the shots of these creatures in the film function as visual metaphors. This is 'parallel montage' which constructs a relationship of similarity between one sign and another. Conversely, while the company stockholders are enjoying a lavish drinking session, Eisenstein cuts to shots of police on horseback charging a workers' meeting. The relationship here is one of contrast or opposition, but again a metaphorical parallel is constructed in the action of one stockholder as he squeezes a lemon. The squeezing of the lemon becomes a metaphor for the exploitation of the factory workers, and this is emphasised by a caption: 'Squeeze hard...and you get juice'.

Eisenstein believed that it was through a 'montage of oppositions', or juxtaposition of contrasting signs, that a new, or third meaning might be created in the mind of the spectator. Montage editing would therefore follow a dialectical principle whereby a thesis, juxtaposed against its antithesis, would create the dynamic conditions necessary for a process of synthetic reasoning. The lavish decadence of the stockholders contrasted with police violence towards the workers might encourage the spectator to make the appropriate political connections. Perhaps similar processes of reasoning might be stimulated by the poster 'Does Life Have Meaning?' where, for example, signs of innocence (the child) are juxtaposed with images of violence, corruption, dictatorship and so on, or where signs of threatened nature (the whale) are placed alongside images of machines and technology (2).

However, as the Soviet film directors also recognised, montage can simply look good. That is to say, it can be used for aesthetic as well as philosophical purposes, for instance in emphasising abstract or formal similarities between one image and another. Montage is generally fast moving, visually dynamic and exciting. The reproduction of the Billy Graham poster in this book does not at all do justice to its aesthetic appearance on a billboard which gave to the campaign additional general connotations of liveliness, social relevance and modernity. For similar reasons, montage is frequently used in pop videos, and in adverts designed to appeal to the young ('You can't beat the feeling'). Edited to music, the frequently striking aesthetic qualities of montage are given rhythmic potential. But the Soviet film makers also exploited this potential (see, for example, the build up of speed in the last section of *Battleship Potemkin*), and this was of course some time before the use of recorded soundtracks.

In general then, as a type of syntagmatic structure, montage works through juxtaposition. These juxtapositions may be emphasising conceptual similarities or contrasts, or they may be used for aesthetic effect, but the crucial point, by comparison with an argument (or indeed a narrative, which we will consider next), is that the connections between signs in a montage structure are implicit, not explicit. A montage structure therefore involves the reader/viewer in an active process of working out the logic (if any) implicit in the inter-connections. Advocates of montage (artists, film makers, designers) sometimes claim that, unlike more traditional forms of argumentation and story-telling, a montage structure empowers the recipient in the process of communication. Unfortunately however, in the Billy Graham example, the intriguing possibilities opened up by the first poster were subsequently closed down by the second – in the form of a general overarching proposition with an (implicit) authoritative justification. 'Life' does 'Have Meaning', after all, because Billy Graham says so.

4   NARRATIVE

Narrative is the third type of syntagmatic structure most commonly found in media texts. It has also been subjected to the most detailed analysis and theory. In particular, narrative has been the focus for the school of thought which, in media studies we know as 'structuralism', which overlaps to some extent with the work of Roland Barthes discussed in the previous chapter. Broadly speaking, following their interest in mythologies, structuralists have sought to discover rules and regularities in the most ancient practice by which cultural meaning systems are commonly reproduced – that is, through the practice of storytelling. There was some excitement in the possibility that the elements of narrative might be a universal human inheritance, which would operate across cultures as well as within them. In Chapter 4, we will look briefly at one attempt (among many) to apply Vladimir Propp's influential analysis of the Russian folk-tale (Propp, 1970) to a contemporary media text. In Chapter 3, we will also consider some aspects of recent film theory, which have also made use of structuralist approaches to narrative, concentrating on the way in which Hollywood narrative cinema seeks to involve and 'position' the spectator.

Different approaches to narrative analysis are, therefore, scattered throughout the pages of this book, and are discussed selectively. In this chapter, my purpose is to provide an introduction to narrative as a syntagmatic structure, a particular way of combining signs, and to make general comparisons between this and the other kinds of structure (argument, montage) previously considered. A generally accepted basic definition of narrative is that it consists of signs arranged, not in a logical, but rather in a chronological order. That is to say, the key signs in a narrative do not have the status of propositions, rather they function as *events*. Propositions are not entirely absent from narrative texts (for instance, they may be spoken by characters) but they have a secondary role in comparison with an argument.

However, although they have a key role, events as such are not the only defining feature of narrative. A general introduction to this type of syntagmatic structure may be provided by considering what is the most basic and common form of storytelling, namely the oral narrative. Short oral narratives (anecdotes) are frequently produced in media texts, particularly in broadcasting, where in interview situations, interviewees are invited to recount experiences or, sometimes, stories they have heard. The following anecdote is interesting, not only because it was aired on a TV chat show (*Wogan*, 17 March 1984), and also because it refers to a TV game show of which the interviewee, Bob Monkhouse, was the host – it is also a fine example of a well-structured oral narrative (Bob has told this story many times), and so we can use this to explore the characteristics of narratives in general:

W: Remember when you used to do *The Golden Shot* live? That was actually my first appearance on British television with you in *The Golden Shot*. Wasn't that a terrifying show to do?

M: I think *The Golden Shot* helped me immensely because I had a kind of glib or flip image on TV. But when I went out and did that show with not just egg on my face, omelettes seen forming on my chin, we had incidents on that – did I ever tell you about the loony priest we had on *The Golden Shot*?

Right, we moved up to Birmingham, I'm talking years ago, 1968, **and this crazy priest starts writing in, Father Pollock.** We didn't always refer to him as that – we found a variation on that. We found two variations, the kinder of which was Pillock.

He starts writing in saying you shouldn't show weapons on television on a Sunday. 'The machinery of death', he said, 'you should not show on television on a Sunday'. **And he said he wanted to come to the studio and wanted to be in the studio.** I think to administer the last rites to someone who had been struck down by a bolt. So the producer at that time suffered fools more gladly than I did and the priest came. **So this particular week, Father Pollock is sitting in the front row,** and as you said, the show is live, it had to be. I should remind perhaps those who don't remember *The Golden Shot* that you had to see the image of a target on your television screen at home in order to say on the telephone . . .

W: 'Up a bit', 'down a bit', and all that.

M: That's right, guide events in a television studio maybe 200 miles away. Great single idea for a show. Now, but once you've done that and qualified and exploded an apple you then come to the studio.

And now a woman comes to the studio who has qualified the previous week. She came from Kelvinside, Glasgow. **And she's got a patch over one eye.** So I said, 'Is there something wrong with your left eye?' And she said, 'Why should there be something wrong with it? It's not there'. 'What do you mean it's not there? You had two eyes in the photograph you sent us when you applied to be a contestant.' She said, 'That was a glass eye; it's not currently in position. The socket is itchy, and I shall place it in position for the show.'

So now – **and then she did that** (Monkhouse twitches). So she's not only one-eyed, she's got a twitch. **She's going to the free-standing crossbow** which is the only one we had any danger to, **and the priest is in the front row.**

We go on air and Father Pollock started praying, audibly in Latin. Now the assistant floor manager's going over trying to stop him. But how do you stop a priest from praying? 'Mmmm' God knows whom he's praying for. **And the woman with the patch and the twitch is out there at the free-standing crossbow. And I'm ad-libbing the jokes,** 'Well anything can happen today, we all make mistakes, that's why they put rubbers on the end of pencils'. **She poom . . . She twitched at the moment she pulled the trigger. The bolt, or quarrel, spun off the metal frame to the target and rebounded into the audience. Guess who it hit?** Here (Monkhouse points to his forehead).

So I've never believed in the power of prayer since then. He went out like a light.

Clearly the number of sentences which are actually concerned with telling the events of this story (bold face in the transcript) makes up a relatively small proportion of the extract as a whole. Events become more significant as the narrative develops and reaches its climax, but these are interspersed with background details, explaining the rules of the game show, and also some dialogue which occurred between Monkhouse and the woman from Kelvinside (incidentally, Monkhouse does a passable, if exaggerated, imitation of a middle–class Glaswegian accent). There is something of an art in sustaining the listener's interest in the chronological sequence of events while pausing from time to time to make digressions. However the listener can follow the structure of the story because whenever Monkhouse returns to the main events he changes tense, usually from past to present, which is a common feature of oral narratives.

We have to conclude I think, that if this narrative was simply a sequence of events, it would not be very interesting or pleasurable. The background details, the asides, the enacted embellishments are as necessary to the narrative as the story itself. In the first place it seems necessary to furnish the narrative with a title (this is 'the one about the loony priest'). Secondly, the background details and explanations provide a context for the action, so that we know all along that this is a kind of cautionary tale about the perils of a live game show. Thirdly, the snatches of dialogue contribute an additional crucial feature of all true narratives – stories contain not only events but also what are conventionally termed existents. This concept refers to the setting in which the events take place, and it also refers to the characters that perform the events. In Monkhouse's story, the existents are introduced as part of the background detail, but characterisation is also enhanced by dialogue.

The result is a complex structure which not only moves forwards chronologically, but also takes the listener into and out of the story, at different levels of involvement. There seem to be at least four levels of involvement which alternate, as Monkhouse tells his anecdote:

1. **Direct address to the listener:** 'Did I ever tell you about the loony priest?'
2. **Background information:** 'We moved up to Birmingham years ago'.
3. **Story events:** 'And this crazy priest starts writing in'.
4. **Quoted dialogue:** ' "The machinery of death", he said.'

Only the last two levels are, strictly speaking, within the story. The background information is necessary to our understanding of the story, but not part of it. The direct address emphasises that this is a storytelling activity, and it seems to establish an ongoing relationship between storyteller and listener or audience.

In narrative theory it is conventional to make a distinction between 'story' and 'discourse' (Chatman, 1978; Kosloff, 1992). 'Story' consists of events and existents. 'Discourse' in this context, refers to the storytelling activity and the relationship between storyteller and audience. This is a useful distinction because it emphasises that stories are told in different ways, with different possibilities for audience participation. At the other end of the spectrum from the live, oral narrative is classic Hollywood cinema, where the only overt discourse comes in the form of a company logo, a brief announcement ('Columbia Presents') a title and a credit sequence (which, if it occurs at the end of the film, many people ignore anyway). The rest of the film is story (though it is possible to argue that an implicit discourse is detectable in its direction). Essentially the audience is constructed as a recipient and it is unusual to interrupt. The audience for an oral narrative, however, can make its own contribution, as when Wogan supplies a few phrases from *The Golden Shot*.

In general terms then, a model for narrative can be constructed as follows:

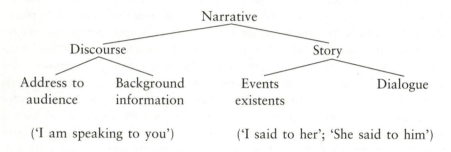

In this model, background information (Birmingham 1968) plays an intermediate role between discourse and story. This is particularly the case in oral and written narratives where its intermediate status, and the fact that it is not part of the story as such, is indicated by a distinctive tense shift – that is the use of the continuous past tense for this information. It is less common to have much background information presented in this way in visual narratives, but it is not unknown in narrative cinema. For example, following the credits, and with the aid of maps, *Casablanca* opens with background information about the refugee trail in Europe during World War II. This provides a historical context for the subsequent story and it establishes the setting in which the events of the film will develop.

Some interesting suggestions are made about television narrative by Kosloff (1992), where she observes that television often seems to want to compensate for the fact that it is an industrial and impersonal mass medium. Television, she argues, in its discourse, seeks to 'personalise the impersonal' through its use of on-screen presenters, or off-screen continuity announcers. In other words, television seeks to return, in this kind of simulation, to the conditions of live storytelling: 'I am speaking to you'; 'We bring you this episode of your favourite soap opera'. Perhaps then, the study of oral narrative is relevant to media studies in more ways than one. It is not just the fact that people like Bob Monkhouse tell stories on television, it is also that television (or broadcasting generally) institutionally reproduces the structure of oral narrative. For example, in a TV news bulletin, like the example considered previously, a live storyteller appears on the screen, supplies some necessary background information, then proceeds to narrate the events of the story, introducing its existents (like Arthur Scargill) who themselves contribute dialogue as they are interviewed.

Which leads on to a major, final point about the way such narratives work. Previously, I have contrasted argument and montage with respect to the way they present information. Arguments may present new information, whereas montage tends to raise critical questions about things we already know. What about narrative in these terms? Clearly, Bob Monkhouse's anecdote provides information which is previously unknown to the audience, unless it has heard this story before. So this is new information; but it is presented, it seems to me, in a way which invites the audience to assimilate it to the already known. 'Guess who it hit?', given the structure of the narrative, is not a difficult question to answer. This is because, although the events are unique, they follow a very familiar formula (troublemaker gets his comeuppance) and they make use of existents, particularly stereotypical characters, with which the audience is also already familiar. Narratives then, reduce the unique or the unusual to familiar and regular patterns of expectation.

To the extent that the storyteller shares a common culture with the audience, those patterns of expectation will be strengthened and even taken for granted. We all knew, didn't we, that this would be the eventual outcome? We all knew, because the narrative reproduces a conventional moral universe of goodies and baddies, normal people (like long-suffering game show hosts) and eccentrics. Stereotypes are all that is necessary for a conventional moral universe, since the function of the story is to confirm what we aleady know. Characterisation becomes necessarily more complex where there is a distance between storyteller and audience, or where the moral universe is complicated. So what kinds of stories are regularly and repeatedly told on television news, with its commitment to 'holding the middle ground'? It is instructive, I think, to reconsider both the structure and content of TV news in terms of its affinity to oral narrative.

5 CASE STUDY: BRITISH DOCUMENTARY FILMS

Many media studies courses look at a group of films made between 1929 and 1945 by the British Documentary Film Movement. These films are useful to study from a variety of different angles. They provide a unique insight into the development of film, in this period, as a means of public communication. They can be used, as they often are in film studies courses, to raise questions about 'realism' in documentary film. However, several of these films are also very interesting in terms of textual structure. They are, or were in their time, highly experimental films in which the film makers seemed to be concerned as much with the properties of the medium itself as with the effective communication of a message. Different syntagmatic structures are used, even within the confines of the same text – but these do generally conform to the structural possibilities which have been outlined in this chapter. Thus, in this case study, I shall make a comparison between three well-known films from 1935–6; these are *Housing Problems* (1935), *Coalface* (1935) and *Nightmail* (1936).

Housing Problems was made in 1935 by Arthur Elton and Edgar Anstey for the British Gas Association. It is a film that promotes the concept of slum clearance, and the rehousing of the inhabitants of the slums in planned, purpose-built, modernist housing schemes, fitted of course with gas appliances. It is interesting to observe that some of the examples singled out by the film have since been demolished (such as the Quarry Hill estate in Leeds) and, in general, the policy of public housing schemes of this kind has been under attack at least since the 1960s. This film, therefore, illustrates a very different attitude to local government than that which prevails today. It does so, however, with confidence, in a 'before and after' structure which is reminiscent of some modern forms of advertising.

The film opens with high-angle shots, some of them pans, across a district which is clearly undergoing some demolition and transformation (see figure 2.3). At the same time, an anonymous voice-over begins:

> A great deal these days is written about the slums. This film is going to introduce you to some of the people really concerned. First, Councillor Lauder, Chairman of the Stepney Housing Committee, will tell you something of the problem of slum clearance.

The role of the voice-over is partly to act as a guide to the various individuals who appear in the film. At the same time, however, the introduction starts with a factual proposition, and this signals the fact that the film as a whole is presenting its audience with an argument.

Councillor Lauder, who is also given a voice-over and is never shown in the film, then begins to speak. As he speaks, the film cuts to give precise illustrations of what he is saying:

> The problem of the slum faces us because in the early days rows upon rows of ugly, badly designed houses were hastily put up to provide accommodation for the ever increasing army of workers which poured in from the country to the towns. Here are some pictures of typical slum architecture. This roof is sagging because the rafters have decayed. No amount of new tiles will put it right. When these houses were erected anyone could

Fig. 2.3. High-angle shots of slums, still from Housing Problems *(1935). By permission of the Post Office Film Library*

> build a factory right outside your front door . . . Here are examples of sheer neglect . . . Many houses have not got water laid on . . . Here's a typical interior of a decayed house . . . [etc]

In short, Councillor Lauder's role is to continue the line of argument. Here, the film develops from its initial factual proposition ('a great deal these days is written') to make an evaluative proposition ('the slum is a problem which faces us'), which is supported by a substantive (causal) justification ('because in the early days'), and subsequently by a great deal of evidence. The role of the camera is to provide visual data to support Councillor Lauder's argument. Ultimately the argument of the film begins to make advocative propositions about what needs to be done.

Today, however, the reputation of *Housing Problems* is based, not so much on Councillor Lauder, as on its use of the slum dwellers themselves, who have been invited to address the camera. This is the first time in the history of documentary film making that working-class people speak about a social problem using their own words. Following Councillor Lauder then, we are presented with a series of 'interviews':

Fig. 2.4 Mr Norwood, still from Housing Problems *(1935). By permission of the Post Office Film Library*

V/O: And now to the people who have to live in the slums. Here is Mr Norwood.

MR N: These rooms which I'm in now I have to pay ten shillings a week for and I haven't got room to swing a cat round. I've also got five other neighbours alongside me with the same predicament as I'm in myself. And I'm not only overrun with bugs, I've got mice and rats. My missus has to send out every little bit of washing there is. Every drop of water we have to go out the yard for to fetch it . . . Coming into these rooms I've had no luck since I've been in 'em. First I lost one youngster in one, then I lost another one seven weeks old.

I have put the word 'interviews' in inverted commas because, as other critics have also noted, these statements by the slum dwellers look peculiar to modern eyes (see figure 2.4). They are delivered continuously (there is some editing) and direct to camera, but the framing is such that the speaker is frequently in long-shot, and rarely in close-up – as would be normal practice for a TV documentary today. The result is what Andrew Higson (1986) has called a 'social distance' between the viewer and the participant in the film, between observer and observed. But this distance is also reinforced by the kind of statement Mr Norwood makes. His role is not to offer further propositions about the problem of slum clearance; on the contrary, he is introduced to provide additional evidence for the ongoing argument of the film. In short, what the slum dwellers provide is not their own opinions, but rather further testimony; they are presented as living examples of the problem.

It is true that other interviewees in *Housing Problems* demonstrate greater 'personality' – particularly a Mrs Attride who tells a story about the killing of a rat. It is also the case that, at the end of the film, Elton and Anstey briefly experiment with a montage of slum dwellers' statements which is used as a voice-over. In general, however, the point to be made about the syntagmatic structure of this film is the main point about any argument: it is strictly hierarchical. The voice-over takes precedence over the image, which functions as a literal illustration. And some voices have priority over others. It is an invisible middle-class voice-over that provides the evaluative and advocative propositions for which working-class witnesses provide further evidence. The same structure is used today in adverts for soap powder, which use the testimony of the housewife to bear witness to the truth of propositions delivered by a male expert or 'voice of God'.

Ultimately, *Housing Problems* should be considered in its historical context, in terms of what approaches could be taken to social problems in 1935. We can note here, however, that some documentaries in the same period, perhaps because they had a less problematic focus, were able to experiment with other textual structures. For example *Coalface* (1935), which was produced by John Grierson for the Empire Marketing Board, begins with a definitive proposition ('Coal mining is the basic industry of Britain'), provides verbal evidence and visual illustration to support this, but also allows an experimental musical soundtrack to develop as a basis for subsequent sequences of montage. Here, shots of miners and machinery are juxtaposed against a background of modernist choral music (supplied by Benjamin Britten). In one sequence, as the miners return to the surface, the music is complemented by a rhythmic visual montage of miners' faces and winding gear which, in its abstract way, seems to be attempting to re-create the psychology of the situation.

At times then, *Coalface* looks and sounds like an art film (see figure 2.5). It introduces an aesthetic, even poetic, element into its portrayal of the mining industry which, we should note, was also a feature of other representations of coalmining in the 1930s, such as George Orwell's famous essay 'Down the Mine' (1937). Whether this gives the film a coherent structure is debatable, but this would seem to be part of its strategy, as the viewer is faced with the problem of making sense out of the juxtaposition of Britten's choral chants, and a mundane recital of facts and figures by the voice-over.

Fig. 2.5. Still from Coalface *(1935). By permission of the Post Office Film Library*

Characteristically, the montage structure presents a challenge; though it has to be said that *Coalface* (like the Billy Graham campaign) finally returns to the safety of its basic proposition.

Nightmail (1936), produced by Basil Wright and Harry Watt for the GPO film unit, begins as follows:

> [*Shots of control room, Euston railway station*]
>
> FIRST WORKER: Here's a departure message for the down postal.
> SECOND WORKER: Right thank you. OK [*picks up telephone*]. Crewe control? Euston telegraph. 157 postal left at 8.30. Class six engine, 340 tons, twelve vehicles.

And we immediately realise, of course, that we are being introduced to some form of narrative. That is to say, that although this is its basic purpose, the film does not start with a proposition such as 'the GPO provides a speedy and efficient overnight delivery service'. Rather, the film immediately introduces an enigma, located in particular existents (a setting, two characters) and invites us to look forward to a sequence of events (see figure 2.6).

To be sure, as a documentary film, the narrative in *Nightmail* is not continuous, though it does contain continuous sequences (continuity editing in narrative film is discussed below, p. 68–9). In the first section, the opening enigma is immediately answered by a voice, over aerial shots of the train:

> 8.30 pm weekdays and Sundays, the down postal express leaves Euston for Glasgow, Edinburgh and Aberdeen. The postal special is a fast express but it carries no passengers. It is manned by forty post office workers. Half a million letters are sorted, picked up or dropped at full speed during the night or carried on for the morning delivery in Scotland.

However, the film then cuts to a second narrative scene (signal man in signal box) and a third (workers on the line) and it becomes clear that the voice-over is not constructing an argument, but rather providing background information for a series of narrative scenarios, connected as a temporal sequence by the progress of the train:

> [*Whistle blows*]. Stand by, stand clear!
>
> FIRST VOICE: That'll be the postal mate.
> SECOND VOICE: Well on time an'all ain't she Joe?

In its more continuous sequences, such as the stop at Crewe, or particularly in the extended scenario on board the train (actually filmed in a studio), *Nightmail* achieves a very different kind of effect from the two films previously considered. This effect is most apparent if we compare the portrayal of working-class people in the various films (recognising of course that working-class people, who were not actors, were appearing in films for the first time). In *Housing Problems*, as we have seen, working-class people appear as witnesses and perhaps as representative social types. In *Coalface*,

Fig. 2.6. Stills from Nightmail *(1936). By permission of the Post Office Film Library*

the miners appear as aesthetic objects in an art film. In *Nightmail*, however, the postal workers, while perhaps they first appear as representative types (as 'typical post office workers'), are ultimately constructed as characters. Characters appear in more than one scene and they are given dialogue to speak. There is, for example, an extended sequence where, in the presence of the supervisor, an experienced worker explains to a novice how to tie up and drop off a mail bag.

Nightmail also has its aesthetic moments. There is perhaps the most famous moment in all 1930s British documentaries where the poem by W H Auden is recited to a montage of train wheels, pistons, and passing scenery. There is a touching moment at the end where the commentary (now, appropriately, Scottish) makes reference to the consumer waiting expectantly for the postal delivery. But what above all, it seems to me, *Nightmail* succeeds in doing, is humanising the postal service. It advertises the postal service, not by making arguments about its efficiency, but by creating, around this national institution, a common culture. It is a situation (waiting for the postman) in which we are invited to include ourselves, to *identify* – for as the voice-over puts it, 'Who can bear to think himself forgotten?'

The conclusion then, to this chapter, amounts to an essential point for media text analysis. For it is crucial to recognise that texts, whatever they may be saying or presenting, as a statement or as a mythology, are involved in the construction of different kinds of experience for the reader/viewer or audience. They construct these different kinds of experience in the way that they organise signs, according to different syntagmatic structures. Clearly, many of the texts considered in this book (and that includes the documentary films) are in the business of advertising or promotion, but there are two considerations here. First, there is the selection of a message, and second there is the question of how to put it across. In this second consideration, argument, montage and narrative are the three basic choices available.

FURTHER READING

The concept of 'anchorage' was introduced by Barthes in his essay 'Rhetoric of the Image' (Barthes, 1977). Accessible introductions to narrative analysis, from a structuralist perspective, are provided by Sarah Kosloff, 'Narrative Theory and Television', in Allen R. C. (ed) (1992); by John Fiske in Chapter 8 of Fiske J. (1987); and by Jerry Palmer in Chapters 2 and 3 of Palmer J. (1991). Otherwise work on narrative and montage tends to be specialised and technical, but readers with a particular interest in Barthes might look at 'The Structural Analysis of Narratives' (Barthes, 1977).

For further discussion of the British Documentary Film Movement see: Andrew Higson, 'Britain's Outstanding Contribution to the film: the documentary-realist tradition', in Barr C. (ed) (1986); Stuart Hood, 'John Grierson and the Documentary Film Movement', in Curran J. and Porter V. eds. (1983); and Aitken I. (1992), which offers a detailed discussion of the intellectual and ideological context for these films.

Modes of address

1 INTERPELLATION

So far, we have considered two key dimensions in the construction of media texts. We have looked firstly at the way sign systems work to construct meanings, and secondly at the organisation of signs within syntagmatic structures. There is, however, a third key dimension to media text analysis, and it is very clearly and explicitly illustrated by the advertisement for Cover Girl International: 'Is that really me?' (see figure 3.1)

Media texts always address somebody – that is to say, they invite the reader/viewer to participate, and seek to engage her or him in specific practices of reading and viewing. They may do this directly ('Let us transform you!'), or they may adopt less direct, possibly more subtle, approaches. In part, the approach adopted will be a consequence of the syntagmatic structure – argument, montage or narrative; but it will also be influenced by the context or situation within which communication takes place – for instance the presence or absence of a storyteller, or the presence or absence of an audience. As we shall see, the way in which an audience is defined, and thus addressed, is also influenced by institutional and economic factors. This is a complex area, and it has given rise to important debates in media studies about the nature of our involvement in media texts. In this book, using a term which is in general circulation, I shall discuss such questions under the heading modes of address.

The Cover Girl advert is actually more complicated than it might first appear. Clearly it does, primarily, make a direct appeal to the reader, and invites her to part with her money. The direct appeal is, however, supported in interesting ways by other elements within the text. Consider the text's syntagmatic structure. There is a certain amount of argumentation around the proposition that the ad is offering to make a dream come true. However, in addition to the professionalism of the make-up artists and so on it is also using, to support the argument, the experience of Sarah Davies which is

"Is that really me?"

YES, IT'S REALLY HER!

When Sarah Davies treated herself to a professional make-over and photographic session at Cover Girl International, she simply couldn't believe the transformation!

For Sarah, and women of all ages like her, achieving the stunning model-girl looks that grace the covers of today's glossy magazines, was a secret dream come true.

And it's a dream that could come true for YOU too!

At Cover Girl International, our professional make-up artists, hair stylists and photographers can transform anyone into a beautiful 'cover girl' look-alike.

All you have to do, is book an appointment to visit our friendly, bright new studios in London.

We'll do all the work.

And you don't even have to worry about 'posing', as all our photographers are female and take great care to help you achieve the look you've always dreamed of.

The session fee is just £95.00 and includes expert consultation, make-over, hair styling and photography. You will then be able to choose as many photographs as you like, as a lasting reminder of your special time as a 'cover girl'. Collections and beautifully framed portrait photographs available from £295.

So go on! Discover the Cover Girl experience for yourself – you'll be amazed at the transformation!

let us transform you!

Relax in our luxurious lounge area, and chat with your consultant about the looks you'd like to achieve.

Make-up is applied by a professional make-up artist and handy hints are passed on!

Photographs are taken by a female photographer to help you feel relaxed with the 'new you'.

Anyone can look like a 'cover girl' and take the end results home for everyone else to see!

Please accept my booking for a personal consultation, make-over/hair styling and professional photographic session at Cover Girl International.

(Please make your cheque for £95.00 payable to Cover Girl International).

I wish to pay by Access ▨ Visa ▨ card (delete as applicable)

Card No. | | | | | | | | | | | | | | | Expiry Date

Signature ———————————— Date ————

I understand you will contact me immediately to arrange a convenient appointment with your studio.

Mrs/Miss/Ms/Other, First name ———————— (Surname) ————

Address ————————————————————

———————————————— Postcode ————

Telephone ————————————   Ref: CS **8**

Please post this booking form, enclosing payment to:
Cover Girl International, FREEPOST 15, London W1E 8XS.

☎ **BOOKING HOTLINE 9AM – 6PM DAILY 071 436 6272** (quote Ref: CS7)

Fig. 3.1. 'Is That Really Me?' Advert for Cover Girl International (1991). By permission of Cover Shots International Ltd

presented as a mini narrative. The story of Sarah Davies is condensed, in the text's most striking visual image, which juxtaposes her photograph 'before' and 'after' her transformation. We might say then, that in the structure of this text, an argument is in dominance, but that it also incorporates elements of narrative and montage. Such combinations are not unusual in media texts, as our analysis of other advertisements has shown.

But now let us turn to consider the appeal which this text is making to the reader/viewer. It seems to work on two levels. On one level, which is dominant, the text is attempting to persuade or convince, by referring to the professionalism, the friendliness and apparent value for money. It also seeks to mobilise the motivational justification that this kind of transformation is every 'cover girl's' dream. This is of course how arguments work: they offer reasons and try to deal with potential reservations. In general terms, the argument seeks to convince you that this is a good deal.

On the second level however, we have the story of Sarah Davies. Interestingly, the opening question (which might presumably be in the potential consumer's mind) is immediately transferred to Sarah Davies, as if it were a quotation from her story – a bit of dialogue which she, at one time, produced. This transfer is achieved by the shift from the first to the third person, as the 'me' in the question becomes the 'her' of the narrative. What is the effect of this transfer, in terms of the general appeal of the ad? It seems to me that, at this level, we might want to use terms like 'recognition' or 'identification' rather than persuasion or justification. The reader/viewer is invited to recognise that Sarah Davies is just an ordinary girl like herself, and to identify with her wish to become a 'cover girl'. This is of course because Sarah Davies is now a character in a story, and the appeal of stories is emotive rather than intellectual.

Mode of address is therefore, to some extent, a product of syntagmatic structure. Argument, montage and narrative engage the reader/viewer in different psychological processes; they invite participation in different kinds of activity. One term, familiar from literary studies, is the 'willing suspension of disbelief' which a narrative text invokes. I can think of several reasons for disbelieving the propositions made by the Cover Girl ad, but the mini narrative, with its exemplary character Sarah Davies, momentarily encourages me to forget my objections. By the same token, the 'loony priest' story told by Bob Monkhouse places its recipient in a similar position. Actually, a moment's reflection might lead us to doubt some of the amazing coincidences in that story, but the story form makes such doubt inappropriate and it would interfere with our pleasure. Unlike arguments, stories (even tall stories) have a 'truth' which cannot be questioned.

So, if the transformation worked for Sarah Davies, then it can work for us too. Identification, in narrative texts, is a powerful hook which supports the reproduction of mythology, because it makes a debatable meaning seem natural and inevitable. In the advertisement for Cover Girl, however, it is not only the story of Sarah Davies that produces this invitation to identify, for there is also a more general sense in which the whole text is constructed to speak to us, to engage our interest and to provoke a positive response, from its initial question to the inclusion of a booking form. It produces arguments and it tells a story, but it also simulates a form of direct inter-personal communication in which 'we' (the Cover Girl Organisation) are speaking directly to 'you' (potential cover girls).

This is the second element in a text's mode of address, that is to say the immediate context or situation in which the text is presented to its intended recipient. The Cover Girl ad organises its meanings and structures in such a way that they address the reader/viewer directly. The direct address of the argument is reinforced by the direct gaze of the 'ordinary' Sarah Davies. It is interesting to observe, however, that when Sarah Davies has become glamorous she no longer looks at us, but, in a rather dreamy fashion, off right, into the middle distance. Somehow then, the 'we' (ordinary girls) who are caught up in the direct, interpersonal exchange, are being invited to observe a newly objectified Sarah Davies. So we can say that the advert contains an exchange of looks, as well as an exchange of words and coupons.

The advert's use of direct address reinforces the identification process. It is now no longer simply an identification with a character in a story, it is an exchange of looks with an individual, and the possibility of direct communication with an organisation. It is on this second level that the Cover Girl advert illustrates a general argument about address and identification which was first proposed by the French Marxist philosopher, Louis Althusser (1971). Writing about ideology (a concept whose relevance for media studies we will consider in Chapter 6), Althusser argued that ideologies (let us say, for now, 'meaning systems') depend, for their effect, on making an appeal to the attention of the individual. Furthermore, this is an appeal which, at some level, cannot be ignored. And if the appeal is successful then the individual might begin to define his or her identity in terms of the meaning system which is on offer. To that extent, Althusser suggested, the individual would become a 'subject' of that meaning system.

Althusser called this process interpellation – the interpellation (not to be confused with interpolation) of individuals as subjects. In this process an address is made to the individual who, perhaps only for a moment, responds. Althusser himself gives two examples of this process, one less, the other more, extreme. The first, a fictitious and amusing scenario, invites us to imagine an individual walking down a street who is hailed ('Hey you there!'), possibly from behind, by another person (possibly a policeman). Such hailings, Althusser argues, rarely fail: whether out of curiosity or guilt the individual will turn round to check – and it is this turning round which constitutes the interpellation, for the hailing has achieved its effect.

Althusser's second example comes from the Bible where God, from time to time, speaks to individuals like Abraham, Moses or Samuel. These individuals are called to serve God and so become His subjects. In so doing they take on a new identity and even (in Samuel's case) a new name.

It can be argued that driving through a modern city, or flicking through a magazine, is very similar to Althusser's imaginary scenarios. From all sides, we are bombarded with texts which seem to say, on one level – 'Hey you there!'. To be sure, there are not many adverts today which directly point the finger, like the classic World War I poster of Lord Kitchener (or Uncle Sam) saying 'Your Country Needs You!' (1). But the general point is that all media texts, in addition to their use of particular meaning systems and syntagmatic structures, are also involved, of necessity, in some form of attention grabbing, to appeal to the potential consumer. Some of these attention-grabbing devices do make an appeal to the identity of the consumer ('Could that be me?' 'Am I that person?' 'Yes it's really me!'). In this sense, the Cover Girl ad is simply making explicit what is implicit in most adverts for cosmetics, or fashion, or stylised consumer goods such as cars.

So there is a double identification with Sarah Davies. She is an ordinary girl like us, but we can also (if we part with £95) look like a cover girl, like her. It can be argued that at this level of looks, which is reinforced by the initial question, the ad is offering a kind of idealised mirror image for the 'ordinary girl'. Interpellation does not then, really need to point the finger at all – it is enough to present idealised images and invite us to identify. We may of course, reject the invitation – this is not the voice of God, or even a policeman. But it may be enough that the invitation has been made. We now know that 'ordinary girls' can look like 'cover girls'. Feminist critics like Rosalind Coward and Judith Williamson have argued that even though a woman might reject this possible version of herself, nevertheless the fact that she is being hailed has to be dealt with, insofar as the promise (and the potential anxiety) remains.

2 DIRECT ADDRESS IN BROADCASTING

Modes of address differ from text to text and from institution to institution. The very direct invitation to the reader/viewer in the Cover Girl advert is only one option from a range of potential modes of address which can be identified in contemporary advertising. This range includes the use of puns, jokes and puzzles, which we have already considered and which I shall discuss further, from a historical perspective, in the final part of this chapter. There is, I think, a sense in which an argumentative structure, employing the direct mode of address ('Hey you there!'), now appears somewhat old fashioned. But if we leave the world of advertising aside for a while, we can now turn our attention to the one media institution which has developed direct address as its pivotal form. That institution is, of course, broadcasting, which is here defined to include both television and radio.

A word of clarification about this institution may be necessary before we proceed. It is possible to classify the different media, commonly included within media studies, from different points of view. For instance, if we take as our key criterion the nature of the signifier, we might conclude that TV, with its combination of visible and audible signifiers, has something in common with (or at least might be compared to) cinema (2); whereas radio, restricted to sound, is quite different. In this book I will argue that such a point of view is misleading, and that there are several reasons why radio and television, as broadcasting systems, need to be considered together. Some of these reasons are historical in that TV (particularly in Britain, because of the BBC) took over and developed many of the functions and formats of radio. But also, crucially for this chapter, radio and TV are alike in their modes of address, and fundamentally different in this respect from cinema.

Consider two essential features of broadcast communication. The first feature is that radio and TV are available as a constant resource – like water or electricity they are constantly 'on tap' for the consumer (even more so now that these media are available round the clock). By contrast a film at the cinema is a discrete event for which special provision must be made (it is, precisely, a 'date'). The second key feature of radio and TV is that they are received in the domestic, or at least the private, sphere. Traditionally, broadcasters have thought of this domestic sphere as a family household. They have transmitted their programmes around presumed family household activities, such as 'teatime', or children's bedtime. They have also, since the 1930s, experimented with different ways of communicating with the domestic audience; consisting, as it does, of people from different social and cultural backgrounds engaged in a variety of domestic activities.

Given these conditions, what mode of address is most appropriate for broadcasting? Several commentators, broadcasters as well as academics, have recognised that broadcasting has had to discover ways of engaging the attention of its audience. But perhaps that's a rather bland way of putting it, since all media need to do this, in one way or another. As John Ellis (1982) puts it, in his discussion of the differences between TV and cinema, the key point about broadcasting is that it needs to engage the attention of its audience continuously. Arguably, once the ticket has been purchased, cinema can guarantee the full attention of its audience. Broadcasting has no such guarantees: because of its conditions of reception it faces competition from other domestic activities, and it can assume only varying degrees of involvement. The domestic sphere is easily interrupted and the audience distracted. To combat this, Ellis argues, broadcasting has invented scheduling – so the audience is able to match its domestic routines to the flow of programmes (we will return to this point, in more detail, in Chapter 4). It also punctuates this flow with recognition devices, such as continuity announcements, jingles and signature tunes. But most of all, broadcasting has discovered that direct address to the audience is the most effective way of securing its involvement – for example Bruce Forsyth's 'Nice to see you'; David Frost's 'Hello, good evening and welcome' etc, etc.

This pervasive use of direct address in broadcasting has two major consequences. I shall discuss the first in this section and the second in the next (and then I shall return to the cinema). The first consequence of its use of direct address is that broadcasting develops what has been called a form of 'para-social interaction' between the institution and its audience (Horton and Wohl, 1956). We have already seen that some kind of social interaction might be encouraged by a mass mediated form of direct address where, for example, the reader of the Cover Girl ad is invited to communicate with the organisation. Horton and Wohl's argument, however, which refers to American TV in the 1950s, suggests that the social interaction encouraged by broadcasting is, in a sense, a sham. It is an 'illusion of intimacy', in what is essentially a one-way process of communication. This illusion they argue, is sustained in various ways: by direct reference to the domestic audience ('viewers at home'); by using a studio audience to trigger appropriate responses from the domestic audience; and, most of all, by constructing a 'persona', or 'personality' for the broadcaster which the domestic audience can come, in some sense, to 'know'.

Horton and Wohl's argument is similar to Althusser's in that they are showing how the domestic audience can easily become interpellated by the strategies of broadcasting. However, what is particularly fascinating about broadcasting is that this interpellation is clearly a manufactured process which happens at a distance. Watching someone address us from a distant studio, via the box in the corner of our living room (which we can turn off at any time) might not seem to have the same force as the policeman's 'Hey you!' to the passer-by in Althusser's example. And yet, suggest Horton and Wohl, broadcasting's construction of 'intimacy at a distance' might be more effective precisely because it can be experienced as an ideal (supportive, pleasurable) form of interpellation, which is not subject to the uncertainties of everyday life.

However, this discussion of broadcasting (particularly television) in the 1950s might need to be modified, to some extent, today. In particular, the assumption that this is essentially a one-way process would seem to be challenged by the many opportunities which now exist for members of the audience to communicate directly with the broadcasters. For example, some interesting forms of para-social interaction are encouraged by the activities of disc jockeys on British commercial radio. These are interesting because they include both the interpellation of the general listening audience and the development of particular forms of dialogue with individual members of that audience (via phone-ins). What then is the relationship between our sense of being part of a general audience, and our (increasingly common) ability to listen in to other people's conversations?

In their study of Radio London's *The Tony Blackburn Show* Graham Brand and Paddy Scannell (1991) argue that DJ talk is essential, not simply to provide information or to fill the gaps between records, but rather to construct an ongoing identity for the show and for its presenter. Such an identity has much in common with Horton and Wohl's concept of the 'persona', it is a carefully contrived public identity; but, at least in Tony Blackburn's case, this includes some (intimate) knowledge about his private life as well (for instance, his divorce from Tessa Wyatt in 1976). Nevertheless, it is to this constructed persona that the audience relates, and Brand and Scannell show how this relationship can give rise to certain forms of verbal interaction in listener's phone calls to the programme. What is foregrounded (preferred) here is a certain kind of verbal banter, which is 'intimate', but also non-serious and playful. In the context of Horton and Wohl's argument, it is possible to speculate that the greater the opportunity for direct intimacy between members of the audience and broadcasters, the more that possibility must be controlled, or deflected, for instance, through the introduction of parody:

TB:	Right. Now, em Garry's in Camden. Hello Garry.
GARRY:	Hello Tony.
TB:	(chat-up voice) Hello, I gather you're getting married tomorrow.
GARRY:	Oh yeah 'n I'm really scared I tell you.
TB:	After all – I'm not surprised – after all you 'nd I have meant to one another as well.
GARRY:	I know but [?] my leader what can I do? We tried to get down 'nd see you last night as well.
TB:	Really?
GARRY:	Yeah we couldn't. We wanted to see your twelve-incher but –
TB:	I'm – Garry!
GARRY:	Ahh.
TB:	I'm amazed that you're getting married. All those times that we spent in the sand-dunes at Swanage together.
GARRY:	Ah d'you remember that time in the Bahamas?
TB:	Yes.
GARRY:	On the beach just me 'nd you.
TB:	When you used to whisper and nibble my ear.
GARRY:	Ahhh.
TB:	Underneath the coconut trees.

GARRY: And you used to show me your twelve-incher.

TB: And you threw it all away and you're getting married tomor-
           row. Don't you think you should reconsider this?

GARRY: I think I should Tone. I think I should mate.

Thus *The Tony Blackburn Show* creates opportunities in which to parody the possibility of 'intimacy at a distance' between the broadcaster and the caller (who is, of course, previously unknown to him). As Brand and Scannell point out, to be an effective participant, the caller must be able to produce the right responses, by knowing the codes, which is yet another version of the 'knowing consumer'. As to what kinds of codes might be operating in the above extract, I will simply observe here that, according to Brand and Scannell, this is radio's equivalent of the tabloid press. We will return to similar examples of parodic intimacy again in Chapter 5.

However, as Martin Montgomery emphasises in his discussion of DJ talk (1986), radio listeners must presumably derive some pleasure from this kind of thing. According to Montgomery, there is, in contemporary radio, not one, but two levels of interpellation. There is the interpellation of particular listeners who are addressed directly, and Montgomery gives examples of a variety of such forms of address: for example, addressing particular listeners by name (Garry), by location (in Camden), by occupation, by star sign, and so on. But at another level there is the more general address to anyone who might be 'listening in'. The result, Montgomery argues, is a discourse with a 'special kind of dynamic':

> On the one hand, it is continuously inclusive with respect to diverse constituencies within the audience in a personalising, familiar, even intimate manner. (Quiz spots, listeners' letters, phone-ins, and so on, may be seen as developments of this strategy.) On the other hand, although the discourse may constitute the audience in fragmentary terms, it also manages simultaneously to dramatise the relation of the audience to itself: as listeners we are made constantly aware of other (invisible) elements of the audience of which we form a part. (p.103)

At this second level of interpellation, broadcasting constructs what has been described as a 'pseudo-community' (see Beniger, 1987) which includes the presenters, the participants and the audience at home. Montgomery argues that Althusser's concept of interpellation needs to be extended to take this into account. We are not just interpellated as individuals, we are interpel-lated as members of an audience ('millions like us') – an identity which is reinforced as we see or hear other members of that audience interacting with the institution by 'having a go'. This is of course, an imaginary community; it is constructed out of the fragments which we see or (over) hear. And it is a community which can be constructed in different ways: as a national community (traditionally served in Britain by the BBC); as a regional community (traditionally served by ITV); and as a local or increasingly (via satellite) international community. So there are several imaginary communities on offer.

Which begins to connect with other arguments about broadcasting. Let us return, briefly, to our argument about the mythology operating in the news bulletin which we analysed in Chapter 1. That was, we recall, a mythology of the 'middle ground' – a set of values supposedly shared by all decent, law-abiding citizens, which is how broadcasting imagines the vast majority of its audience. Now, though he is discussing a particular type of radio programme, I believe that Montgomery's argument about the interpellation of the listener to an imaginary community shows how that mythology can be reinforced. In this argument, such 'middle ground' values are right and proper, not just because they are preferred by the BBC, but also because, as we sit at home, we imagine ourselves to be part of the general community in which everybody shares these values. So an imaginary consensus of values and beliefs is constructed through the para-social interaction which revolves around broadcasting's direct address.

What happens when new delivery systems, like satellite and cable, allow for the construction of new (local and international) communities? The basic argument about broadcasting remains – it uses particular forms of direct address which have certain para-social consequences. However, there is at least the possibility that a fragmentation of audiences might produce a fragmentation of 'middle grounds'. For instance the values shared by members of the audience for *The Tony Blackburn Show* are probably not the same as the values shared by the audience for BBC Radio 4. It would be interesting to see if the preferred reading of incidents in the Nottinghamshire coalfields in March 1984 was the same on BBC1 and Local Radio Trent. The general point is that, for a preferred reading to gain the status of an imaginary consensus it must successfully interpellate the audience. But different audiences may be interpellated into different preferred readings, which may begin to have profound consequences for the middle ground of national broadcasting and indeed for the construction of national identities. We will return to these questions later.

3 THE REGIME OF BROADCASTING

For the moment, let us return to the second major consequence of the use of direct address in broadcasting. I have previously suggested that direct address is 'pivotal' to the way broadcasting works, and I now want to argue that this is quite literally the case, in that the direct address of the presenter, or anchorperson, acts as the central point for a whole institutional system or regime. Through the years, broadcasting has evolved its own particular way of doing things – covering world news or sports events, or bringing us comedy or drama. But whatever the type of programme, it is introduced by direct address, even if this is just an invisible continuity announcer. That direct address, in its most 'intimate' forms, appears to be 'live', and so broadcasting constructs a situation of temporal 'co-presence' between the institution and its audience. Moreover, in the vast majority of instances, this live direct address comes to us from a special place, a kind of sanctum, which is the studio. Studios are so important to broadcasting, as the privileged space through which all its events are relayed, that sometimes (for example at some sports event) artificial studios are constructed, high up in the stands, and we can enjoy the spectacle of the fans outside, waving to their mums.

A moment's reflection then, will confirm that, for radio as well as television, its direct address is embedded within an institutional regime. This is a regime which revolves around the mode of address itself, but also the time (live present or recorded past) and the place (in the studio or on location), as its three main variables. It is a regime which establishes a hierarchy of positions for the participants in broadcasting. Some participants introduce others, some interrogate others, some make comments and pass judgements on others' actions and statements. Those who appear in the studio, live, and have the right to direct address (always the broadcasters themselves) are at the top of this hierarchy of positions. Those who appear on location, recorded, and who are not permitted to look at the camera (such as the ordinary people filmed in interviews, or simply going about their business) are at the bottom. Significantly those at the bottom have no control over the regime; their appearances or statements are always subject to editing, analysis, commentary and so on, by others situated further up the hierarchy.

And there are intermediate positions: such as the reporter who appears live, has the right to direct address, but is situated on location (and thus is always obliged to report 'back to the studio'); or the documentary maker whose filmed report is recorded on location, but who nevertheless has the right to direct address (a right which is denied to others in the film). Some idea of the structure of this hierarchy, and its possible permutations is provided by the tree diagram below. It should be read from left to right, as well as from top to bottom, as a map of the distribution of structural power in broadcasting:

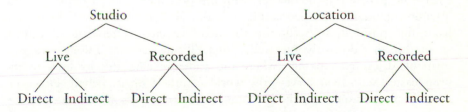

What are the effects of this regime? We can begin to explore these by applying this diagram to the TV news bulletin analysed in Chapter 1. Clearly at the top of the tree, in this model, sits John Humphreys, the newscaster, who is in the studio, live, and has direct address. There is a sense in which these newscasters are seen as 'authors' of the news – an effect which is sometimes reinforced by shots of them shuffling papers and editing scripts. But also, as we saw, Humphreys frequently passes his narrative to reporters situated on location, and who may or may not be live (in this bulletin, John Fryer is clearly not live, since he has been filmed in daylight; Michael Sullivan might be live, since it is dark, and note the attempt to achieve temporal co-presence with his use of the word 'tonight' – but at nine o'clock? It is unlikely). However, these reporters are permitted the use of direct address, and this in itself places them in a superior position to other participants in these filmed reports (like Arthur Scargill) who are not. It is from this superior position that Michael Sullivan is able to pass speculative comment on Mr Scargill's possible course of action and establish his preferred reading of Mr Scargill's state of mind.

As an experienced politician, Mr Scargill knows that his statements, which have now entered the public arena, are immediately subject to the rules of this regime. Potentially they will be referred to, quoted, picked apart, mulled over, and speculatively assessed by others, like Sullivan, who occupy positions which are further up the chain. His statements may also, at a later date, be thrown back at him, by an interviewer claiming to represent the public's 'right to know' ('On the 24th March, Mr Scargill you said . . . What do you say now?'). So perhaps this structural fact, rather than sheer bloody-mindedness is part of the explanation as to why Mr Scargill, or any other politician, is somewhat evasive with his answers. More generally, perhaps, there is an art to producing repeatable or quotable public statements which the broadcasters can subsequently get their teeth into and chew over. Perhaps this is why some politicians (Denis Healey, Norman Tebbit, of recent memory) succeed in becoming media 'personalities'. What this suggests I think, is a need for further research on the different forms of public statement appropriate to the different positions we can identify within the hierarchy of broadcasting.

There are also at least two further interesting effects of this structure. Consider the position of the interpellated viewer or listener. He or she may engage in 'para-social interaction' with the presenter, and participate in the 'pseudo-community' of 'people like us'. But also, he or she will be invited from this position, to scrutinise the activities and statements of others, situated further down the hierarchy. John Ellis argues that TV encourages a form of 'delegated looking', where the audience delegates its look to the broadcaster, who then surveys the world of others on its behalf. However, in many programmes, it is the function of the anchorperson to shift our gaze, as he or she turns away from the camera to face the third party interviewee or 'guest'. 'I am speaking to you' (direct address) thus constructs a 'we' who look at 'them' (who of course are not permitted to look at the camera and are restricted therefore to third-party status). Direct address is in dominance, but there is actually a hierarchy of looks between first, second and third persons, particularly between 'we' and 'they'. As Ian Connell (1980) suggests, from its position as a non-participating onlooker, a bystander, the audience is interpellated as a 'witness' to whatever events or conversations television wishes to stage.

In the previous chapter I suggested that there might be certain affinities between some aspects of television (such as TV news) and the conditions of live storytelling. Now it is possible to suggest that it is the regime of television which simulates the structure of oral narrative – insofar as the storyteller appears on screen, in direct address, to narrate the events and existents 'in the news'. And if we pursue this comparison we can see the potential here for the regime to construct its third parties as characters, just like the loony priest and the woman from Kelvinside. Furthermore, we saw that the characters in an anecdotal narrative are not constructed with any psychological complexity or depth; on the contrary, they are offered up as stereotypes, with a limited set of traits (the accent, the twitch) which the audience can easily recognise, and with restricted patterns of behaviour which the audience can predict. Later (in Chapter 7) I shall explore some other ways in which stereotypes are constructed in the media, but here, with reference to the regime of television I am suggesting it is possible to offer a structural explanation as to why certain participants (like politicians) are frequently caricatured. From our position of bystander to the world's events we are invited to recognise their already familiar and predictable behaviour: 'there they go again', television seems to say, 'what else did you expect from them?'

4 'DOMINANT SPECULARITY' IN HOLLYWOOD CINEMA

Cinema, John Ellis reminds us in *Visible Fictions* (1982), offers a very different kind of experience to that of watching TV. Some of the reasons for this difference have been mentioned earlier, but it is not just that cinema offers discrete experiences, similar in some respects to the theatre. What is crucial is that the cinematic mode of address, its process of interpellation, is quite distinct from that constructed in broadcasting. As noted in Chapter 2, the so-called 'classic' narrative film (the model developed in Hollywood) appears to minimise or efface the level of 'discourse' in storytelling, and so has largely eliminated the need for direct address (if it is used at all in the cinema, direct address usually has a comic effect, as in certain Woody Allen films). Instead, following the title sequence, members of the cinema audience are typically plunged into approximately two hours of unfolding events, interpellated, in a darkened auditorium, by an intense beam of light passing over their heads.

These peculiarities of the cinematic experience have been intensely debated and analysed since the late 1960s. For some reason, there is much more theoretical work on the characteristics of cinema than on broadcasting, though the latter is possibly catching up today. Much pioneering work was developed in France, associated with the writings of Christian Metz, and with the journal *Cahiers du Cinema*. In the 1970s, this work influenced a group of British film theorists, associated with the journal *Screen*. In this section, I look at some of the arguments developed by this group, particularly the work of Stephen Heath, in what I consider to be his key essay, 'Narrative Space' (1976). As usual however, I will be selective, for two reasons: first because, in its theoretical detail this work is very complex; but second, there are other accessible summaries of much of this work (3). I will then focus this discussion on the cinematic mode of address and, in particular, on its processes of interpellation.

It is common to start by acknowledging the immense influence of Colin MacCabe's (1974) essay on 'Realism and the Cinema'. In fact, given our previous discussion of the regime of broadcasting, it is interesting to observe that MacCabe also applies the principle of hierarchy to classic narrative film. He suggests that these films, like classic novels (such as *Middlemarch*) operate as 'classic realist texts', in which there is a 'hierarchy of discourses'. In essence, this means that the perspectives adopted or personified by different characters in the narrative, will always be subject to evaluation through a 'meta-language', which in novels may be carried by the voice of the narrator or an 'authorial voice' which addresses the reader directly. In films, of course, there is no authorial voice as such, but there is the camera which is, for instance, able to draw the spectator's attention to details which the characters may have overlooked. To this extent the spectator may come to occupy a position of superior knowledge, and therefore judgement, with respect to the characters in a film. MacCabe calls this a position of 'dominant specularity'.

This model proposes that, for cinema, it is the look of the camera (rather than any dominant voice) which organises the interpellation of the spectator. MacCabe's essay has, I think, been particularly influential on subsequent film theory for two reasons. First, it insists that narrative films are 'realist', and there has been a great deal of subsequent debate as to what that term might mean. Second, however, the notion of dominant specularity suggests that the realism (the credibility, the plausibility) of a narrative film is organised so as to engage with the 'look' of the spectator (a look which, we recall, is particularly intense, given the technology involved). This perspective then opens up for detailed analysis the precise ways in which the text has been constructed (filmed and edited) to maintain a sense of realism while simultaneously interpellating the spectator. MacCabe's notion of the 'classic realist text' has been criticised for being too general and monolithic (4), but in placing 'dominant specularity' at the top of its agenda, this essay did provoke some further, very fruitful work on the construction of spectatorship in Hollywood cinema.

For instance, in his essay 'Narrative Space', Stephen Heath makes two key propositions about this form of spectatorship, allied to a third argument which (as we shall see later) is more debatable. Heath's two propositions basically relate to the technology of cinema as 'moving pictures'; that is, photographs, printed on a length of celluloid, projected at twenty-four frames per second. What is demanded by this technology is: (i) a certain definition of what constitutes an acceptable photographic image, and (ii) a set of acceptable editing techniques for relating images to each other (acceptable that is, both to the cinematic institution and to its audience). Heath argues that Hollywood cinema has found its definition of the acceptable image in a western tradition of visual composition which dates from the fourteenth century (the 'quattrocento'). The acceptable editing techniques were pioneered by Hollywood itself, and they differ in some respects from other editing techniques (such as those used by Soviet film in the 1920s).

As the term suggests, 'quattrocento' refers to a style of painting developed in Italy in the early Renaissance. It has since become the dominant style of western visual culture, but it has been challenged by some artists (such as Picasso) in the twentieth century. It is organised in terms of perspective; that is to say, the composition of the image must follow certain geometrical principles which give the impression of depth (a third dimension) in a two-dimensional image. Other, more aesthetic, conventions of composition follow from these basic principles, such as 'harmonious' relationships between foreground and background, and 'pleasing prospects' for the eye. It is interesting to look at pre-quattrocento painting where, for instance, the size of figures is determined not by their position in the frame but by their divine status, or where the lines of buildings appear, to us, to be 'wrong'. These paintings resemble the untutored drawings of small children, and they remind us that perspective is an arbitrary convention which has to be learned. It is also argued by Heath that perspective represents a shift in point of view from a divine to a human order; that is, it represents 'space' as perceived by a human spectator located at its centre.

'Dominant specularity' in Hollywood cinema reproduces this essentially humanist field of vision. It is, of course, not inevitable that cinema must follow this convention, and some experimental or avant-garde films have constructed images in other ways (for example, certain abstract images in British documentary films like *Coalface* and *Nightmail*). But it would seem that photographic perspective is an essential component of Hollywood's claim to realism. Furthermore, this is a construction of space which inter-pellates the eye of the spectator, insofar as the image is composed for the spectator as its point of intelligibility. But now the second of Heath's propo-sitions comes into force, for these are moving images, and so the space they construct is never static:

> From the very first, as though of right, human figures enter film, spilling out of the train, leaving the factory or the photographic congress, *moving* – this is the movies, these are moving pictures. The figures move in the frame, they come and go, and there is then a need to change the frame, re-framing with a camera movement or moving to another shot. The transitions thus effected pose acutely the problem of the filmic construc-tion of space, of achieving a coherence of place and positioning the specta-tor as the unified and unifying subject of its vision. (p.38)

The problem of filmic space is illustrated by our common experience that the still image, held for a certain length of time, becomes intolerable. More precisely, it draws our attention to itself, because we are anticipating the 'need to change the frame' (some students' videos unfortunately have this effect – the images are held too long). This is because, in the moving picture, the image has become a 'shot' – that is, a composite of several images, flick-ering by at a speed too great to be perceived by the spectator. Characteristically, argues Heath, Hollywood has solved this problem by narrativising the image. So in the shot, the movement of the figures is from somewhere, and towards somewhere else and, at a certain point, we desper-ately need the next shot to reveal their destination. In the shot, the image becomes an event, and 'space' is reconstituted as 'place'. This is now, perhaps, doubly realistic, for it is realistically composed space, located in an equally realistic (insofar as it seems plausible) temporal sequence.

The key issue here, which Hollywood had to confront, was how to retain the effective interpellation of the spectator. Heath makes this point above where he suggests that the need to re-frame – move the camera or move to another shot – might disturb the position of the spectator as its point of intel-ligibility. Thus, classic Hollywood cinema developed its system of 'continu-ity editing' to combat this potential disruption (5). It is a system that consists of conventions such as the '180 degree rule' (whereby the action is filmed from one side of an imaginary line) and the '30 degree rule' (whereby if, in shot (B), the action is re-framed from an angle at least 30 degrees from shot (A), a perceptible 'jump' is avoided). The effect of such techniques is to construct an apparent 'flow' from shot to shot which maintains a continu-ity of position for the spectator. Ideally, in continuity editing, the editing itself should go unnoticed, and the spectator who 'goes with the flow' should be able to devote his or her entire attention to the unfolding sequence of events.

However, these events do not simply unfold 'before our eyes'. The experience of watching a narrative film is intensified by further techniques of editing which place the spectator in and among the events it portrays. In this respect the comparison with theatre becomes misleading. The auditorium may look like a theatre, and (like the proscenium, but unlike theatre in the round) the action is viewed according to the 180 degree rule; but cinema is also able, as it were, to position the audience on the stage. It can do this by showing the events from the perspective of an imaginary (but silent) character at the scene; or it can show the events from the point of view of an identifiable character in the story. The technical means for achieving these effects involve breaking down the scene as a whole (the 'establishing shot'), into sequences of shot/reverse shot editing, where the camera takes different (usually complementary) angles, allied to (but not usually identical with) the perspectives of different characters. The result is a form of spectatorship which has greater potential for visual subjectivity than the theatre; but, as Heath points out, even with the use of 'point of view' shots, where the spectator is placed temporarily 'in the eyes' of a character, the overall position of 'dominant specularity' is retained.

Film theory, in the 1970s, thus produced a complex and detailed account of the mechanics of interpellation which are characteristic of classic narrative film. What emerges from this analysis is an account of the rhetoric of narrative film: the way it transforms 'space' into 'place', and yet retains a central position for the eye of the spectator. Any Hollywood film, 1930–60, could be taken to exemplify this rhetoric (and the simplest method is just to turn off the sound and observe both the camerawork and the editing). Once we are aware of this rhetoric, it becomes instructive to observe how some films either fail to achieve, or sometimes deliberately manipulate its conventions. For example, *Nightmail* does contain narrative sequences but, of course, it is not a classic narrative film and, looked at from a Hollywood point of view, the visual continuity in these sequences (when the workers are sorting letters, for example) leaves much to be desired (not disastrous however, because in this film the voice-over maintains continuity). More to the point perhaps, a late film in the classic Hollywood tradition is Hitchcock's *Psycho* (1960), a film which seems to illustrate every possible rhetorical variation. Here, in addition to scenes which deliberately break the 180 degree rule (such as the famous shower scene), there are radical shifts in point of view (for examples from Marion to Norman as the central character) and some very clear deviations from the standard angles of shot/reverse shot editing (as in the lengthy scene in the office of the Bates Motel).

However, there is a further level of argument in what became known as 'Screen Theory' in the 1970s. Having discussed, in interesting detail, the interpellation of the spectator by classic narrative film, several writers, such as

Heath himself, go on to speculate about possible limits to that interpellation. There is an interest here in the ways in which 'dominant specularity' can possibly be undermined, or in the ways in which its dominance can, nevertheless, be revealed as fragile and unstable. There are problematic links here with Althusser's original concept of interpellation, and we will consider these later, in Chapter 6, insofar as they relate to problems with a particular 'empiricist' version of the Marxist theory of ideology. Furthermore, in some 'Screen Theory' (in some of Heath's other work), there is a turn towards psychoanalysis as a theory that can, it is suggested, illuminate that which 'dominant specularity' has subordinated or repressed (I shall return to this in Chapter 7). In 'Narrative Space', towards the end of the essay, Heath discusses the possibility of some (avant-garde) films 'de-constructing' the unified position of the spectator which classic narrative film constructs: 'the relations of the subject set by film – its vision, its address – would be radically transformed if the intervals of its production were opened in their negativity, if the fictions of the closure of those intervals were discontinued . . .' (p.62–3). In other words, by revealing and precisely not concealing its editing techniques, the avant-garde film would construct another form of spectatorship.

Perhaps the problem here lies in the notion of 'radical transformation'. Clearly it is possible to discover other rhetorics in other kinds of film. It can be argued that the use of montage editing by Soviet films of the 1920s offers one kind of alternative to the dominant specularity of Hollywood cinema. By posing questions about the possible relations between different shots, montage editing obliges the spectator to construct rather than simply to occupy, a unified position. But such alternatives (Heath himself discusses Japanese cinema) have not radically transformed, or even interrupted, the appeal of the most powerful cinema in the world. Different techniques of editing, and different modes of address, can certainly be located in other cinemas of various kinds, but these do not, in themselves, transform the power relations which sustain the dominance of 'dominant specularity'.

5 CASE STUDY: MODES OF ADDRESS IN TV ADVERTISING (1956–90)

I do not mean to say that transformations in modes of address, even in powerful institutions, do not or cannot occur. We have already considered the possibility that technological and political changes to the structure of broadcasting might be creating greater diversity in its modes of address. In this, the final section of this chapter, I want to explore a similar set of arguments with reference to television advertising. In some ways, such advertising is paradoxical: it is, on one hand, highly transitory and ephemeral, punctuating the seemingly real business of watching programmes; and yet, as the imperative of the commercial break reminds us, the real business of television is to deliver audiences to advertisers. As regards its textual structures, TV advertising might seem to be parasitic, since it has borrowed formulae from broadcasting and cinema, as well as from a host of other media, from comic strips to fine art. However, in Britain at least, and particularly since the 1980s, there seems to be a feeling that TV advertising is becoming increasingly sophisticated. Certainly the industry now has its own annual awards for creative achievement in which some British agencies (such as Bartle, Bogle, Hegarty) have gained international reputations (6).

In this case study I want to investigate these possible developments by looking at TV advertising in a historical context. My immediate source of data for this project is a television programme broadcast in 1990, as part of a series on the history of advertising, entitled *Washes Whiter* (BBC2), which was primarily concerned with images of men and masculinity in TV advertising. The programme presented a montage of clips from ads since the 1950s, organised into different categories (such as advertising to men, or advertising featuring men but targeted at women), strung together by a voice-over, but also, interestingly, interspersed with the comments of advertising executives. The overall impression was one of historical development, insofar as this was presented as a story of progress; and, for some of the advertisers at least, early TV adverts could not be looked at without a certain cringe factor creeping in:

> [*Man cast as expert, in suit and tie, sitting behind desk with packet of Persil in foreground*]
>
> EXPERT: Millions and millions of women use Persil They know it and they trust it. Because Persil has always washed whiter (1957).

As a starting point, it is worth considering where this cringe factor comes from. Interestingly, it is a factor which seems to be more associated with forms of broadcasting than with cinema (it is still possible to enjoy repeats of old films). Early broadcasting is now consumed either with a feeling of nostalgia, or, as in this instance, with amused embarrassment. The *Washes Whiter* programme deliberately constructed an anachronistic image of early TV advertising by starting with a montage of 'good evenings' from male 'experts', such as the one above, using direct address (from behind their desks) to the camera. Perhaps, because of its simulation of co-presence, such direct address is particularly vulnerable to a process of historical distanciation. But here is how one of the advertising executives, Barry Day, vice-chairman of Lintas, explained the situation in the 1950s:

> Before the war authority figures – doctors, lawyers, bank managers – if they said it, you believed it, you were brought up that way. After the war I think we were all anxious to get back to that sort of normality even

though it was less applicable. And so when advertising came in on television where nobody knew much about how to do it at all, which is the key point, you just went back to what you were used to. So you showed the people who were meant to be the authority figures and put them up as a shorthand way of saying 'Well, don't take it from us, take it from them because if they say so you know it must be true don't you?

It would seem then, that there is more to the cringe factor than the use of direct address as such. Rather, this use of direct address is now seen as particularly awkward because it is embedded within an argumentative structure which uses authoritative justification (see pp. 30–3, above). It is this whole textual strategy which is now criticised as naïve ('nobody knew how to do it') by executives like Barry Day.

At this point it will be useful to turn to the accessible and systematic survey of (North American) magazine advertising provided by William Leiss, Stephen Kline and Sut Jhally (1990). It is clear that, in the *Washes Whiter* programme, the cringe factor is initially associated with what they term the 'product-information' format: that is the kind of ad that gives us argumentative reasons why we should purchase a product. As Leiss *et al.* put it:

> The demand for reason-why advertising was closely connected with the needs of national advertisers to elicit demand for their new product. Especially in the realm of food, personal-care, and household products the nature of the new item and the way it should be used were often unfamiliar . . . Breakfast foods, toothpaste, canned foods, polishes and an endless series of previously unknown products had to be carefully introduced into the daily patterns of life, and the reasons for using them explained in detail. (p.138)

This 'product-information' format is actually the first in a series of four major strategies which Leiss *et al.* discovered in their survey. Subsequent formats are defined and illustrated as the 'product-image' format (where the product is associated with a desirable setting or context); the 'personalised' format (where the product is associated with personal qualities or can effect personal transformation); and the 'lifestyle' format (where the product is associated with a desirable lifestyle). The development of each format is related by these authors to the history of the advertising industry, and particularly to the impact of new media (such as radio), the influence of psychological theory and the development of sophisticated market research. A key factor has been the shift towards market segmentation, using 'psychographic' data to delineate different 'lifestyle patterns' – hence the growth of the 'lifestyle format' (7). Leiss *et al.* make the point, however, that later formats do not simply replace earlier ones; rather the advertiser has available an increasing variety of formats, developed in the course of the century.

Fig. 3.2. The 'product-information' format in a TV advert for Persil (1957)

It is interesting that the 'product-information' format, which Leiss *et al.* identify as the earliest and most basic form of advertising (they give dates of 1890–1925) should still be so prevalent on British TV in the 1950s (see figure 3.2). Soon, however, according to *Washes Whiter*, this format was seen as problematic by the advertisers themselves, and the use of direct address in advertising became more inventive. Its personification began to change – from the authoritative 'expert' or scientist, to the friendly shopkeeper or more familiar TV personality. During the 1960s, on British television, there was the advent of musical direct address, where TV personalities now began, literally, to sing the praises of the product they were presenting to the camera. More recently we have grown familiar, at one end of the spectrum, with working-class or cartoon characters performing song and dance routines ('You can't get better than a Kwik-Fit fitter'); and at the other, with film stars (Rutger Hauer, Jeff Goldblum) adopting an ironically cultivated persona as they extol the virtues of particular beers and lagers. Direct address then, remains an option, but it would seem that it is no longer acceptable as a textual strategy without some changes to the manner of its performance.

I think that some versions of the 'personalised' format have suffered a similar fate. Consider what Leiss *et al.* refer to as the 'self-transformation' ad, where 'people change – make themselves better – through the possession or use of the product' (p.254). Traditionally, this kind of advert has used a narrative structure (as in the 'before/after' scenario of the Cover Girl ad). If there is an argument, it is not directed at the viewer, but at the character in the story, coming frequently from an unseen voice-over (or 'voice-of-God'). *Washes Whiter* illustrates this with a 1957 advert for Brylcreem, entitled 'Broken Date':

> [*Shot of young man outside cinema*]
>
> v/o: So she's broken your date. Well can you wonder with dry, lifeless hair like yours?
>
> [*Young man observes hairdresser's window; cut to point of view shot*]
>
> v/o: Yes, what you need is Brylcreem.
>
> [*Cut to shot of couple meeting*]
>
> v/o: For a truly handsome appearance use Brylcreem every day.
>
> [*Cut to shot of product*]

By the 1970s, as *Washes Whiter* illustrates, the performance of this kind of advert had also changed. Typically, it had become a comedy which exaggerated, and thus parodied, the possibility of personal transformation. The magical powers of the product were now too potent to be believed (the wimp who experiences new levels of irresitability to women in adverts for Hi-Karate aftershave, for example). Of course, gender may be an important factor here: it may be that parody is one way of making cosmetics palatable to men. However, I also think there is a more general sense in which the kind of 'self-transformation' advertising which invokes personal anxieties (a strategy which is related to psychological theories of need and motivation) is no longer as acceptable as it used to be. Such ads still appear in down-market magazines (one thinks of ads for slimming aids and cures for baldness) but they are by no means characteristic of modern television advertising.

What these two advertising formats do have in common is a certain set of assumptions about the consumer. Essentially, at least in the straight versions of 'product-information' and 'self- transformation', the consumer is 'talked down to'. It is assumed, either that the consumer has to be educated, or that he or she is a victim of deeply personal needs or psychological drives. It is the first assumption that underpins the strategy of direct persuasion; and the second that produces narrative scenarios which are designed to encourage consumer identification (as in the use of cinematic point of view in the Brylcreem ad). To modern sensibilities, both strategies feel like versions of the 'hard sell' – but there are, of course, alternative formats associated with

Fig. 3.3. The 'personalised' format in a TV advert for Brylcreem (1957)

'soft sell' which have also been available to advertisers since the 1950s. Interestingly, although these soft-sell formats have developed technologically, and have modified (to some extent) their meanings and mythologies, they do not seem to have faced the same problems of cringe and credibility as the strategies we have so far considered.

For instance, the final clip in the *Washes Whiter* programme comes from an advert, which some readers of this book may recall, for Gillette shaving equipment. It uses a montage of images signifying a mid-1980s 'thirtysomething/yuppie' lifestyle, cut to a familiar signature tune: 'Gillette: the best a man can get'. The signs include the successful business man, the romantic lover, the sportsman and the father (with both baby and young son); and the montage works, not to set up contrasts between these images, but to establish their unity and equivalence within the overall lifestyle ('For all a man can be', as the song goes). It is not surprising that *Washes Whiter* concludes with this ad, for it represents, of course, the mythology of the 'new man', which serves (in the context of this programme) to show how far advertising to men has progressed since the 1950s. Actually I think the key point is that the mythology of masculinity can now confidently include signs of personal life and self image, which are no longer issues for potential anxiety or embarrassment.

However, confident masculinity in itself is nothing new, nor indeed is the 'lifestyle format' which the Gillette advert exemplifies. For instance, *Washes Whiter* includes a British Petroleum ad from 1965 which features the lifestyle of a photographer – as one of the trendier professions of the time (see figure 3.4). Here, images of our hero taking photographs are intercut with shots of him driving (there is some use of point of view) and with external shots of parts of the car, in a fast-moving montage which eventually delivers him to the garage with the BP sign. Meanwhile a voice-over intones:

> See this man. This man sees action. This man gets around, gets a job done. This man and the car in his life. Together. With it. Against it. Confident. Backed up by this sign.

On this evidence, it would appear that the range of images which are available to signify confident masculinity (we might call this the masculinity paradigm) is more restricted in the 1960s, by comparison with the 1980s. It is also the case that in the contemporary ad, the strident tones of a voice-over have been replaced by a quasi-pop song. However, as regards what Leiss *et al.* describe as the format of the ad, and the construction of its appeal, I think there are clear continuities. This 'lifestyle' advert is not designed to persuade, nor does it really invite self-identification; rather, its mode of address is directed towards what one advertising theorist (quoted by Jhally, 1990) has described as the creation of 'resonance':

> Tony Schwartz (1974) has given the most eloquent expression of this discovery in his 'resonance' theory of communication . . . Schwartz's concern is not with the message itself as a communicator of meaning, but rather with the use-value of the message for the audience . . . Advertisers, according to Schwartz, should be in the business of 'structured recall'. The purpose is to design commercials that create pleasurable moments that will be triggered when the product is viewed in the market place. As Schwartz . . . says: 'I do not care what number of people *remember* or *get* the message. I am concerned with how people are affected by the stimuli'. (p.129)

I think this quotation captures the essence of soft-sell advertising. It is, as Schwartz puts it, a process of communication without a specific message, and it represents a shift away from persuasion or psychological manipulation, towards a more generalised affective appeal. How is the consumer interpellated by this form of advertising? Surely when Schwartz talks about 'stimuli' he is, in our terms, referring to signs, where the stimulus is constructed through the ability to associate signifiers with signifieds, and the

Fig. 3.4. The 'lifestyle' format in a TV advert for British Petroleum (1965)

consumer is interpellated as a decoder of signs. What he calls 'resonance' is derived from our recognition of pleasurable connotations. The crucial shift here, is from the denotative to the connotative level of the sign, and in this respect, as regards the categories defined by Leiss *et al.*, I see little to distinguish between the 'lifestyle' format and the earlier 'product-image' format (which they discover in American magazines from the 1920s). Here again, as they argue, 'products are presented less and less on the basis of a performance promise, and more on making them "resonate" with qualities desired by the consumer – status, glamour . . .' and so on (p.155). What might have occurred, under the influence of modern market research, is an increasing focus on the glamorous lifestyle, but this is offered to the consumer within a well established semiological strategy.

Plus ça change . . . What this analysis seems to suggest is that there is nothing particularly new about 'new man' advertising, at least insofar as we are concerned with its textual structures and modes of address. In fact, this is a common perception in media text analysis – the more we familiarise ourselves with the basic working of texts, the less innovative (or 'progressive') new developments often appear. However, I now want to turn very briefly to a new advertising format which is not discussed by Leiss *et al.*, and which is not illustrated in *Washes Whiter*. This is the format we have already seen illustrated by the advert for Gordon's gin, and which, in Britain at least, may be found more often in magazines, on billboards or in the cinema (where the Gordon's campaign has also appeared) than on television. That it has the capacity to construct a new mode of address for television advertising is suggested by evidence from the USA, as provided by Robert Goldman's (1992) analysis of the 'not-ad' – that is, the advert which addresses the consumer by saying 'this is not an ad'. As Goldman comments:

> The name of the game in advertising today is to differentiate one's sign from others. This is done by visually differentiating the look of one's ad – seizing the eye of the viewer . . . Advertisers are also motivated to produce ads which are unpredictable and whose meanings are opaque, if not impenetrable, because they *arrest* the attention of viewers. If viewers spend more time pondering the meaning of an ad, if they make more of an investment in interpreting it, then perhaps they will be more likely to recall the product name. (p.171)

Goldman describes a US TV advertising campaign for Levi's 501s, which, in its use of documentary realism, and its 'knowing wink' to the viewer, seems much more 'arresting' than its (admittedly stylish, but nonetheless conventionally mythological) British counterpart. It would seem that to arrest the attention of the viewer in this manner is to offer a form of interpellation in advertising which is quite different from those we have considered so far. For Goldman, such not-ad advertising may be deliberately obscure, but it also has the capacity to become self-reflexive – drawing attention to its own status as advertising, or posing questions about what advertising is, or should be, doing. Here again, we are back in the territory of the 'knowing consumer', who now not only knows about products (and so does not need to be educated), but also knows about (has grown very familiar with) the more conventional formats of advertising. Perhaps we could say then that in not-ad advertising the consumer is now not simply interpellated as a decoder of signs; rather he or she is now addressed as an expert in forms of signification and so interpellated, at least potentially, as a semiologist.

Undoubtedly the most notorious example of the not-ad in the British context has been Benetton's controversial use of (shocking) documentary photographs (new-born baby, terrorist bomb, dying AIDS victim and so on). Again it is significant that the Benetton campaign was directed at billboards and magazines rather than British TV. Clearly, there are economic and institutional conditions which set limits to such forms of experimentation. Not-ad advertising is a product of the principle of market segmentation, which connects with the point previously made that British television is only just beginning to explore its potential to appeal to diverse audiences. But perhaps

there are some (much less radical) not-ads on TV: I have mentioned Jeff
Goldblum's knowing wink to the viewer in recent ads for Holsten Pils; before
that we had Griff Rhys-Jones edited into scenes from old movies in 'Holsten
Pils Productions'. Generally such forms of humorous inter-textuality appear
to be the preferred strategy for current British television.

The general point then, to conclude this chapter, is to confirm that historical changes and transformations in popular media texts can and do occur,
but these always depend on broader social and economic conditions. Textual
structures are open to experimentation – and we have noted some innovative ways of delivering persuasive arguments in advertising. Equally, new
modes of address may be developed, particularly where there is a shift in
definitions of the audience. Ultimately however, and at its most radical, I
think not-ad advertising is raising a further set of questions, which will point
us forward to the next part of this book. Where questions are raised about
the purpose of advertising as such, or about what is, or is not 'appropriate'
in advertising, such questioning begins to focus on the definition of advertising as a genre. Certainly Benetton's advertising has provoked such
questions, at the same time as it has generated unprecedented numbers of
complaints. And it is interesting that these complaints have led to censure,
not only from 'watchdogs' like the Advertising Standards Authority, but
even, in one notorious case, from the very media which might otherwise be
profiting from the advertising. Here, at the editorial board of *Elle*, it would
seem that generic sensibilities, as well as ethical misgivings, were at stake:

WHY THESE PAGES ARE BLANK

This space was reserved for a double page advertisement, but after
discussion between the editorial and advertising departments we feel
that the image supplied by the advertiser is too distasteful to run. For
ethical reason we have never run fur, cosmetic surgery or cigarette
advertising in ELLE and all ads are carefully vetted before appearing.
In this case, the debate rests on whether the images of some real-life
subjects are too personal and upsetting to be hi-jacked for advertising
purposes. A line of decency has to be drawn between freedom of
journalistic reportage and purely promotional intentions. Rather than
risk offending our readers we have taken the decision to leave these
pages blank, if you wish to know more, please write to The Editor,
ELLE, Rex House, 4–12 Lower Regent Street, London SW1Y 4PE.

Maggie Alderson Editor

FURTHER READING

Most of the recommended reading relating to this chapter has been cited previously: such as John Ellis (1982) on modes of address in cinema and television; Pam Cook (ed) (1985) on cinematic spectatorship; and William Leiss *et al.* (1990) on modes of address and the history of advertising. However there are also some useful American essays on modes of address in television: by Jane Feuer (1992) 'The Concept of Live Television: Ontology as Ideology', and by Robert Stam 'Television News and its Spectator' both in Kaplan EA (ed) (1983); and by Margaret Morse, 'The Television News Personality and Credibility' in Modleski T. (ed) (1986), and 'Talk, Talk, Talk – The Space of Discourse in Television', *Screen* Vol 26 No 2 (1985). An earlier version of the arguments presented in Section 3 of this chapter can be found in Tolson A (1985).

2

CONTEXTS

4

Genre

CHAPTER ONE

NOT again!

Bernadette's teeth clenched in sheer frustration as she stared at the sheaf of red roses in the delivery boy's arms. She knew, without having to count them, that there would be twenty-four this time. 'Miss Bernadette Hamilton?'

'Yes', she bit out, unable to respond to the fatuous grin on the boy's face.

She inwardly winced over the curtness of her acknowledgment as his grin disappeared. The boy was only doing a job. He wasn't to know that the beautiful blooms gave her more torment than pleasure. She offered an appeasing smile as he gravely handed her the roses and the gold-embossed envelope – sealed, as it had been every year, with wax.

Bernadette didn't bother to ask who was the donor. She had pursued that track three years ago and the florist knew no more about the mystery man than she did. The envelope was sent with a typed note of instructions and a blank cheque – untraceable.

She dragged her gaze up from the wax seal and caught the sparkle of suppressed laughter in the delivery boy's eyes. 'Thank you', she said with almost frigid dignity, instantly realising that the curious once-a-year incident was probably a source of amusing gossip at the florist shop . . .

. . . This was the sixth time. She almost hated the man who was doing it to her, whoever he was. The roses she could have dismissed. Anyone could be sending her roses on her birthday – one for each year of her age since she had turned nineteen – if only the gold embossed envelope did not come with them.

> What he was doing to her – what he had done to her – with his tanta-
> lising messages was diabolical. They had completely undermined her
> relationships with Scott and Barry and Trent; made her wonder about
> every other man who had apparently been attracted to her . . . whether it
> was for her own self, or because of their potential prospects as Gerard
> Hamilton's future son-in-law. Even if she was illegitimate, it seemed that
> any foot inside her father's door would do.
>
> Bernadette had suffered too many lessons in disillusionment to accept
> much at face value any more. But this insidious seige on her heart and
> mind . . . why didn't he make himself known to her? Why taunt her with
> words of love if he had no intention of meeting her . . . openly declaring
> what he secretly and mysteriously professed?

The problems faced by Bernadette Hamilton in her attempts to understand
the significance of this gift, run deeper than any we have encountered in this
book so far. Clearly, she understands the meaning of the red roses, insofar
as she recognises their fairly obvious connotations. Because she is disturbed
by them, she is also in a position to question their preferred reading, but her
disturbance is not based on a critical perspective which is sceptical of the
mythology of romance. Rather, Bernadette's problems derive from her inability to interpret the motivations of the sender. While she derives some
'resonance' from this gift, Bernadette has major problems with what some
theorists would term its communicative intentionality. Are these connotations
for real? Are they sincere? Or is this some perverse form of deceit and manipulation?

The theory of communicative intentionality derives from a particular
philosophy of language (H. P. Grice) which has been developed within a
branch of linguistics known as 'pragmatics' (see Levinson, 1983). We will
not be concerned here with the details of this approach, merely to observe
that it is founded upon two key propositions. The first proposition states
that, in any act of communication, or 'utterance', there is a level of meaning
beyond the semantic (which we have analysed here using the methods of
semiology). That further level of meaning concerns the import of the utterance, which is a product of the manner in which it is produced and (potentially) consumed – sincerely, sarcastically, ironically, humorously and so
forth. The second proposition is based on an assumption that all communication is essentially co-operative, and so the import of any utterance is interpreted on that basis, and according to an implicit code of ethics (or
'maxims'). Unless there are very good reasons not to do so, utterances should
be produced according to maxims of truthfulness, clarity, relevance and
sincerity – and if they do not demonstrate these qualities, then speakers may
be held accountable. For instance, if someone is found to have lied, we
typically want to know why – it may be that they are deceitful, or even, as

Bernadette also suspects, psychotic. If a politician lies to the House of Commons, or if he is 'economical' with the truth, or even if he produces utterances in interviews which are obtuse or evasive, then he could have a lot of explaining to do.

Bernadette's problems are of this kind. She cannot read the true import of this gift, she needs an explanation, but she is bound to be frustrated, at least for another 170 pages. However the fact that this frustration, though a problem for Bernadette, is not ethically intolerable for the reader, raises a further key issue for media text analysis. It is possible, like Bernadette, to question the personal motives of individuals suspected of behaving badly ('What did you mean by this?'); but it is also possible, by attending to the context, to discover good reasons for the apparently bad behaviour. In some contexts a certain economy with the truth might produce effects which are ultimately pleasurable and entertaining. In this context, Bernadette may be bound to be frustrated; but we, the readers, are prepared to suffer and even enjoy her frustration because we are confident that, in the end, a pleasurable outcome will ensue.

Our confidence, of course, comes from our understanding of the rules of the game being played. Not only in media texts but also in everyday life, we are prepared to accept some deviation from the ethics of co-operative communication if we understand (not necessarily beforehand) that particular rules apply. So there is no problem with insincerity if we discover that the context is a joke (consider the 'April Fool'); and there is no problem with deceit, if someone is acting deceitfully in a play. In short, our willingness to tolerate 'deviant' communication is related to our understanding of the genre within which the utterance is produced. This key concept refers, in the first instance, to our knowledge that there are different types of communication, and that this will influence the way we interpret any media text.

For example, as readers, we will all have some prior knowledge of the generic context within which these roses are delivered to Bernadette. At the outset, we can see that this is a narrative, but that it conforms to the conventions of the novel, rather than, as previously discussed, the oral narrative (the key conventions here are adherence to the third person, and past tense, mode of narration). Moreover, how many readers of this book were able, without being told, to recognise precisely the type of novel within which these events occur? Is it obvious to any reader, in this culture, that despite the suggestion of a psychotic donor, these events will not lead on to a horror story, or a murder mystery but, in fact, they are the opening skirmishes in a romance? It certainly would have been obvious if I had included the information, which any reader of course would have, that this is an extract from the first two and a half pages of a novelette entitled *The Power and The Passion*, by Emma Darcy, published in the Mills and Boon 'Favourites' series (1994).

The romantic novelette is a prime example of a mass mediated genre. Although it is not transmitted by what we conventionally define as 'the media', it is, as Deborah Philips (1990) emphasises, produced and marketed in conditions of mass cultural production, and sold, like any other commodity, on supermarket shelves. In part, the 'rules of the game' for this genre are well understood by readers because they are well established in the history of the novel (going back to classics of English literature like *Pamela* and *Pride and Prejudice*). More particularly, however, these rules are carefully adhered to by the authors who write for Mills and Boon – and the publishers themselves issue 'tipsheets' on what ought to be included, as well as rejecting manuscripts deemed to be unsuitable. It is also interesting that the mass production and marketing of these novelettes is influenced by continous market research, and the authors are encouraged to write with the typical reader in mind. Thus, readers' views and expectations feed back into the production process which, as long as it remains conventional, will serve to reinforce a 'game' which is well understood by all concerned.

I will turn to theoretical discussions of genre in my next section. Here I just want to explore the kinds of knowledge which the reader might be expected to possess as soon as she (for a female reader is, of course, assumed) picks up a Mills and Boon. Tania Modleski (1982) has provided an outline of what she terms the 'formula':

> Each book averages approximately 187 pages, and the formula rarely varies: a young, inexperienced, poor to moderately well-to-do woman encounters and becomes involved with a handsome, strong, experienced, wealthy man, older than herself by ten to fifteen years. The heroine is confused by the hero's behavior since, though he is obviously interested in her, he is mocking, cynical, contemptuous, often hostile, even somewhat brutal. By the end, however, all misunderstandings are cleared away, and the hero reveals his love for the heroine, who reciprocates. (p.36)

If this is a fair representation of the prior knowledge of the reader of *The Power and The Passion*, then presumably there will be a strong suspicion that the flowers will have been sent by the hero who is currently, insofar as this is tormenting Bernadette, behaving with his customary ambiguity. In fact, he is revealed to be Danton Fayette, who is indeed a powerful financier, from a French family, approximately ten years older than Bernadette, and who possesses all the necessary physical attributes. Bernadette herself is twenty-four, relatively inexperienced (given her misfortunes with Scott, Barry and Trent) and potentially well-to-do as the illegitimate daughter of an equally rich and powerful father. Furthermore *The Power and The Passion* is 189 pages long and, by the end, the necessary 'reciprocation' has occurred. Modleski's 'formula' would seem to be in place – so are these novelettes entirely predictable?

Other features of the 'ideal' romance are discussed by Janice Radway (1984). Interestingly, she bases her account not on an academic description of the formula, nor even on a publisher's tipsheet, but on the preferences expressed by readers she has interviewed. However these preferences do not contradict Modleski's formula, rather they add to it – conforming the sense of a well regulated industry which takes its readers into account. Thus, in the ideal romance, the heroine should show signs of 'spirit': she should be intelligent, capable of independence and able to stand up for herself. She should be highly attractive to men, and capable of uncontrolled sexual response, but unaware of this in her innocence. Meanwhile, the hero's bad behaviour must be revealed to be a mask which conceals a true identity which can finally be understood by the heroine. Ideally, according to Radway, his ambiguity is the product of a previous emotional hurt, which the love of the heroine can put to rights.

In these respects, Bernadette is certainly characterised as a highly 'spirited' heroine, who has recently qualified as a doctor, and who will not accept her father's charity, or any other form of male condescension. She cannot, however, avoid responding to Danton. On the other hand, his bad behaviour is revealed to be, not the sign of an emotional problem, but rather an elaborate stratagem to woo Bernadette, based on his knowledge of her suspicion of men. So it turns out that Bernadette must make peace with her father (he has a heart attack) at the same time as she accepts Danton. In so doing, she discovers the truth of her illegitimacy and so reconciles herself to her father, to his current mistress, and to the image of her own dead mother. At this point, perhaps, things are becoming a little complicated!

Let us review therefore, the generic knowledge the reader possesses which allows her to make sense of this text. Beyond a general knowledge of what to expect from a novel, there are three particular kinds of knowledge which pertain to the romantic novelette. First there is, most obviously, knowledge of character, of what to expect from a hero and heroine. This can be extended (see Chapter 2) to include all knowledge of the 'existents' which typically feature in this genre; and this would include typical settings as well as characters. Thus, in *The Power and The Passion*, the sexual consummation takes place on a Tahitian island (owned by Danton) where the exotic tropical scenery and the lack of cultural inhibitions both contribute to Bernadette's seduction.

Second, there is some prior knowledge of the sequence of events which is typical of the genre. It is this knowledge which allows the opening to be read as an enigma (who is the donor?) which it is the purpose of the narrative to reveal. Also we know that we are about to embark on a journey from an unhappy to an ideal state of affairs. This is part of our general knowledge of typical plots; and we know that, in a romance, the plot will resolve the problems it introduces at the start. Moreover, Janice Radway

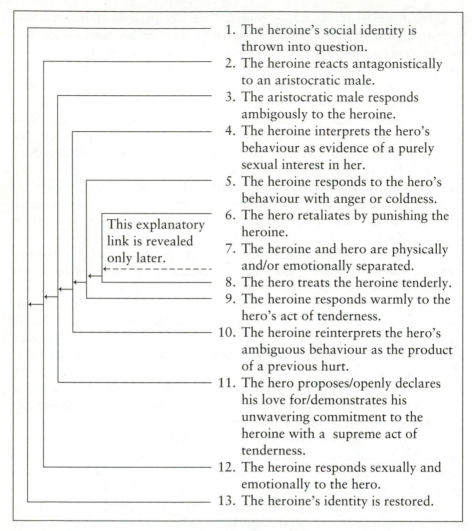

1. The heroine's social identity is thrown into question.
2. The heroine reacts antagonistically to an aristocratic male.
3. The aristocratic male responds ambiguously to the heroine.
4. The heroine interprets the hero's behaviour as evidence of a purely sexual interest in her.
5. The heroine responds to the hero's behaviour with anger or coldness.
6. The hero retaliates by punishing the heroine.
7. The heroine and hero are physically and/or emotionally separated.
8. The hero treats the heroine tenderly.
9. The heroine responds warmly to the hero's act of tenderness.
10. The heroine reinterprets the hero's ambiguous behaviour as the product of a previous hurt.
11. The hero proposes/openly declares his love for/demonstrates his unwavering commitment to the heroine with a supreme act of tenderness.
12. The heroine responds sexually and emotionally to the hero.
13. The heroine's identity is restored.

This explanatory link is revealed only later.

Fig. 4.1. The Narrative Logic of the Romance, from Janice Radway, Reading The Romance, Verso (1984), p.150. *By permission of the author and Verso Publishers*

claims that it is more or less possible to chart the progress of the plot in an 'ideal' romance, which she does in the diagram set out above. This is an illustration of Propp's narrative theory, where the plot is a sequence of typical events or functions, but where Radway has discovered a rather neat 'logic' in which each function is balanced by another and a narrative equilibrium is produced (see figure 4.1).

To a very large extent, the plot of *The Power and The Passion* does indeed correspond to this model. Bernadette is illegitimate (function 1), and she reacts antagonistically to Danton (functions 2 and 5), whose behaviour is certainly ambiguous (function 3) and open to all kinds of interpretation by Bernadette (functions 4 and 6). However, such is the complexity of Danton's approach that the 'punishment' (function 6) which involves enticing Bernadette to his tropical island, is also ambivalently desired by the heroine herself (he makes her an offer she cannot emotionally refuse), and is revealed (as in function 10) to be a strategem on his part, not the product of a previous hurt. It is a strategem where punishment and tenderness (function 8) alternate at bewildering speed, but after a period of separation (function 7), where the heroine nurses her father, functions 11, 12 and 13 are all fulfilled in the final chapter.

It is consistent with Propp's theory that there can be some variations and unexpected twists in the development of a plot, as long as the essential narrative functions are completed. Moreover, these functions can be fulfilled by any existents and not necessarily, as Radway implies, solely by the hero and heroine. In *The Power and The Passion* there is, in effect, a sub-plot built around Bernadette's relationship with her father. So far as she is concerned, he is another ambiguous man who cannot be trusted and against whom she must establish her independence. At the back of this problem are the circumstances of her birth and the identity of her mother – in fact, what a psychoanalyst would regard as an unresolved Oedipus complex (we will return to this concept in Chapter 7). The upshot however is that it is the father, not the hero, who fulfils function 10 in the narrative logic – for Bernadette's mother died during her birth and the hurt which Gerard has suffered since is the source of his ambivalence towards her.

But this existence of a sub-plot also points to a third level of knowledge which the reader may be bringing to this novel. This can be defined as knowledge of sub-genre: that is to say, the reader has prior expectations, not only of the romance in general, but also of specific types of romance and variations on the romance theme. In her discussion, which is informed by a historical perspective, Tania Modleski distinguishes between the 'Harlequin' and the 'Gothic' romance, as two distinct sub-genres. The former is the typical Mills and Boon (Harlequin is the equivalent Canadian publisher) which focuses on the heroine overcoming her resistance to the hero. The latter (e.g. Daphne du Maurier's *Rebecca*) focuses on the fears of the heroine after her marriage, given the ambiguous behaviour, and mysterious family history, of her husband. Thus, Modleski suggests:

> The reader of Harlequin Romances finds herself . . . desiring the subversion of the heroine's attempts at self-assertion; and the reader of Gothics identifies with a heroine who fears hereditary madness or who feels literally possessed by the spirits of other women from out of the past. (p.37)

Modleski turns to psychoanalytic explanations for the Gothic sub-genre: where the husband is also (symbolically) a father-figure and the 'woman in the past' (or in the attic) invokes the heroine's relationship with her mother. Here I am drawing on this theory only insofar as it would suggest that there might be elements of the 'Gothic' in *The Power and The Passion*. Knowledge of this sub-genre might allow for the reader's acceptance of a narrative logic where the identity of the mother is a central question and where (in Bernadette's mind) the romantic hero and the father are, at times, interchangeable. Indeed, at one point, in the plot Bernadette suspects Danton and Gerard of colluding against her – which would seem to be a case of the 'paranoia' Modleski associates with the Gothic romance.

At any rate, the complexities we can discover, even in a conventional romantic novelette, do suggest some important points about genre, which we can take further in the course of this chapter. They suggest, for instance, that if genre is concerned with readers' expectations of texts, then these must be open to novelty and variation. No one, not even the Mills and Boon reader, wants to read the same plot, with the same characters over and over again – which further suggests, I think, that if these books are written to a formula (Modleski), we need to be clear what we mean when we use this term. Stephen Neale (1980) points out that genre as an aspect of film production is quite different from, say, the notion of the 'model' in the production of commodities like cars. Genre admits, indeed requires, difference; whereas the model turns out the same product (albeit in different colours). Even Deborah Philips, who is most concerned to stress the mass-produced character of romances, recognises this – where she observes for instance that changing reader expectations (such as a tolerance of more explicit eroticism), as discovered by market research, has led to some diversification of sub-genres by the publishers of romantic fiction.

However, despite such differences and variations, the writers on romance are agreed that there remains a basic unity to the genre which defines it as such. The theoretical question, which we will go on to consider, is where to locate that unity; that is to say, where do we discover the principle that allows us to recognise the romance, or any other genre, as a genre? As we shall see, this theoretical question has been answered in different ways, but one key aspect of the recent work on romance has been the recognition that this genre, in certain fundamentally conservative ways, speaks to the experience of women. As Janice Radway puts it, 'the romance is an account of a woman's journey to female personhood *as that particular psychic configuration is constructed and realised within patriarchal culture*' (p.138, her emphasis). At the heart of this psychic configuration is the problem of men ... 'in learning *how to read a man*, the romance tells its reader, she will reinforce his better instincts, break down his reserve, and lead him to respond to her as she wishes' (p.148). This is, of course, a fantasy; but it is this fantasy which motivates the narrative logic of *The Pride and The Passion*, and which is announced in the gift of the roses to a confused Bernadette Hamilton.

2   THEORY OF GENRE

Perhaps more than any other area of contemporary media studies, the theory of genre remains in a state of uncertainty and confusion. Certainly, as regards the theoretical question we have posed, about the basis on which genres might be recognised, there is an apparent difference of opinion. There is an argument, for instance, that the task facing media studies is to emulate the history of literary criticism, where critics would impose their own generic categories on the apparent diversity of media texts. This is seen as analogous to the process of classifying species of flora and fauna – as in the science of biology, where these are located within a taxonomy or theoretical scheme (see Feuer 1992). In *Marxism and Literature* (1977), however, Raymond Williams has criticised this approach, arguing that it is both 'empiricist' in its assumption that texts are fixed and given entities, and also 'idealist' in its theoretical invention of categories. One question which might be asked, therefore, is whether it is appropriate for media studies to adopt this kind of pseudo-scientific approach.

In a moment we will see where this kind of questioning might lead. First however, we must acknowledge that both the 'empiricist' and the 'idealist' perspectives, as defined by Williams, have had some influence in media studies, particularly in film theory. Perhaps the influence of the empiricist approach derives from the rather 'obvious' fact that one can recognise a certain type of text when one sees it. Thus, film theory has found it possible to categorise the major genres of classical Hollywood cinema (the western, the gangster film, the musical, the melodrama, the *film noir* and so on) on the basis of its recognition of typical textual features. Such features have ranged from aspects of content (basic subject matter, thematic preoccupations) to aspects of style (for example, the lighting techniques which characterise *film noir*).

Undoubtedly the most interesting contribution from this perspective has been its concept of iconography. Iconography refers to typical signs whose connotations have, through routine use, become fixed. It thus becomes possible for a spectator who is well versed in the conventions, to recognise immediately the meaning of signs such as costume, setting and what Buscombe (1970), in a discussion of westerns, calls the 'tools of the trade' (for example, certain typical weapons and forms of transportation). This concept of iconography seems to have particular relevance to highly coded cinematic genres such as westerns and gangster movies of the 1930s and 40s.

But this recognition of typical signs in Hollywood genres has also been supported by a further historical argument. It is the case that some generic categories have been mobilised in several ways within the film industry itself. Thus there is a familiar line of argument which runs from the 'obvious' existence of genres, through the way the film industry was organised in its 'classical' period (1920s–1950s), to the continuing importance of genre as a marketing device. For instance, different Hollywood studios have specialised in producing different genres (such as the MGM musical and the Warner Bros gangster film). As Steve Neale (1990) has demonstrated, generic categories such as the western, were being used in the trade press to classify films for exhibition purposes from as early as 1912. And, as John Ellis (1982) argues, the genre of a film is one major aspect of its selling point, featured in the posters and publicity which constructs what he calls a 'narrative image' for a film in the minds of its potential audience.

Such arguments are interesting because they begin to indicate something of the complexity of this key concept. Clearly, the more the discussion proceeds in the directions suggested by Neale and Ellis, the more the concept of genre begins to extend beyond the simple recognition of textual features. Genre is now a category which mediates between industry and audience, through particular procedures for the distribution, marketing and exhibition of films. As Deborah Philips has pointed out, a similar industrial process exists in the marketing of Mills and Boon romances, so we might speculate that this might be true for all mass media and popular cultural texts. Genre then becomes a difficult concept because it extends beyond the text itself to a number of different sites for textual production and consumption, and it is not easy to specify how all these aspects relate to each other.

In any case, the empiricist attempt to categorise the different genres according to their textual features, soon runs into additional practical difficulties. In many film texts, even of the classical period, there is a perceived combination of generic elements such as the melodrama which is filmed in *film noir* style *Mildred Pierce* (1945) or the melodrama which is also a western *Duel in the Sun* (1947). Certainly, by the 1950s, it becomes necessary to recognise the production of 'hybrid' genres, such as the musical westerns *Calamity Jane* (1953) and *Oklahoma!* (1955). Towards the end of the classical period, a comedy film like *Some Like It Hot* (1959) can not only make fun of traditional genres (in this case, the gangster film) it can also begin to parody classical acting techniques (as in the impersonation, by Tony Curtis, of Cary Grant's acting style). This points the way forward to the generic spoofs produced in the 1970s by Mel Brooks *Blazing Saddles* (1974) and *High Anxiety* (1977). The general point is that genre may remain a relevant concept, but it must be recognised that generic categories are fluid and flexible, and that they are subject to historical change and development.

This recognition of the importance of history, certainly to the analysis of film genres, has led some media theorists to question the relevance of the other tendency discussed by Williams, namely the 'idealist' perspective. The main difficulty here is that, in literary studies, where it is most developed, this perspective is resolutely ahistorical. Descended from the Greek philosophers Plato and Aristotle, it has sought to identify a few key factors which can account for the differences between all conceivable texts. For Plato, such factors were discovered in the poet's enunciative voice (which Williams calls a 'stance'), which classified all texts into the categories of lyric (where the poet speaks in his/her own voice), dramatic (where the poet assumes the voices of characters), and narrative (a mixture of the two). In Aristotle's *Poetics*, these factors were extended to incorporate classifications based on subject matter, from which were derived the dramatic genres, tragedy and comedy, and the narrative genres, epic and parody. Thenceforth, there has circulated throughout the history of literature, a theory of ideal types of texts, which has had a prescriptive as well as a descriptive influence. For instance, in the sixteenth century, playwrights such as Shakespeare were influenced by Aristotelian principles of what constituted 'proper' tragedy and, in the eighteenth century, the theatre was governed by equally prescriptive principles of manner and decorum.

A basic distinction between 'historical' and 'theoretical' approaches to genre continues to operate in literary criticism (see Todorov, 1976), and this has exerted some influence on the development of media studies. For example, some literary theorists, most notably Northrop Frye (1970), have sought to extend the theoretical approach of the ancient Greeks to encompass modern forms of literature, such as the novel. On the other hand, media theorists have questioned the relevance of such universal categories and, indeed have disputed their 'theoretical' status (see Palmer, 1991). In general, media studies has seemed more 'at home' with an empirical and historical approach, which recognises generic flexibility. However, I am not so sure that the theoretical approach should be regarded as entirely redundant, at least in the sense suggested by Williams with his use of the term 'idealist'. For all its historical focus, I think there remains a sense in which a prescriptive emphasis, on ideal-types, remains relevant to the theory of genre in media studies.

For instance, the ghost of Aristotle can be seen to walk even in some empiricist accounts of genre. In an (admittedly early) essay, Tom Ryall (1970) considers, but rejects as too prescriptive, the argument that film genres should follow 'ideal forms'. Here, he is criticising the notion that there is such a thing as the 'classic' western or gangster film, which all other examples of the genre should try to emulate. However Ryall still wants to restrict, in this essay, the use of the term 'genre' to texts which can be defined as properly generic. There are films, Ryall suggests, and there are

'genre films'. To qualify as a genre film, the text must exhibit certain qualities, and these imply, among other things, certain intentions on the part of
its producers:

> A crucial notion in any definition of genre, must be that the genre film is
> one which exhibits a relationship with other examples of the genre. This
> also implies a consciousness of this relationship on the part of the man
> [*sic*] who makes the film and on the part of the audience who go to see
> it. If we consider the western, the relationship will be in terms of a
> *complex* of basic material or subject matter, of thematic preoccupations
> and of iconographical continuity. This complex provides the directors of
> genre films with a basic 'given' to work upon and it also provides an
> audience with a set of expectations which they will carry to the film.
> (p.26)

There are two major problems in this quotation (which probably can be
accounted for by the fact that it was written in 1970) but I do not want
these to detain us here. Briefly then, the first problem is the sexism of the
language and the second is the very debatable notion of 'consciousness' – as
we shall see later, more recent media theory radically questions the assumption that the producers of texts are necessarily 'conscious', in this sense, of
what it is they are doing. Nevertheless, I think Ryall's point is interesting
because it locates a sense of propriety (what can or cannot be called a 'genre
film') not simply within the text itself, but again within a wider context in
which genre is a mediating term between industry and audience. Once again,
there is a sense here in which the term genre refers to a body of knowledge
which is not derived (in empiricist fashion) from the texts themselves, but
which accompanies the production, distribution and consumption of texts.
And, if Ryall is to be believed, it is in this body of knowledge that there
remains a space for some discussion of 'proper' generic characteristics.

However, it seems to me to be crucial that this body of knowledge is not
the invention of philosophers or even media critics, rather it is located in
everyday life. In this context, let us also return to Radway's discussion of
the 'ideal' romance. In fact, the narrative model for the romance which
Radway has produced (see above) is difficult to apply to all romances
precisely because it is an ideal type, rather than the product of an empirical
survey of the genre. However, Radway is making a virtue of the fact that
this is a model of the ideal romance as perceived by the readers she has interviewed. In other words, this is a prescriptive definition which is part of their
body of knowledge, and it is on this basis that they distinguish between
'ideal' and 'failed' romances. Clearly then, Radway is taking an 'idealist' or
'theoretical' approach to what constitutes a good or proper example of this
genre, but her warrant for so doing is that this is precisely the approach
adopted by the readers themselves. The idealist perspective remains relevant

to the theory of genre in media studies because it is one aspect of the range of expectations which readers or audiences are bringing to media texts.

Once again then, the theory of genre becomes complicated. If the empiricist approach points us towards the wider context within which texts are produced and consumed, consideration of the idealist approach would suggest that some lingering interest in ideal types is one feature of that wider context. So where does this lead us? I think it leads, ultimately, to a fundamental shift of perspective in media text analysis. It suggests that there are factors which are relevant to this analysis which cannot be derived simply from studying media texts. In other words, the theory of genre shows that there are limits to the applicability of semiology. Genre is not simply a feature of signs, structures, or textual modes of address; it is an aspect of the wider context to which we have referred. However, we also need to account for the fact that this wider context, in exercising its influence on the production and consumption of texts, does have some effect on the signs which texts contain – allowing some signs, for instance, to be recognised as generic iconography.

Perhaps the most suggestive of the recent discussions of the theory of genre in media studies is that provided by Steve Neale in his essay 'Questions of Genre' (1990). As we have noted, in this essay Neale shows how generic categories have been used to classify films (in company catalogues, for purposes of sale and distribution) since the earliest days of the cinema. He argues (with reference to Todorov) that such categories imply the existence of generic 'systems' or 'regimes', where genres are defined and differentiated with reference to each other (a bit like the notion, in semiology, of a system of differences). In different periods in the history of cinema, different generic systems have prevailed; however, Neale's key point is that at no time has the film industry simply invented its own categories. Rather, it has made use of terms (comic, mysterious, scenic etc) already in public circulation, and which have been incorporated into what Neale wants to call 'institutional discourses':

> Clearly, generic conventions and knowledges do not emanate solely from the film industry and its ancillary institutions; and clearly individual spectators may have their own expectations, classifications, labels and terms. But these individualised, idiosyncratic classifications play little part, if any, in the public formation and circulation of genres and generic images. In the public sphere, the institutional discourses are of central importance. Testimony to the existence of genres, and evidence of their properties, is to be found primarily there. (p.52)

In this highly condensed passage, Neale is introducing additional key concepts for media text analysis, which will be explored in subsequent chapters of this book. In particular, what is meant by the term discourse, and what it means to speak of discourses as 'institutional' will require further clarification (in Chapter 7). Here, it seems that Neale is referring to a body of knowledge, which is 'public', and which is again located between the media industry and its audience, in that it is irreducible either to the industry itself or to individual expectations which members of the audience might have. However, in thinking about the precise location of this knowledge, I am not sure that I follow Neale's dismissal of the relevance of 'ancillary institutions', particularly because he goes on in his essay to look at trade magazines and catalogues. What his essay shows, I think, is that the wider context that influences the production and consumption of media texts is, in fact, occupied by a further network of texts, which might seem to be parasitic, but which are necessary to their circulation.

We are obliged then, by questions of genre, to extend the range of texts which we must consider. Genre prompts us to analyse, not only particular books, adverts, films and programmes, but also the publicity materials, catalogues, programme guides and reviews that announce their presence and accompany their circulation. Clearly, this latter body of material is 'public' in Neale's sense, for its function is precisely to make public, to public-ise, the products of the media industries. But what, exactly, is implied by Neale's insistence that this material is 'institutionalised'? Is he suggesting that the consumption of media texts, which at first might seem to be a personal and often private activity, is actually governed by institutional priorities and constraints? Do the media industries serve the purposes of some more general social institutions, which use categories, like genre, both to define their requirements and to organise the behaviour of consumers? Clearly we are not forced to consume media texts in quite the same way as we are obliged, by law, to attend school – but nevertheless the implication of Neale's discussion is intriguing: it suggests that our relationship to the media is not quite as casual, or perhaps as innocent, as it might at first appear.

In the remainder of this chapter, and in subsequent sections of this book, I want to explore the possibility that media consumption can be understood as a social activity which is governed by institutional pressures and conditions. That is to say, in our reading practices we have been socialised, educated, to consume media texts in particular ways, determined by the kind of society in which we live. At the most obvious level, we need to find time for our consumption of the media, which relates to the way in which we prioritise our activities, and define certain areas of our lives in terms of 'leisure' and 'entertainment'. Within these areas there are texts (like the *Radio Times*) and people (like Barry Norman, film critic for BBC television) who define what media texts we might be interested in and also, to a large extent, how to consume these texts in appropriate ways. This is where genre comes in: it is part of a kind of cultural 'know-how'; it implies that we are already experienced, indeed highly trained, in our responses to media texts.

It also assumes that we know how to organise our lives and 'get our priorities right' – issues which can be most clearly illustrated with reference to genre and television.

3 GENRE AND TELEVISION: READING THE *RADIO TIMES*

There are different ways of studying genre and television. The most common approach begins with a description of the characteristics of genres, but avoids 'empiricism' (Williams) by also offering theoretical explanations for their continuing success and popularity. Thus the continuous serial, particularly the soap opera, has been widely discussed as a narrative structure which is distinctive to broadcasting, with its familiar characters and multiple storylines, achieving a particular resonance with the cultural experience of women (1). Another genre which is equally characteristic of broadcasting is the situation comedy, but there is also now some considerable work on police and crime series, on quizzes and game shows, on children's programmes and on televised sports (2). Indeed it is possible to find interesting discussions of most television genres, and these have been informed in recent years by a growing interest in their historical evolution (3). However my concern here, following on from my previous discussion, will be less to do with the characteristics and the histories of particular genres (though I will refer in passing to the history of situation comedy), and will be more directed towards the way in which television uses generic categories – or what it might mean to say that a 'generic system' has been 'institutionalised' in television.

For instance, on Thursday, 21 April 1994, the BBC introduced a new serial drama called *Cardiac Arrest*. Of course, any new programme requires publicity, which it is the function of the *Radio Times*, and rival TV guides (which are now not only similar magazines like *What's On TV* and *TV Quick*, but also inserts and supplements in national newspapers) to provide. So (since this was a BBC programme) the *Radio Times* gave it the treatment: a caption on the front cover, a full-page interview with the writer, a full page photograph of the main characters, and a smaller photograph of characters alongside a 'choice' Thursday listing. The listing introduced the programme as a 'new six-part drama series about working in the NHS . . . filmed in an almost documentary style'. Clearly then, at least this amount of generic classification was felt to be of assistance to the potential viewer. In fact it is routinely supplied, in British TV guides, for all feature films; and some guides, particularly the *Radio Times*, offer generic descriptions of some TV programmes: 'a collection of comedy sketches', 'last in the documentary series', 'the weekly current affairs series', 'comedy drama series', 'a new seven part drama series' – all appear in the *Radio Times* listings for Thursday 21 April 1994.

The interview, with scriptwriter John MacUre, adds further levels of generic classification. Much is made of the fact that MacUre is himself a former junior hospital doctor, and he is photographed in uniform, complete with stethoscope. The interview begins with an account of his basic idea for the programme:

> It was buried next to the adverts for Famciclovir (a powerful new alternative in shingles) and chest infection seminars. There in the back of the *British Medical Journal* was a four-inch plea for comedy writers. 'It was the only interesting advert in the history of the *BMJ*' says Dr John MacUre, who as a result was chosen to pen – legibly – a new sitcom about general practice. 'I thought however, that it would be better to do a hard-hitting drama about junior hospital doctors – with lots of laughs – instead of a sitcom. So in *Cardiac Arrest*, patients are portrayed as junior doctors see them, not as patients see themselves. It's unashamedly biased. And unashamedly jaundiced'. (p.42)

Perhaps some of these remarks are the BBC's way of fending off potential political criticism, which this series did indeed attract. (There are also some interesting theoretical implications in what MacUre is saying about the doctor's point of view, to which, in Chapter 7, we will return.) More to the point here, however, is the relevance of generic distinction – indeed a generic system of differences – to both the process of production, and, in this article, to the generation of publicity. Thus the article proceeds:

> Television has never seen anything like *Cardiac Arrest* (Thursday BBC1). It's not *Surgical Spirit* (hardly made to talk about the NHS was it?'). And it's certainly not *Emergency Ward 10*. 'There have been good medical dramas that have satisfied BBC production values', says MacUre, 'like *Casualty*. But in *Casualty* what you see is the workings of a department. In *Cardiac Arrest*, even the nurses are seen from a junior doctor's perspective . . .

Here the publicity for the programme not only differentiates it from other current hospital dramas, it also refers to a long defunct series which is thirty years old! (*Emergency Ward 10* was made by ATV, an ITV company, in the 1950s and 60s). Thus it presumes, at least in some members of the audience, a memory, which we might call a popular memory, of what is effectively a sub-genre in the history of British television drama.

In fact the caption on the front cover of the *Radio Times* also stresses: 'Casualty it isn't . . . Hospital drama as you've never seen it before'. And both the comparison with the more conventional programme, and the emphasis on generic (or sub-generic) experimentation, were echoed in newspaper reviews of *Cardiac Arrest*, the following day. Thus, writing in the *Sun*, in 'What I Watched Last Night', Gary Leboff observes that 'sharing none of *Casualty's* softness, warmth or compassion, BBC 1's blistering new drama is bound to stoke the fires of controversy. For Virginia Bottomley and her Department of Health mandarins, *Cardiac Arrest* guarantees heart failure'. For Suzanne Moore in *The Guardian*, the comparison with *Casualty* confirms the same political point, that 'anything that veers towards realism on television . . . is by its very nature anti-government propaganda'. Thomas Sutcliffe in *The Independent* makes a similar political reading but goes on to discuss more particular generic issues: 'there were some rough gear changes between comedy and issue drama last night'. And, perhaps predictably in the *Daily Telegraph*, Theodore Dalrymple, invited to give a doctor's view of 'the blackest hospital drama series ever', produces a less sympathetic account of its generic instabilities:

> Clearly the life of a junior doctor is a fitting subject for the blackest of black humour. Misanthropic Swiftian savagery would hardly be misplaced in the circumstances; but *Cardiac Arrest*, in its eagerness to escape the sentimental view of medicine, falls uncomfortably between social realism and bitter satire. (p.19)

Thus, some TV critics, in these reviews, have felt obliged to make aesthetic evaluations of the programme. However, I think it is more interesting to observe that, whether they are positive or negative, these evaluations are governed by the very same agenda that has already appeared in the programme's publicity, namely: that here is a hospital drama with a difference; which can be compared with other (more conventional) hospital dramas; which is making some generic experiments (combining comedy with documentary realism); which might have political consquences. There is then a popular-critical frame of reference within which this programme is produced, defined and presented to the audience, exploiting and recycling its assumed generic knowledge. Here, perhaps, we might begin to see some evidence that an 'institutional discourse', which Neale discusses in relation to cinema, might also have constructed a similar 'generic system' for television.

Moreover, there are additional arguments which would suggest that such a regime is institutionalised in other, more practical, ways. For instance, there seems to be an interface between this kind of critical commentary, and the more specific business of building audiences for television. As we have just seen, generic definition is one way of attracting potential viewers; but it has also influenced the way programmes are scheduled and, to some extent (which might be declining), the assessment of their success in terms of ratings. In his discussion of programming strategies in the 1970s, Richard Paterson (1980) shows that the construction of the schedule around presumed family activities, reinforced by programme guidelines issued by the (then) regulatory authority (the IBA), had particular consequences for the transmission of certain categories of programme; '"Serious" drama becomes a non-starter in peak viewing time, whereas the popular quiz show and the situation comedy – both highly accessible to the desired audience – can aggregate a large audience with significant buying power' (p.81). He goes on to emphasise, however, that the schedule does not simply determine when particular programmes will be watched; rather the 'art' of scheduling is about attracting, and then retaining an audience across an evening's programming. Consideration must then be given to the appropriate generic mix, through peak viewing time and into the mid-evening and late viewing slots. As a 'serious' drama series, *Cardiac Arrest* was scheduled to follow the Nine O'Clock News, and was placed prior to an adult comedy show (*Harry Enfield*, at 10pm) and a current affairs discussion programme (*Question Time*, at 10.30).

The success, or otherwise, of particular programmes in particular slots in the schedule, is also the focus of William Phillips' weekly review of the ratings in the trade magazine *Broadcast*. Ten years ago, the ratings league table in *Broadcast* routinely referred to programme 'type' (using categories like 'soap', 'drama series', 'sitcom', 'comedy', 'quiz' and so on). Now this detailed classification has disappeared, though drama, children's TV and sport still merit separate league tables of their own. However generic categories remain relevant to Phillips' assessment of the strengths and weaknesses of programmes as they compete against each other in the schedule. For instance *Cardiac Arrest* was mentioned in the review of the week ending 8 May 1994 (its third week) where, despite some fall in ratings (and a position at number 48 in the top 70), it was cited as evidence of BBC 1's drama showing 'a few signs of life' (*Broadcast*, 27 May 1994, p.20).

Here is evidence then, from a variety of sources, that the television industry does operate through an institutionalised system of genres. It is a system which is very much part of the industry, but at the same time stretches beyond it, to include the journalists and the commentators, and ultimately to influence the audience itself. Now I want to discuss the nature and extent of this influence, which I believe can be investigated very much along the lines suggested by Neale, namely that there is a historical dimension to the development of generic systems. Some recent historical work (see Corner 1991a) has suggested that the construction of new generic categories was part of the establishment and acceptance of television, as a new mass medium, in the 1950s. So what was television like before these categories were invented? Consider two pages from the Radio Times published in April 1954 and April 1957 respectively.

To contemporary eyes, there are several oddities about the schedule and the programme notes, from April 1954 (see figure 4.2). Of course, throughout the 1950s and 60s, there was no breakfast or morning TV – transmissions

Fig. 4.2. BBCTV *listings, Monday 12 April 1954, from the* Radio Times *9 April 1954, by permission of the* Radio Times

began in the late afternoon, here with a film which we might assume is targeted at a youth audience. There is then a gap in the schedule of 45 minutes before the start of children's television, and then a further gap of over an hour before the evening's viewing begins. Where are the teatime soaps? Where is the early evening news? There are no teatime programmes of any description because it was felt that this would interfere with family routines, particularly the business of putting young children to bed (hence this period of emptiness, between 5.50 and 7pm, known as the 'toddlers' truce'). There is no evening news because, quite simply, there is no news – at least, no TV news as we recognise it today. That is to say, in Britain the genre of TV news had not yet been invented (it began with the advent of ITN in 1955). So the 7.30 *Newsreel* was similar to a cinema newsreel: film, voice-over and music. The 10.45 news was sound only, like radio.

Meanwhile, what television was providing in 1954 has been described as essentially a 'relay function', transmitting events, usually live, from the outside world. So on Monday 12 April 1954 the BBC audience was treated to dancing from a ballroom in London, drama from the Theatre Royal, Windsor, and a recording of last Saturday's soccer match. The only programme which looks as if it has been produced, rather than adapted, for television, comes from the USA, and is accorded the rather quaint label 'a televised controversy' (not a current affairs programme, not an interview, not a debate). Thus, in 1954, the generic regime of British television did not yet exist. And a glance at the *Radio Times* will confirm that, at that time, television was regarded very much as the poor relation of radio. For each day, the TV programme guide appears following several pages of radio listings, almost as an afterthought. Occasionally TV programmes are included in 'Programmes To Note', but they appear alongside radio programmes and in categories devised for radio (for example, *See It Now* is advertised under the heading 'Talks and Discussions').

By 1957 the situation has completely changed, and the *Radio Times* presents us with something that looks like a modern television service (see figure 4.3). The schedule begins at 3pm with *Mainly For Women*, followed immediately by *Watch With Mother*. There is a break from 4 to 5pm, and the start of children's television, but there is then continuous transmission until close down. The 'toddler's truce' has been broken by *Tonight*, the BBC's pioneering news magazine, and there are other regular news bulletins. Moreover *Tonight*, and all the subsequent programmes (except perhaps the boxing), look like TV programmes (the drama for example, is no longer relayed from a theatre but is made for television), and they occupy slots in a schedule which is roughly consistent with Paterson's account (for example the popular talk show *This Is Your Life* and the situation comedy *Hancock's Half Hour* transmitted in peak viewing time). Now it is true that, by comparison with today, generic categories are used minimally in the actual listings, but this is how the new series of *Hancock's Half Hour* was announced, on 29 March 1957:

Fig. 4.3. BBCTV listings, Monday 15 April 1957, from the Radio Times 12 April 1957, by permission of the Radio Times

Writing the new series are Alan Simpson and Ray Galton, who have been associated with Hancock ever since his first *Calling All Forces* programme in 1952. To date they have completed four Hancock radio series, and one TV series and they now know their subject so well that

> they can put words into his mouth four times more quickly that they
> could when they started.
>
>   Tony Hancock dislikes following a formula too closely and is always
> liable to change his programme about, but a few things will remain
> constant. The theme will be situation comedy, but there will be a new
> awareness by Hancock that he is being looked at – so expect a few asides
> thrown at the camera.

Peter Goddard (1991) has discussed the pioneering significance of *Hancock's
Half Hour*, in terms of its break from the genres of radio comedy, dominated
as they were by music-hall and stand-up comedy routines. In this connection,
it is interesting to observe the *Radio Times* itself emphasising the distinctively
televisual nature of the programme. However I think it is also clear that, by
1957, there is in place at the BBC a whole new understanding of television,
not just as a new medium, but also as a social and cultural institution.
Television programmes are no longer an adjunct to radio and the TV section
of the *Radio Times* now precedes the radio section. Moreover, television now
has its own genres (like situation comedy), its own personalities (like Tony
Hancock), and its own popular memory (developing out of, but irreducible
to, radio) which allows a form of publicity to be constructed for *Hancock's
Half Hour* which is not unlike that produced for *Cardiac Arrest*.

    In considering the possible implications of these developments we might, at
first, want to return to the arguments about television's mode of address,
made by Horton and Wohl. For instance, in the *Radio Times* of April 1957,
I think we can detect a new confidence in the 'para-social interaction' between
institution and audience, which is illustrated by the photograph of Derek Hart
(a presenter of *Tonight*). This new confidence relates particularly to a new
perception of the 'television personality', which is a concept I shall discuss in
detail in my next chapter. However, it is also the case that this mode of
address is both constructed and differentiated generically, as different types
of programmes are slotted into different times in the schedule, according to
a newly assumed continuous pattern of family viewing. Thus we have
programmes for women (housewives, mothers?) in the afternoon; programmes
for children after school; 'light' and then 'serious' programmes for adults in
the evening. And, as the announcer of the close down used to say: 'Don't
forget to turn off your TV set before you retire to bed'!

    Richard Paterson's article on scheduling (1980) is subtitled 'Planning the
Family', for television has now (by 1957) become an institution which, in very
practical terms, reinforces a particular kind of daily routine. In the nicest
possible way, its mode of address is related to a form of time management.
From its inception (and perhaps more than any other medium) television has
been an object of suspicion and anxiety: would it destroy the art of conversation, would its attractions prove to be addictive, especially to children, as

the modern term 'couch potato' suggests? In the schedule, as presented by the *Radio Times*, we see the BBC's attempt to find a balance between programme publicity and a notion of the socially responsible, family-orientated, discriminating viewer. And it is implied, I think, that knowledge of genre is a key factor in this exercise of discrimination – as consumers should know which types of programme are appropriate for which slots, and for which categories of viewers, at different times in the course of an evening's 'family viewing'.

4 'GENERICITY' IN THE NEW HOLLYWOOD CINEMA

As we have seen, the development of the theory of genre in media studies has been particularly associated with the analysis of cinema. In that context, the concept has been most frequently applied to Hollywood, in its so-called 'classical' period, dominated by the studio system (4). However, in the post-war era, both the organisation and the output of Hollywood cinema has been forced to change in response to a wide variety of factors – political, technological, social and economic. These factors, which range from American anti-trust legislation in the 1940s, to the global impact of new electronic technologies in the 1980s, are outlined in an informative essay on 'The New Hollywood Cinema' by Thomas Schatz (1993). In this section, using Schatz as a starting point, I want to look at the changing face of contemporary Hollywood film production, with particular reference to the concept of genre.

I am interested, for example, in the kind of publicity that contemporary Hollywood films receive:

THE FUGITIVE

Warner 15 Thriller Starring Harrison Ford. Tommy Lee Jones

Hunky Harrison Ford takes on the role that David Janssen made famous in the hit sixties telly series, putting in a breathtaking performance as the Chicago surgeon who's wrongly convicted of his wife's brutal murder.

It was one of last year's biggest box-office hits – and no wonder! The film opens in spectacular style as Dr Richard Kimble (Ford) makes a break for freedom after an escape bid in a prison van causes chaos. The van veers into the path of an oncoming train and causes a devastating crash which has been acclaimed as one of the most amazing in film history.

Ford's determined to find his wife's real killer to prove his innocence. But tough cop Tommy Lee Jones is on a personal mission to track him down and what follows is a spectacular series of stunts and action before the real villains are finally unmasked. Don't miss the chance to see one of the year's best thrillers – it's out NOW.

Not on satellite or TV for at least a year.

This quotation was taken from *1st On Video* (Issue 27, April 1994), a free magazine distributed through video rental outlets in the UK. In this issue *The Fugitive* was not only the month's 'star release', it was also number one in the video rental charts. In fact, according to the full-page advert which faces the 'star release' publicity, this was 'the biggest video release of 1994'. I think this publicity highlights very clearly a number of important issues for contemporary film production. Most significant is the critical importance of the video rental market: as Schatz points out, by the late 1980s, home video revenues were exceeding box-office revenues, contributing some 40 per cent of total income. But total income for whom? This video was published by Warner Bros – no longer, however, simply a Hollywood film studio; but rather a subsidiary of the Time-Warner Corporation, with interests in the music industry, television and cable, and print publication, as well as the film industry *per se*. As the publicity for *The Fugitive* makes clear, this video is entering a market-place for home entertainment where it is in competition with other products, such as television, in which the parent corporation also has financial interests. We are in a situation today where the film industry is forced, by economic necessity, to cater for more diverse contexts of consumption, and thus more varied forms of spectatorship, than was characteristic of Hollywood in its classical period (5).

How has the Hollywood film industry responded to this situation? In this context *The Fugitive* is the exception that proves the rule. Unusually, it is directly based on a hit TV series of the 1960s (which has been truncated into a two-hour feature film). However, the rule which is proved here is that contemporary cinema generally has an ambivalent eye focused on its principal competitor, television. Thus on the one hand, cinema needs to differentiate itself from TV (and we will consider how it tries to do this in a moment). But, on the other hand, cinema is now tied into television, not just as a source of plots, but also of stars, and more generally as a frame of reference with which the cinema audience is familiar. One of the most significant factors here is that the cinema audience now has access, through television, to Hollywood's own 'back catalogue'. Through judicious home taping, it is possible to construct one's own classical film archive. It can also be assumed that the audience for *The Fugitive* will have seen Harrison Ford in previous films – *Raiders of the Lost Ark*, *Bladerunner*, *Witness* – all of them repeated as feature films on TV.

As regards the kinds of films produced within this new context, I think the publicity for *The Fugitive* illustrates the central point very well. Consider the focus for this publicity, the kinds of language it uses – and note, in particular, the emphasis on action and spectacle. Actually, the original TV series had a much more psychological focus: it ran for four years (1963–7), and it raised the possibility that Richard Kimble would be on the run forever. The film version however, as described here, 'opens in spectacular style', with one of 'the most amazing [crashes] in film history', and it develops into 'a spectacular series of stunts and action'. It is here, in this shift towards the spectacular, that cinema identifies its key difference from television. Schatz defines the characteristic product of the new Hollywood cinema as the 'blockbuster', where 'the emphasis on plot over character marks a significant departure from classical Hollywood films'. In 'blockbusters', 'particularly male action-adventure films . . . we see films that are increasingly plot-driven, increasingly visceral, kinetic and fast-paced, increasingly reliant on special effects, increasingly "fantastic" (and thus apolitical) and increasingly targeted at younger audiences' (p.23).

The point about the younger audience opens up a veritable can of critical worms. It is widely recognised that it is Hollywood's cultivation of youth audiences, attracted to blockbuster films in multiplex cinemas, that has enabled the industry to survive. On the other hand, as Schatz's point about their supposedly 'apolitical' character would confirm, this new cinema has had its critics. Schatz himself describes the new youth audience as 'a generation with time and spending money and a penchant for wandering suburban shopping malls and for repeated viewings of their favourite films' (p.19). Parallels have been drawn between the often serial and repetitious narrative structure of these films, and the format of the video game – with only the most rudimentary distinction between goodies and baddies (humans and aliens), and where success is achieved by zapping one's way to victory. Indeed, it would seem that the new action cinema, like the video game, has aesthetic links with cartoon and comic-book traditions – where the Terminator meets Sonic the Hedgehog, meets Batman. If this is the case, it would again emphasise the significance of an intertextual, inter-technological market for home entertainment, dominated by a youth audience, which might be in the process of transforming the whole experience of cinema spectatorship:

> Even more than video, the computer game seems perfectly cast in the role of cinema's cuckoo in the nest: the ugly duckling kid whose facility with the latest technology unlocks a wholly different way of relating to moving images – one based less on identification with a character and more on direct interaction with the screen: less on the experience of unravelling linear narrative and more on controlling the branching scenarios of the game.
>
> (Bode, 1993, p.8)

However, as Schatz also points out, there is something very dubious about 'middle-aged movie critics', brought up on classical film theory, bemoaning the direction taken by the new Hollywood cinema. In fact, several recent discussions have emphasised the semiotic and generic complexity of many blockbuster movies, and have acknowledged, with less antagonism, their potential political implications. Schatz argues, with reference to *Star Wars* (1977), that its 'lack of complex characters or plot . . . opens the film up to other possibilities, notably its radical amalgamation of genre conventions and its elaborate play of cinematic references' (p.23). In the same volume of essays, Jim Collins (1993) coins the term 'genericity' to refer to a new awareness, a 'sophisticated hyperconsciousness', related to the reworking of traditional generic conventions in contemporary films. And in the most sympathetic account of the action cinema of the 1980s, Yvonne Tasker (1993) finds evidence of a new kind of audience orientation to the way traditional genres are 'performed':

> *Young Guns* offers a self-conscious *performance* of the western . . . The film has a strange quality which stems from its combination of the 'historically authenticated' western narrative with the teenage rites of passage movie. *Young Guns* can be seen as a teen movie that performs the western in a similar way, though without the same ironic quality, to John McClane's [Bruce Willis'] performance of the role of the hero in *Die Hard*, a performance which self-consciously chooses its popular cultural reference points. Perhaps this indicates how we, as film audiences, understand genres. Our recognition takes place not in relation to particular films, but to a total field which includes a range of contemporary forms, including MTV. It is not so much that *Young Guns* points to the effective disappearance of the western from the cinema of the 1980s, but that its aesthetic strategies indicate how the kind of generic classification implied within film criticism by 'the western' have become increasingly problematic. (p.67–8, my parenthesis)

Clearly, Tasker has a problem with traditional 'empiricist' descriptions of classical genres, which are no longer appropriate to the 'genericity' of action cinema. Thus, in the first instance, *Young Guns* (1988) is a generic hybrid, where one element (the teenage rites aspect) establishes a critical distance from the classical western. (This process is a general characteristic of 'hybrids'; for example, *Calamity Jane* can be said to be 'performing' the western in this way.) However, further levels of irony are made possible by the intertextual, popular cultural context in which the action cinema is consumed – Tasker refers to Willis' playful adoption of the Roy Rogers persona in *Die Hard* (1988). And, more generally still, the generic conventions associated with classic narrative cinema are subject to various reworkings and transformations in the pursuit of 'spectacle'. Tasker's reference above to MTV relates to her observation that, in *Young Guns*, there is some borrowing of techniques from music video. Schatz also discusses the 'intermingling' of cinematography with techniques from TV advertising, as film making strives for a visual impact which is appropriate for the small (video rental) screen.

As we have seen, the emphasis on the spectacular in the new Hollywood cinema has been the focus for some negative criticism. Tasker, however, addresses herself to this criticism in two interesting ways. Firstly, on the aesthetic level, if it is true that spectacle disrupts some traditional narrative pleasures; it also, Tasker argues, extends them. Thus, psychological identification may be minimal and narrative continuity is disrupted by the kind of fast-moving, discontinuous montage editing associated with pop video (usually to the accompaniment of a pop music soundtrack). On the other hand, according to Tasker, narrative pleasures may be enhanced by 'the enactment of narrative as spectacle' (p.6), where these two aesthetic principles achieve a new synthesis. Perhaps this point is illustrated by the 'breathtaking performance' of Harrison Ford, as Kimble, in *The Fugitive*.

Second, Tasker makes some interesting (political) points about representations of gender in the new action cinema (and we will consider their significance in more detail in Chapter 7). Briefly then, if the traditional action-adventure has operated with conventional gender roles (the male hero; the female victim/reward), the current representation of these roles in increasingly spectacular forms makes them unstable, even parodic. Arnold Schwarzenegger, for example, has become an exaggerated, comic-book parody of the muscular action hero, which Tasker discusses in terms of a new 'musculinity', in which she detects both a self-awareness and an anxiety around conventional masculinity. In some movies this new musculinity extends to women, as action heroines – Sigourney Weaver in *Aliens* (1986) – and as hard-bodied gunslingers – Linda Hamilton in *Terminator 2* (1991). If the pleasures of spectacle have the capacity to reduce narrative complexity, they also have the potential to disturb some conservative generic conventions from the classical tradition.

Thus, the new Hollywood cinema raises a number of questions for film theory. It questions, as Tasker points out, the emphasis placed on narrative as the driving force in cinema's traditional mode of address. It also calls into question the traditional generic categories, not simply to replace them or make them redundant; but rather, to recycle them (Collins), or 'perform' them in new ways (Tasker). In this recycled performance, the traditional genres are reproduced self-consciously, knowingly, ironically etc – as appropriate to the audience's awareness of 'genericity'. But, as we began by saying, this awareness is the product of a new industrial situation, itself created by a revolution in patterns of leisure and entertainment, and the consequent search for new audiences.

In this last respect, I am fascinated by an advert which appears on the final page of *1st On Video* (see figure 4.4). It is an advert for Hitachi CinemaSound – a domestic sound system, which reproduces 'the sound you get from films in the cinema – at home'. In this advert, a composite, cartoon-like, photo image depicts a man, a woman and a boy (a family?) sitting on

TURN YOUR FRONT ROOM
INTO THE FRONT ROW.

Now, sitting in your front room can be can sit back in your comfy chair and other systems it's designed so that, to music and sport. Visit your local

just like sitting in the cinema. Thanks enjoy stunning sound quality. (Matched, wherever you sit in your room, you'll dealer who'll happily show you how

to the new Hitachi CinemaSound tele- of course, by stunning Hitachi picture enjoy the full, dramatic **HITACHI** Hitachi CinemaSound

vision with Dolby Surround Pro Logic. quality.) The system comes as a effect. Not just from **CINEMA SOUND** makes them all sound

It's one of the very first systems complete package, consisting of a your favourite films. But the way they're meant

developed to play back four-track Hitachi television with a built-in from videos, television and satellite to sound. In fact, there's only one other

Dolby Stereo – the sound you get from Dolby Surround Pro Logic amplifier broadcasts too. And from a wide thing you need to remember when

films in the cinema – at home. So you and four external speakers. Unlike variety of programmes, from cartoons you buy your system. The popcorn.

Fig. 4.4. Advert for Hitachi CinemaSound (1994), by permission of Hitachi Sales (UK) Ltd

a sofa, watching TV (interestingly, the woman possesses the remote control), in a room devoid of any other furniture than four speakers, a standard lamp, and (behind the sofa) three rows of cinema seats. The caption reads 'Turn Your Front Room Into The Front Row'; and the accompanying text goes on: 'Now, sitting in your front room can be just like sitting in the cinema. Thanks to the new Hitachi CinemaSound television with Dolby Surround Pro Logic'.

What does it mean to transform your front room into a cinema? Clearly it is no longer a traditional domestic space, for the futuristic domestic space envisaged here incorporates a theatre, and the conventional opposition between broadcasting (domestic) and cinema (theatrical) has been transcended. The Hitachi advert seems to want to address some of the anxieties this situation might invoke, for clearly this might represent the final realisation, in the 1990s, of all those early worries associated with television. Here we have a family whose entire domestic space has been invaded and reduced to accommodate new electronic technologies; except, bizarrely enough, they remain a family – and watching the TV/cinema/video is the one thing which holds them together.

There is an image on the TV screen in front of this family of the future. It is not easy to see (and impossible to reproduce here), but it appears to be somewhat strange. In the foreground, with his back to the camera, stands a native (American?), with, in the middle distance, a tree to the left and a vehicle (some kind of minibus?) to the right, all in a fairly barren desert landscape. So what kind of media text is this family watching? Is it a western (if so, the minibus doesn't fit with traditional western iconography)? Is it an anthropological documentary (another genre, which again we will discuss in Chapter 7 – here, the presence of the minibus could signify the 'disappearing world' of native Americans)? Or is this an advert for the minibus itself (high-tech product invades low-tech environment – a common scenario in car advertising)? Are these people watching cinema or are they watching TV? It is impossible to know for, as the text tells us, 'wherever you sit in your room, you'll enjoy the full dramatic effect. Not just from favourite films. But from videos, television and satellite broadcasts too.' Thus, the Hitachi advert affirms a brave new world of technological convergence, in which what is on offer is generically indeterminate, distinguished, most of all, by its dramatic and spectacular qualities.

5 CASE STUDY: GENRE AND PHOTOGRAPHY – FROM 'FASHION' TO 'GLAMOUR'

In principle, the theory of genre can be applied to any mass medium, and not only popular fiction, or cinema, or television. In any instance, the analyst

words, the theory of genre might readily apply. Other writers on fashion photography have recognised this, but under the sway of the notion of photography as an art form, the theory of genre has not been taken very far. Consider for example Nancy Hall-Duncan's introduction to her classic *History of Fashion Photography* (1979), where she attempts to distinguish the fashion photograph from other forms of photography:

> It is in fact sometimes difficult to distinguish photographs taken for the theater from those taken for fashion, though the theatrical shots generally show their sitters in more theatrical poses and include more stage props, such as leopard heads and bearskin rugs. During the 1910s when it became fashionable for society celebrities... to indulge in fashion modeling, fashion photographs were strikingly similar to society portraits. Recently fashion photography has begun to resemble another type of photography – pornography . . . For our purposes however, the distinguishing feature of every fashion photograph – and the common denominator in the great diversity of style and approach – is the fashion intent. (p.9)

Thus, for want of a theory of genre, Hall-Duncan falls back on a resolutely empiricist, even circular, argument. A theatrical photograph looks 'theatrical', a fashion photograph . . . is a fashion photograph, and each type of photography is directly and functionally related to its purpose. *The History of Fashion Photography* then becomes a series of chapters featuring 'great' fashion photographs, which have usually been influenced by the movements of modern art (modernism, surrealism and so on). But perhaps this is doing Hall-Duncan an injustice, for she also gives us the beginnings of another, more interesting, definition of what makes a fashion photograph. Here we are introduced to a type of photography which incorporates ideal, as well as empirical, elements:

> The content of the fashion picture is not the clothes alone but also the attitudes and conventions of the people who wear them; it is an index in miniature to culture and society, to people's aspirations, limitations and taste . . . It reflects the self images of people as well as their dreams and desires.
>
> The fashion photograph is not a statement of fact but an ideal; it does not deal in commonplace subjects but with created illusions, flattering garments and flawless models. The success of a fashion photograph depends not only on the desirability of the clothing but on our ability to believe in and identify with the subject. (p.10)

Other critics and historians have concerned themselves with these notions, central to fashion photography, of idealism and identification. There is, in fact another way of writing the history, which is to put less emphasis on the affinity with modern art, and more on a progressive interrogation of definitions of the ideally fashionable. Thus, in this account, fashion photography began as a relatively cheap and realistic alternative to the idealised tradition of fashion illustration (see Craik, 1994). The 'progressive' photographers of the 1940s and 50s (Parkinson, Penn, Avedon) took their models out of the studios, introducing movement within dramatic and documentary scenarios. The 1960s destabilised the world of *haute couture*, and placed the model in an explicitly sexualised encounter with the photographer. This interrogation of the ideal continued through the 1970s, in the work of Newton, Bourdin and Turbeville, where the emphasis was on the artificiality of the scenario, and the difficulty of identification (see also, Brookes 1992). Hence, in this view, the 'great' photographers represent a variety of attempts not simply to reproduce, but to critically reflect on the fashionable image. The interesting thing however about this history of fashion photography is that certain ideals, which seem to have been first defined in the 1920s and 1930s, remain pivotal to its continued development. Whatever new angles the 'great' photographers might have found, their subject, in a sense, remained the same. Jennifer Craik quotes Maynard (1986) on this point:

> By the end of the 1930s, the history of the fashion print [that is, illustration] was almost played out. Their [*sic*] role had been taken over by the fashion photographer. Occasionally fashion impressions appear in glossy magazines as a faint memory of the influential past they once had. They live on only in the working drawings of the great fashion houses. Strangely enough what remains in fashion photography today is to a large extent the legacy of the situational fashion print . . . and the impression of a fashion ideal – the concept of chic – a far more tantalising and marketable idea than a precisely detailed photograph. (p.98, my parentheses)

There are other (art-schooly) arguments which suggest that fashion illustration, far from being redundant, may have made something of a comeback in the 1980s (see Smith 1988). But my interest in the Maynard quotation concerns the concept of 'chic', or, as we might put it less colloquially, 'glamour'. For surely it is glamour that defines the 'created illusion' of the fashion photograph, which is at once an object for empirical observation and an aspirational ideal. Moreover, as we shall see shortly, glamour is a concept in institutional circulation. Thus, if there is something distinctive about fashion photography, as Hall-Duncan would prefer, in my view it is because it represents, or, better, constructs, the concept of glamour. It is glamour that defines the truly fashionable, but it is not restricted to this definition, as we shall see.

Take a look at the *Vogue Book of Fashion Photography* (Devlin 1979). The points I am about to make could be made with reference to almost any page, but I have opened the book at pages 76–7 (see figure 4.5). These pages

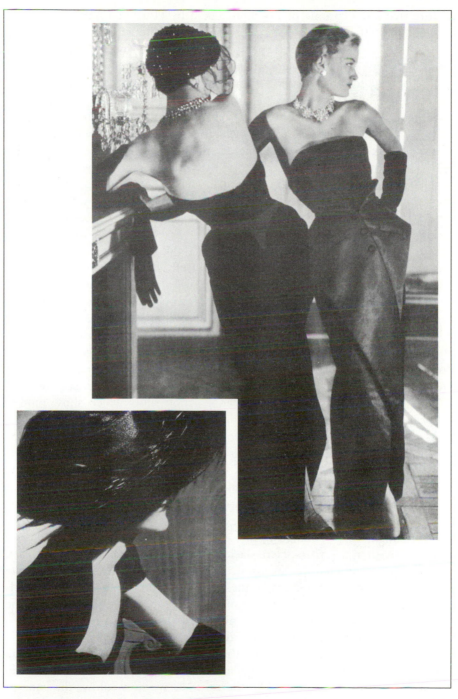

Fig. 4.5. Photographs taken by Horst P Horst for American Vogue (1940s).
Copyright © 1979 by Conde Nast Publications Ltd

feature two monochrome photographs taken by Horst for American *Vogue* in the late 1940s. On page 77, a woman's face is almost entirely covered by a black feathery hat, and she appears to be wearing a low-cut black evening dress with elbow-length black gloves. The photograph has an abstract, geometric (modernist?) quality – emphasising the contrast between black clothes and white skin. Opposite, on page 76, is a full length photograph of two models, one facing, one with her back to the camera, both wearing the same (?) off-the-shoulder evening gowns (by Dior) and similar black gloves. The models are also wearing seemingly expensive jewellery, and the one with her back to the camera a hat, also studded with sequins or jewels, and with a veil. The studied pose involves both models looking right, while resting their arms on a mantelpiece on which appears some kind of crystal candelabra. The luminosity of the candelabra matches the glitter in the jewellery around the models' necks.

Flicking through the pages of this book, I think we can recognise a veritable iconography of glamour. Traditionally, it consists of evening wear, jewellery and elaborate accessories. Hats with veils, or brims which partially cover faces (while shoulders and arms remain uncovered) are very much in evidence. In many shots, fur and feathers accompany the jewellery. There is a typical setting, for which 'palatial' might be an apt description: hence, columns, statuettes, candelabra and so on. There is also a typical way of posing which is angular and aloof and which is often accentuated by a low angle of vision. This idealised image is a certain vision of 'high society', and it is only modified, not broken, by those action shots which show models 'at play' in swimming costumes or horse-riding gear.

As the *Vogue Book of Fashion Photography* illustrates, this iconography remains a constant feature of the genre, right through to the 1970s – in the work of Newton for example. There, it is certainly treated with some irony and disturbance, but its generic centrality is not disturbed. What does occur, in the post-war period, but only fleetingly (given its market) in *Vogue*, is the emergence of a less remote, more accessible version of what 'glamour' might be. This might be personified by the early Marilyn Monroe in her 'cheesecake' or 'sweater girl' years. Here slacks, skirts and sweaters (ready-to-wear), as well as the ubiquitous swimsuit, replaced evening dresses and *haute couture*; and the engagement with the camera was more direct – the models even smiled! Such images do not seem to have appeared in *Vogue* until the emergence of Twiggy in the 1960s, and even then they are treated with a certain irony, as if disturbing to a high fashion magazine.

I would then distinguish between the classical or 'high' glamour of *haute couture*, and a more accessible 'popular' glamour which became available in the post-war consumer society. Furthermore as we now know, the concept of glamour can be extended to refer to forms of soft pornography, and even certain formations in popular music/youth culture ('glam rock', for example).

It is not therefore a concept which can be neatly tied to a certain field of texts; rather, in its wider circulation, it points to interesting shifts, borrowings and intertextual references which, however, can be generically named. It is indeed instructive to consider relationships between fashion photography and portraiture and pornography, which the conventional histories would rather repress. In the terms which we have previously discussed, glamour is a type of 'genericity': that is, an intertextual framework through which producers and consumers make sense of a variety of media texts.

In case this concept is beginning to appear rather nebulous, let me offer a further, very interesting definition of glamour. It comes from Michael Hiley's *Seeing Through Photographs* (1983), in a chapter where he is mainly concerned with the history of the pin-up. Like other accounts, he points out that the earliest fashion portraits featured well-to-do women and 'society celebrities'. There was a transitional period around the turn of the century where (to considerable moral disapproval) glamour photographs were taken of well-known actresses and showgirls. However, according to Hiley, a further development had to occur before glamour photography, as such, was established:

> Glamour is divorced from any consideration of worthiness or talent and is often to be found when the women on display in photographs are 'professional beauties' and little else. Glamour lies at the heart of the process used extensively by the modern mass media in which attention is diverted from people who could be described as famous because they are praiseworthy, towards those who have gained the dubious distinction of being famous through being a 'personality'. They owe much of their prominence to the camera and take care to make use of whatever photogenic qualities they can muster because of the crucial importance of their image in the photograph or on the screen. (p.120–2)

Hiley's reference to 'personality' here points us towards the next chapter, where this concept will be more extensively considered. At the same time, however, I would suggest that he has identified something very basic about glamour photography, which is to do with the type of subjectivity constructed for the model. Indeed, what does it mean, to 'model'? In her fine furs and feathers, swimsuits, or in various stages of undress, the model is essentially *an object to be looked at*. Many models are anonymous but, even when we know their names, their notoriety stems from their moments of objectification. What does it mean therefore to be 'glamorous'? It seems to me that this clearly involves dressing up (or down), but on the condition that one is prepared to pose, to be looked at, to constitute oneself as an object. As Hiley points out, the availability of photography as a mass medium has both encouraged and commercialised this kind of activity.

Glamour is thus a combination of iconography, settings, scenarios and forms of looking, which is both common to a range of visual imagery (including

Fig. 4.6. Advert for Pretty Polly Nylons (1991). By permission of Pretty Polly Ltd

fashion photography) and, of course, to certain everyday practices (such as 'clubbing'). As a generic concept, it is in circulation, and one doesn't have to look very far to find evidence of its institutional use. An interesting body of recent research (Gaines and Herzog (eds) 1990; Herzog and Gaines 1991) has examined the ways in which, from the 1930s to the 1950s, 'tie-ups' were established between chains of department stores and the Hollywood film industry, in publicising and promoting new fashions for women. Central to this process was the star, or star image (Lombard, Shearer, Crawford), enhanced by the publicity portrait. The star-as-model was, however, supported by a vast ancillary literature, in the form of advice to local exhibitors, and pressbooks designed to feed publicity and information to local newspapers (Herzog 1990, p.135). Some films were made specifically to feature a 'fashion show' element, and film-orientated magazines, such as *Photoplay*, featured articles on fashion. What provided common currency was the concept of glamour: as in the publicity for *Lovely To Look At* (1952) which proposed to give its female audience 'an eyeful of glamor' and an 'Oriental oomph ... that housewives were expected to swoon over', (Herzog 1990, p.157).

A similar effect, presumably, is to be derived from the Pretty Polly advert, featuring Rita Hayworth (see figure 4.6). It seems to me that we are invited, required, to read this advert on two levels. On the first level, semiologically, the advert presents glamour as its *mythology* – that is, as the meaning system to which its connotations refer. Here glamour seems to be tinged with nostalgia, perhaps looking back with fondness to the time when nylon stockings first made their appearance in Britain. However at a second level, which is generic, I think we are invited to recognise and respond to the conventions of a glamour photograph. That is to say, we can see that this is an advert, but also that it is a star portrait – a species of classical glamour photography, which in this instance has been hijacked to become a fashion photograph (in the currently fashionable 'retro' style). That is to say, this advert mobilises, not only our popular memory (of the 1940s etc), but also our ability to identify and classify types of photographic texts. It is this second level of knowledge that is properly defined by the concept of genre, and which this chapter, in various ways, has attempted to elucidate.

FURTHER READING

Apart from the works cited in the course of this chapter – in my view Neale S. (1990), and Tasker Y. (1993; Chapter 3) are crucial and the very thorough review of genre criticism in film theory, in Cook P. (ed) (1985); perhaps the most useful further reading on genre is contained in discussions of popular fiction such as Palmer J. (1991) Chapter 7, and Bennett T. and Woollacott J. (1987) Chapter 3.

5

Stars and personalities

1   DIMENSIONS OF STARDOM

In the previous chapter we considered the concept of genre largely from the point of view of its institutional significance. From this point of view, generic considerations have influenced the production of media texts, have evolved into a system which regulates their distribution and availability, and have defined audience expectations and thus the way that media texts are read. Genre is not, however, the only concept in media studies which has this kind of institutional significance. Equally important, in the history of the mass media, has been a critical interest in quality of performance, and a fascination for the identities of performers (actors, stars, personalities etc). *The Fugitive* for example, can be classified and publicised generically, as an 'action-adventure' film; but it can also be categorised as a 'Harrison Ford' movie. In these terms, the film's producers will have budgeted for the involvement of a well-known star, in the expectation that the cinema audience, familiar with his work, will be attracted by his presence. Indeed, the publicity magazine *1st On Video* (No 27, 1994), contains a 'star profile' of Harrison Ford, and the video release of *The Fugitive* is taken as an opportunity to review his track record, some of which you might have missed:

> It's official! Harrison Ford is the 'Movie Star of the Century' – beating legends like Humphrey Bogart, John Wayne, Clark Gable and Clint Eastwood in the box-office stakes.
>
> US movie bosses gave Ford the honour recently for bringing in a staggering £1.25 BILLION worth of business during his career, which includes seven of the 20 biggest blockbusters of all time. His latest video, *The Fugitive* is one of the movies on that list. It's brought in over £112 MILLION at worldwide box-offices. And you can see it on video NOW.
>
> Ford's on top form in his latest role as runaway Dr Richard Kimble, on the run from what seems to be the entire Chicago police department

as he tries to prove his innocence after being found guilty of his wife's murder.

In real-life too, Ford is a hot property and constantly being sought by producers and directors who know that his name means mega-bucks.

Ironically, in his new movie *The Fugitive*, the action is set in Ford's home city of Chicago. He's come a long way since leaving the Mid-West nearly 30 years ago to forge a glittering career.

Two of Ford's first big breaks came in the early '70s with the cult classic *American Graffiti* – who can forget him in the Stetson as the sexy lone rider? In 1974 he teamed up with director Francis Ford Coppola for the acclaimed thriller *The Conversation*.

But it was still a few years before he could give up his tool-box in his daytime job as Hollywood's carpenter to the stars. He'd built up quite a reputation for his woodworking skills on the days he was 'resting' as an actor. But the step was made thanks to the huge success of the 1977 sci-fi blockbuster, *Star Wars*.

As handsome Hans Solo his career hit stratospheric heights and he continued to dazzle in the smash-hit sequels, *The Empire Strikes Back* (1980) and *Return Of The Jedi* (1983) . . .

In many respects, this extract is typical of the conventional popular interest in film stars. We can observe to begin with, the economic basis for the Harrison Ford 'legend', for it is primarily as a marketing phenomenon, at the worldwide box office, that Ford gains the accolade of 'movie star of the century'. That accolade is particularly instructive, because it illustrates the intertextuality of stardom, which works on two levels: firstly, to allow us to compare one Harrison Ford film with another, in his 'filmography'; but secondly to situate Ford in a tradition of action-orientated male stars, from Gable to Eastwood. Again, as with the concept of genre, the mobilisation of popular memory is evident. Thirdly, there is an interest here in Ford's own capabilities as an actor, in the quality of his performance (where, for instance, he is described as being on 'top form' in *The Fugitive*). But perhaps most significant are the references to Ford's own biography – to his Chicago origins, and to his well-documented struggle to gain acceptance as an actor, while working as a carpenter in Hollywood. The Harrison Ford story is not exactly 'rags to riches' (for he was brought up in comfortable middle-class circumstances) but, in his perseverance to succeed, he does illustrate some aspects of the American dream.

Richard de Cordova (1985) has suggested that it is only when the popular interest is extended in this way, in terms of a paradigm of 'professional life/personal life', that we can begin to speak of stardom as such. De Cordova's remarks are situated in a historical context, where he traces the emergence of the concept of the star in the American film industry. Here, in much the same way as the concept of genre, stardom emerged gradually in the first decade of the cinema, to appear as a fully institutionalised concept around 1914. This institutionalisation was achieved, not only by actors' appearances in films, nor even at box-offices (in publicity displays and so on), but most importantly by the publication of subsidiary texts, such as the fan magazine *Photoplay*. According to de Cordova, the concept of the film star was preceded by two earlier developments: first, screen acting had to be recognised as such (in the earliest forms of publicity it was described as 'posing') and thus granted a status which was equivalent to acting on a stage; and second, screen actors had to achieve identities which extended beyond their performances in particular films. It was this latter development which produced the shift from the 'picture personality' (known only by his or her appearances in films) to the star with a public biography and 'persona'.

In this respect, Harrison Ford may not be the best example to take. Clearly *1st On Video* is doing all it can to establish his star credentials, insofar as a career which has 'hit stratospheric heights' enables him to take his place among the legends of Hollywood. But there is really more to stardom than a commercially successful 'sexy' image. As Yvonne Tasker has argued, 'Harrison Ford, whilst [he is] a star who has appeared in a variety of action roles, has, as his career has progressed, inceasingly been seen as an actor' (1993, p.74). In other words, there is a distinction to be made between film star and film actor; and if Ford is to be classified primarily as an actor, this is to introduce a number of qualifications to his 'stratospheric' significance. First, as Tasker points out, following films like *Witness* and *Mosquito Coast*, Ford's acting ability, rather than his star image, has been foregrounded in critical commentary. Second, however, though something is known of his private life, this is minimal compared to other (past and present) film stars, who will be discussed in this chapter. Off the set, Ford does not live in the glare of publicity; he is described in one biography as a 'reluctant star' (1). To that extent, his identity remains closer to that of the 'picture personality' than the fully-fledged star. Let us then leave him and *The Fugitive* behind, and follow Tasker's own interest in the major male movie star of the 1980s.

For many people, critics as well as fans, the personification of the male action-adventure cinema remains Sylvester Stallone. Hugely successful in box-office terms, particularly with youth (and international) audiences, many of Stallone's films are exemplary of the genre (as outlined in the previous chapter). Thus, seriality and repetition are evident in both the Rocky and Rambo cycles; video techniques are used extensively; but most of all, Stallone's image has acted as a sign for a certain mythology of masculinity which, for many viewers, these films represent. As Rambo in particular, Stallone is the quintessential comic-book hero: hair flowing, muscles bulging, automatic machine gun at the ready (see figure 5.1). The original 'action man'. But as we have already noted, some critics, like Tasker, have suggested

Fig. 5.1. Sylvester Stallone as Rambo. Uncredited publicity still for Rambo First Blood Part 2

that this image is perhaps not quite as straightforward as it might first appear.

In terms of their narrative and generic structures, a most interesting aspect of many action-adventure films is the way the hero is placed outside, or beyond, institutional legality. That it to say, whatever his moral rectitude (allied, of course to his spectacular prowess), the male action hero of the 1980s does not often represent the established social order (unlike the cops in gangster films, or the sheriff in the traditional western). Rambo, for instance, is an outcast, as signified by the 'wildness' of his hair, his semi-naked body, and the setting in which he performs. Closer to nature than culture, Rambo thus represents a critique of the 'civilised' status quo. Moreover, in his hyper-masculinity (his 'musculinity' according to Tasker), Stallone-as-Rambo seems to indicate some uncertainty about gender. On one level, the Rambo image can be seen as a classic example of the 'instability' of the male pin-up: that is to say, of the difficulty, in our culture, of representing the male body (see Dyer 1992). But on another level, there is perhaps a sense in which, as well as being 'wild', the body of Rambo is somehow feminised. 'Rambo is a pussy', remarks Stallone as Ray Tango *in Tango and Cash* – at least, as our illustration shows, his body is produced as a spectacle, to be looked at (and the construction of 'spectacular bodies', including male pin-ups, will be examined in further detail, in Chapter 7 of this book).

In some ways then, the image of Rambo represents trouble – a troubled relationship with authority, but also an excessive preoccupation with masculinity. However, as any fan of Stallone will know, such trouble has been, and remains, a feature of his own biography, or at least his public star image. As Tasker again points out, the story of Rocky was originally publicised as a sort of parallel to Stallone's own biography: 'the themes of rags to riches, achievement through struggle within a white immigrant community, determination to succeed against all odds ...' etc (1993, p.84). Subsequently, as Rocky gave way to Rambo, and the construction of hyper-masculinity grew more excessive (and eventually less successful in box-office terms), Stallone expressed public dissatisfaction with his star image, and attempted to change it. Thus, the experimentation with comedy, and a more articulate version of action-adventure ('from pecs to specs' as Tasker refers to *Tango and Cash*). In this way, Stallone's own troubled backgound, and his subsequent concern with different versions of ethnic and gender identity, seem to reinforce, to make more authentic, some of the themes in his films. This is clearly quite different from the (relatively untroubled) image presented by Harrison Ford, and is much closer to the relationship between professional life and personal life which, for de Cordova, defines the identity of the star.

Furthermore, Stallone is rarely out of the news. Tasker refers to his much-publicised marriage to, and subsequent divorce from, Brigitte Nielsen. It just so happened that as I was preparing to write about him, Stallone was in the news again, this time at the launch of a Planet Hollywood restaurant in Miami (a venture co-owned by Stallone, Bruce Willis and Arnold Schwarzenegger). The press interest in this event centred on Stallone's current 'love-life' – a somewhat complex situation involving two ex-mistresses and a new 'mystery 5ft 10in blonde' (according to the *Daily Star*, 17 May 1994). A picture of 'Stallone with the new girl in his Rocky love-life' actually made it on to the front page of the *Star*. The *Sun*, throughout the same week, preferred to elaborate on the context – Stallone's £10 – million mansion in Miami (Casa Rocko), and the stars, such as Madonna, Whoopi Goldberg and Patrick Swayze, who were present at the £250,000 bash (of course, Andy Coulson of the *Sun* was present too). Ian Connell (1992) has written about this peculiar and contradictory fascination, in the tabloid press, with the lives of the rich and famous. He suggests that, while the glamour defines the horizon of popular aspiration, the trouble (and Andy Coulson's column in the *Sun* is entitled 'Bizarre') reassures the ordinary reader that it is not all it is cracked up to be.

This surely is stardom, in all its glory – and it is partly what sells movies. It is, like genre, an institutionalised frame of reference, reinforced by a publicity machine, and by public commentary and gossip, which accompanies our readings of media texts, particularly (in this case) Hollywood films. However, though its primary function may be to publicise the film industry, and to attract paying customers, I want to suggest that it also achieves something more profound. Here, I am following Richard Dyer's suggestion that 'stars articulate what it is to be a human being in contemporary society' (1986, p.8). In this respect, I want to argue, stars serve to legitimise the mass media (in this case, cinema) as popular cultural institutions. We read media texts through their signs, structures and modes of address, and through our mobilisation of a general knowledge of genres. But that reading is predicated on the possibility that, at least some of the time, these texts will have a cultural importance, a human significance, which the presence of a star can reaffirm.

The basic point here is that Rocky and Rambo, particularly Rambo, were not just characters in films. Tasker's book goes on to discuss the 'Age of Rambo' – for, in the 1980s, Rambo became a metaphor for a certain type of masculinity; or, more generally, a concept which featured in a debate about masculinity. At its lowest level, the Rambo metaphor functioned as part of a 'moral panic', in the press and general public debate, about increasing levels of violence, particularly mass murder and serial killing. At a higher level, the Rambo concept functioned as a contrast to the 'new man' (which we have previously described). Here were two alternative masculinities, alternative ways for men to respond to social change – 'new man' versus 'retributive man' as one discussion put it (2). To this extent, this cinematic character clearly featured in a debate about 'what it is to be a human being' (or, at least, a man) in contemporary society. But Dyer's point is that such characters, as particular combinations of signs and traits, are embodied in stars. And the important thing about stars is that we know, on one level, that these are indeed *real* human beings.

In his star image, Stallone confirms the human significance of the characters of Rocky and Rambo. There is a trivial aspect to this, insofar as Stallone will always be 'Rocky' for the tabloid press, at least as long as his 'rocky love-life' continues. However, there is also a more serious point which is indicated, in passing, by Andy Coulson's revelation (in the *Sun*, 20 May 1994) that Stallone's Miami mansion contains a giant painting of himself as Rocky in one of its 'three enormous lounges'. The serious point is that Stallone's public image remains haunted by the Rocky and Rambo versions of masculinity. His career has been focused, at times, on a need to critically engage (or disengage) with this image, which, nevertheless, he cannot leave behind. Rocky and Rambo remain culturally significant representations of masculinity and, in his continued (ambivalent) relationship with these images, Stallone authenticates their significance and indeed their power. Later in this chapter I focus on Marilyn Monroe, the essential movie star – who, as Norma Jeane Baker, had an even more troubled relationship with the image of 'Marilyn'.

When star images achieve this kind of cultural significance – a representative significance which absorbs the humanity of the person who is the star – they become, as we might say, 'iconic'. The image of Stallone as Rambo is an icon of contemporary masculinity. There are some definitions of this concept which (following the semiotic theory of C.S. Pierce) simply equate it with the motivated sign (3). In this discussion I am going much further than this – to suggest that the image of Stallone as Rocky or Rambo has many of the same qualities as the religious iconic paintings to be found in Italian and Byzantine churches. It may not, exactly, be an image to be worshipped; but it is (in the old-fashioned sense of the word) an awesome image. It has cultural resonance and power. It reaches out from the film in which it is located, and touches our cultural experience, just as it remains the key reference point in representations of the man himself, Sylvester Stallone. In this sense too, there is a distinction to be made between Harrison Ford as Richard Kimble and Sylvester Stallone as Rocky or as Rambo. The latter is, comparatively, much more interesting and much more humanly problematic – which is why it helps to sell newspapers, like the *Sun*.

2 STARS, PERSONALITIES, CELEBRITIES

The concept of stardom in media studies is often related to another key concept – that of personality. In this area, like the theory of genre, there remain some unresolved ambiguities and problems, but again I think there is some current work which is beginning to point a way forward. The central difficulty is that, in much conventional media studies, the concept of the film star is sharply contrasted to that of the 'TV personality' (see, in particular, John Langer 1981). Here the term 'personality' is more or less exclusively reserved for broadcasting, where it seems to have a particular institutional significance. However, there is a problem in making this distinction too rigid, in that the 'personalities' of some film stars are also of interest, particularly to the tabloid press, as we have seen. So in this section I will try to work through some of these conceptual problems, with reference to the wider context within which all media – cinema, broadcasting and the press – are consumed, and I will introduce a further concept which, hopefully, will provide a way out of these ambiguities.

A starting point for this discussion is, once again, provided by the work of Raymond Williams. In *Keywords* (1976), he points out that 'personality' has acquired two meanings: the first, a general meaning, which refers to an attribute of any human being; the second, a more specific meaning, which defines 'personality' as a quality possessed and displayed by some human beings but not others. In the first sense, as psychologists might say, everyone has a personality (strong/weak; extrovert/introvert etc). In the second sense, which is much less scientific, and more the kind of evaluative comment which might be made by a layperson, it is possible to speak of someone as having no 'personality'. Conversely, it is possible to say that some people are full of personality, or that they are in fact 'personalities'. As Williams also points out, in the twentieth century, being a 'personality', in this sense, has become a career (particularly associated with the development of the mass media). So we now recognise the existence of professional 'personalities'; and clearly only a few select people have, or are, personalities in this sense of the word.

Film stars of course, just like anyone else, have personalities in the more general, psychological sense. Indeed, the more they 'articulate what it is to be a human being', the more exalted and iconic their status, the stronger the interest in their 'real personalities' becomes. In his essay on *A Star Is Born*, Richard Dyer (1991) describes an almost obsessive interest in the performance of Judy Garland, particularly in her singing, which can be read as an indication of her supposedly real (neurotic) personality. It can be read in this way, if the spectator subscribes to what Dyer calls a 'rhetoric of authenticity', which is the dominant criterion in the twentieth century by which such performances are judged. In an interesting historical sketch, Dyer argues that there has been a shift in the criteria governing public performances of this kind: whereas once (in the eighteenth century) performances were assessed according to aesthetic and moral precepts (including idealised concepts of genre) in terms of 'manner' or 'propriety'; today they are judged to be authentic according to whether or not they demonstrate qualities of 'sincerity', or personal truth. Thus, the fan of Judy Garland will scrutinise her films for those moments of sincerity which are discovered in gestures which appear to be unpremeditated, uncontrolled, or even 'private' (though of course these are public performances, of a particular kind). The interest is in the way Garland betrays herself, her 'real personality', while acting out her role.

More generally, and perhaps more usually, this kind of interest is also sustained through what John Ellis calls 'subsidiary forms of circulation' (1982, p.91). These are the press reports, the photographs, the interviews in fan magazines and on chat shows etc, which serve to maintain the hype surrounding the activities of film stars, and serve to publicise their relatively rare appearances in films. We have looked at some examples of this, in the previous section, in relation to Sylvester Stallone. Here the rhetoric of authenticity again focuses on the unpremeditated and uncontrolled (for example, when questioned by a fan about his current love-life, Stallone snaps back 'Why don't you get a job that pays?'); and of course on the private sphere (sex lives, parties, lifestyles of the rich and famous). All this serves to construct, for Ellis, a particular paradox: stars are ordinary and extraordinary at the same time. On one hand, in terms of lifestyle, they are larger-than-life, glamorous and remote; on the other hand, in their 'real personalities' they are capable of anger, disappointment and perhaps occasional personal happiness – just like any 'real' person might be.

But in the face of all this interest in what the stars are really like, perhaps we need to remind ourselves of a simple and obvious point – that we will never really know. For the 'real personality' of the star is just as much a media construction (albeit in different media) as his or her appearances in films. Thus, what we are looking at in Ellis's paradox is a relationship between two practices of media signification: on one hand, the cinematic performance; and on the other, the 'subsidiary circulation' of press reports etc. The most sophisticated attempt to theorise this relationship, in my view, is provided by Christine Gledhill (1991) in her account of the construction of the star's persona. This construction assumes the relevance of Dyer's 'rhetoric of authenticity', but essentially it is an amalgamation of the media fragments which constitute the star's public image:

> The components I am concerned with here include the 'real person', the 'characters' or 'roles' played by the star in films and the star's 'persona' which exists independently of the real person or film character, combining elements of each in a public 'presence'. The real person is the site of amorphous and shifting bodily attributes, instincts, psychic drives and experiences. In contrast the film character or role is relatively formed and fixed by fictional and stereotypical conventions. The persona, on the other hand, forms the private life into a public and emblematic shape, drawing on general social types and film roles, whilst deriving authenticity from the unpredictability of the real person. (p.214–5)

It seems to me that 'Sylvester Stallone' is a star persona of this kind. The film roles (Rocky, Rambo) are clearly stereotypical, but they merge, in the persona, with a public biography sustained through 'subsidiary circulation'. The unpredictability which occasionally surfaces in this circulation (in the tabloid press) serves less to reveal the 'real person', than to authenticate, by humanising, the persona. In addition, I have suggested that the star persona of Stallone is iconic, insofar as it has a representative (or 'emblematic') significance, and in so far as it says something (symbolically) about what it means to be masculine in contemporary culture. The real Stallone (whoever he is) can only live with this persona (we can only guess how) which by now escapes his control, but remains the key public image against which he is condemned to be judged.

In her essay, Gledhill makes a most interesting connection between this concept of the star persona and the history of what she calls 'the melodramatic project'. Here, the term 'melodrama' is being used in two ways, both to refer to a particular theatrical genre (dating from the nineteenth century), and to characterise the moral philosophy which that genre articulates. Thus, as a theatrical genre, melodrama displaced certain classical dramatic conventions, in particular its code of ethics. It moved away from the emphasis on propriety and conformity to external moral codes, and towards the notion of an inner personal conscience. This notion of conscience (first developed in the protestant religious tradition) assumed internal conflicts and contradictions within the person which could only be resolved through the discovery of a 'true identity'. In these circumstances, the concept of character acquired new psychological dimensions, and the traditional theatrical stereotypes (heroes, villains) now displayed through gesture, the signs of their inner torments.

The star persona can be interpreted in this light, as a similar 'melodramatic' construction. The difference is that the search for a true identity is no longer contained within a particular play, or film (or series of films) – it is now extended to encompass what is known of the life of the star. Thus, argues Gledhill, 'the melodramatic demand for clearly defined identity has shifted from fictional to star personae who offer the advantage of authenticating the moral drama in reference to a real person outside the fiction' (p.218). In this reading, stars are interesting because in their personae they demonstrate a personal engagement with their (stereotypical) roles, in terms of a perpetual search for some way of 'being themselves'. This connects with Gledhill's second, and wider, concept of melodrama, as a contemporary philosophy of 'personhood'. In contemporary culture it is often assumed that a person's 'true identity' is concealed, or is problematic and difficult to achieve. This establishes an intense interest in what a person is 'really like', or where their essential self might be discovered.

In this respect then, Gledhill is again pointing to a wider conceptual framework, which influences the way in which media texts are read. In this framework, knowledge of genre is accompanied, not simply by a knowledge of the stars themselves and their past performances, but by a general philosophy of personhood which allows us to make judgements of their 'personae' (as true, or sincere, or not as the case may be). Arguably, the more interesting the star, the more complex and contradictory (the more 'melodramatic') the star persona – which is why Judy Garland, and not Lauren Bacall, has attracted particular critical attention, and why Sylvester Stallone provides more press coverage than Harrison Ford. Now, however, perhaps we can begin to detect some ambiguity, or at least instability, in the use of terms like 'star' and 'personality'. For insofar as the 'persona' is not the real person, but a construction; and insofar as some star personae have greater cultural resonance than others – then the concept is beginning to look like Williams' second definition of 'personality'. It is a quality exhibited to a greater extent by some individuals than by others. It is even, potentially, a career in its own right: Elizabeth Taylor remains a public 'personality, even though she has not made a significant film for years.

As I mentioned in my introduction to this section, the difficulty here for media studies is that, in some accounts, a fairly rigid distinction is made between film stars and other media 'personalities', associated particularly with radio and TV. Thus, in this argument, it is in broadcasting that we find the professional personalities such as Oprah Winfrey and Johnny Carson, Cilla Black and Terry Wogan. Such individuals may well be public figures, leading comfortable lives, but they do not have the exalted status of Hollywood film stars. Indeed in British broadcasting, many presenters have cultivated precisely the opposite kind of image, appearing as down-to-earth, ordinary, 'people like us'. Such qualities are often associated with particular class and/or regional origins: Cilla Black, for instance, belongs to a tradition of northern, working-class 'homeliness' which goes back at least to the 1940s and the emergence, as a radio personality, of Wilfred Pickles. But more generally the concept of personality has been defined as a systematic tendency in broadcasting, and has been contrasted sharply with the paradoxical, enigmatic figure of the film star. For example, John Ellis (1982), mentioning Patrick Moore and Robin Day, concludes that:

> These are personalities or celebrities rather than stars in the cinematic sense. Their notoriety results from their fairly constant presence on the medium rather than their rarity; they are familiar rather than remote; they are present in the actuality of the television image rather than the photo effect of the cinema image; they activate no conflict of meaning and no real enigmas; they bear a fairly minimal relationship to the desire of the spectator; the subsidiary circulation of material about them is more concerned with discovering if there is a personality separate from that of the television role than it is with the paradox of the ordinary-but-extra-ordinary. (p.107)

There are times, in *Visible Fictions*, where Ellis seems to want to minimise the significance of broadcasting, as compared with cinema. However, even if we take a less negative view, we must concede that he has some valid points. In particular, in our previous discussions we have seen that broadcasting and cinema have distinctively different modes of address, relating to the conditions in which these media are consumed. Moreover, broadcasting operates through a regime, a hierarchy of positions – and it has been argued that a down-to-earth, conversational approach is appropriate for a style of presentation which is designed to stimulate 'para-social interaction' (4). To this extent, a particular kind of 'personality effect' may be associated with broadcasting's mode of address; but it is also, as Ellis points out, an effect of the schedule, and of routinely repeated, and therefore familiar, appearances. TV personalities have none of the exclusivity of film stars; and furthermore, because broadcasting systems have been, until now, nationally (or regionally) located, few such personalities have an international reputation.

All this may serve to diminish the possibility of the broadcasting personality achieving iconic status. Rather than defining an era, like the persona of Sylvester Stallone, the role of the broadcasting personality is reduced to providing comment and interpretation or, at most, interviewing the star on his or her rare public appearances. But, though less exalted, it is not true to say that the broadcasting personality lacks a persona altogether, or as Ellis suggests, that this activates 'no real enigmas'. For if the melodramatic philosophy of the person is indeed universal in our culture, then it can be applied to any individuals with whom we become familiar, through their appearances in any mass media. 'What is the true identity of this person?' is a question we can bring to any media persona – whether that of the film star or the TV personality.

And in fact applying this question to the TV personality gives rise to a whole series of enigmas which Ellis does not consider. For the interest in a 'true identity', implying the possibility that this is concealed or problematic, becomes paradoxical when applied to the down-to-earth persona of the broadcaster. Surely these are people who, in their very ordinariness, are simply being themselves? Surely their identities can be taken at face value? But I have two sorts of evidence to suggest that this is not, in fact, the case, and that the TV personality is increasingly perceived to be another kind of constructed persona. My first evidence is purely anecdotal, but it arises from discussions with students, who when asked to define the qualities shared by TV personalities frequently mention words like 'glib' or 'smarmy'. Smarminess is artificial sincerity – a sincerity which is perceived to be a construction. For many viewers, it has been personified on British television by Bob Monkhouse who, in the same interview where he tells his funny stories about *The Golden Shot* (see Chapter 2), also engages in a dialogue with Terry Wogan about his own (and Terry's) mediated personae:

WOGAN:	You've done your chat show series for BBC2. How do you like being an interviewee rather than an interviewer?
MONKHOUSE:	I found being an interviewer very very difficult. I have watched this series of course I have, and the last one and the previous one. And I think you are, I hate to do this, I think you're very good [*laughter*]. I really do . . . I found it very difficult. I find the biggest problem for me is, that my admiration for my guests, because they were all comedians, is so considerable that I can't disguise it, I can't hide it, and therefore it's possible to appear, erm, obsequious and, er, overenthusiastic about a guest when

	that is a genuine emotion, and that's been criticised. I noticed, er, (W: Yes). Well I should develop the same contempt that you obviously have for your guests.
WOGAN:	No, only for some of them.
MONKHOUSE:	[Laughs] Adsum.
WOGAN:	Do you think then that, erm, being honest or showing honest emotions on television is not a good idea, if they could be misinterpreted, as they have been in your case, they're called smarm which is genuine admiration?
MONKHOUSE:	[*Laughs*] Yes, er, I don't think er, television is a place for me to show my genuine emotions. I think it's a place for, I would rather, I'm much happier, er, Joan Rivers when you interviewed her the other week so, so excellently, said the cabaret stage was her psychiatrist, er, that she regarded her job as to entertain, to get laughs. And that's the way I feel I, I came into the business in eighteen hundred and forty five in order to get laughs but that meant inventing a persona, offering something which is not necessarily me, it's an invention, it's a construction.
	I, I've known you long enough to know that there are er, inconceivably deeper parts of you than are actually visible on the TV screen. There are parts of you which have never been seen on the TV screen [*audience laughter*]. I for one hope that they will never be seen.
WOGAN:	You nearly got into a compliment there. And you decided to duck out of it. Because a little bit of the real Bob came out there and you quickly shoved it back again.
MONKHOUSE:	Yes, yes I don't really want to, no, exposing myself on the TV screen is not my idea of fun.

(Wogan, 10 March 1984)

Here is some evidence that the concept of the persona, and indeed the melodramatic interest in a true identity ('the real Bob'), is perceived to be relevant to the television personality, by some personalities themselves. It is significant that this perception should be so self-consciously (if ironically and flippantly) foregrounded in a chat show, and I shall explore some further implications of this shortly. For the moment, however, I want to use this evidence to support my claim that the melodramatic philosophy of the person, as outlined by Gledhill, is a general feature of our culture. Film stars and TV personalities appear in different media, and reach their audiences in different ways, but they all have personae which we are encouraged (by the culture) to interpret according to this philosophy. But this is not, it seems to me, a phenomenon which is limited to media stars and personalities.

Politicians too, in our culture, have personae, constructed in the media, and through the public relations industry, which are similarly interrogated. So now, to conclude this section, let me offer a further twist to this tale.

In his book *All Consuming Images* (1988), Stuart Ewen argues that the construction of personae, in all walks of life, is a feature of modern consumer societies. Specifically, he suggests that there has been a transformation in concepts of personhood, from 'character' (a concept which includes moral criteria) to 'personality' (which, for Ewen, is closely associated with the notion of 'style'). Recall that the persona is a public self, constructed out of diverse public appearances and what is known of the private life of the person. According to Ewen, in the 'personality' persona, this public self can be cultivated, enhanced, made-up and 'stylised': 'the idiosyncracies of character are forged into the market-tested gleam of personality' (p.89). Ewen refers to practices of salesmanship and image management in 1930s America – Dale Carnegie's *How To Win Friends And Influence People* (1936) – where it was essential to cultivate a marketable 'extrinsic self'. He quotes psychoanalyst Erich Fromm (1941) to the effect that:

> Friendliness, cheerfulness and everything that a smile is supposed to express, become automatic responses which one turns on and off like an electric switch. (p.94)

Here then, the persona is not just a media construction; rather it is a general condition of human (or at least middle-class) existence. Now, the melodramatic philosophy of the person is subjected to market forces, that both, on one hand, make the notion of a true identity even more problematic, and also, on the other, offer new opportunities in terms of the development of 'lifestyle'. In short, the construction of 'personality' is expressed through the use of consumer goods. It remains the case, however, that though the American Dream projects this as a general possibility, it is in the lives of celebrities that it is truly realised. In Ewen's account, the term 'celebrity' subsumes both the film star and the television personality, just as it includes others (such as royalty) who have not, in the first instance, become 'rich and famous' through the media:

> In a consumer society, the lives of the celebrities are not merely guideposts from which people take their stylistic cues. They also embody every consumer's dream of what it would be like if money were no object. In 'the magnifying glass of the mass media', wrote C. Wright Mills in 1956, we see 'all the expensive commodities to which the rich seem appendages . . . money talking in its husky, silky voice of cash, power and celebrity.' The luminaries, their clothes and cars and villas and vacation yachts, represent a consumerized interpretation of personal freedom – a 'middle class' ideal – multiplied exponentially; beyond comprehension, but never

so far as to undermine a glimmer of hope in the mind of the spectator. The dream of abundance, the principle of appearances, circulates in the lives of celebrities as it circulates in the desires of those maintaining – or attempting to construct – the semblance of a 'middle class' life. (pp.99–100)

Ewen's concept of the celebrity, whose 'personality' is expressed through conspicuous consumption, adds a further dimension to the theory of stardom in media studies. It suggests that the familiar distinction between film stars and TV personalities is too limited, tied to observations about the different communicative practices in these two media. As we have seen, Gledhill's argument, which suggests that stardom is constructed in terms of a melodramatic philosophy of the person, can be extended to encompass TV personalities. Now Ewen is arguing that this philosophy has been infected, in the course of the twentieth century, by consumerism – so that both film stars and TV personalities, in their status as celebrities, have adopted 'personality' personae. That is to say, the philosophy through which we now judge a person has to accommodate the 'principle of appearances', and the significance of 'lifestyle' – and this is the case not only in the rarified lives of Hollywood film stars (Stallone's 'Casa Rocko') but also in the 'ordinary' (and therefore more accessible) world of TV personalities, as my next section will illustrate.

3 PERSONALITY AND TELEVISION: READING THE *TVTIMES*

As if to confirm Ewen's theory of celebrity, in which film stars and television personalities are interchangeable, the *TVTimes*, on 23 April 1994, included a profile of Sylvester Stallone. In 'Tamed At Last?' (pp14–15), the usual references were made, to the developments in Stallone's love-life, to his exotic lifestyle in Miami, and to his problematic attempts to shake off the 'Rocky/Rambo label'. Unlike the tabloid press, however, the *TVTimes* profile also emphasised Stallone's professional self-discipline. Thus despite the distraction of his mistresses and love-children, Stallone was 'trying to concentrate on his job', and was interviewed on the set of his current film, *The Specialist*. Having reluctantly accepted that the action-thriller was his genre, Stallone had 'no plans to relax his disciplined lifestyle'. He remained dedicated to his 'high-protein, low-fat diet', with the result, as the article reassuringly put it, 'the muscles are back'.

This profile appeared in the *TVTimes* to publicise a showing of *Rocky IV* on ITV. It also reminds us that genre is not the only institutional system for packaging and publicising television programmes – even if this is an example of a feature film on TV. For the profile of Stallone appeared alongside other profiles, of the actor Timothy Spall for example, who has appeared in films (such as *The Sheltering Sky*, 1990), but who is best known in Britain for his performances in television series (in particular, the hit comedy drama, *Auf Wiedersehn Pet*). More generally this issue of the *TVTimes* was littered with shorter pieces ranging from the love-lives of actresses (Jayne Ashbourne, Lesley Dunlop), and the 'real life friendship' between Letitia Dean and Susan Tully (of *EastEnders*), to the practical traumas of individuals featured in 'human interest' documentaries. All of this amounted to a mass-mediated life-world of stars, personalities and 'ordinary people'. And the assumption is clearly that this life-world is enticing to the potential audience, whether our interest is in the real lives of familiar celebrities, or the human problems of individuals who are 'just like us'.

In the *TVTimes* this focus on personality is the most upfront form of publicity for forthcoming television programmes. Any issue of the magazine contains twenty or so pages of such material, followed by a film guide and the TV programme listings, and rounded off by a '*TVTimes extra*' – a further ten pages of lifestyle items, including, on 23 April, 'At Home' with TV presenters Paul Coia and Debbie Greenwood, and 'Tasty low-cal recipes inspired by Oprah Winfrey's amazing weight loss'. In Britain, since 1991, the publication of TV guides has been deregulated, so that the traditional duopoly of the *Radio Times* and the *TVTimes* now faces competition from cheaper magazines like *TV Quick* and *What's On TV*, as well as from weekly supplements in national newspapers. Overwhelmingly, the popular formula is similar to the *TVTimes*, with the emphasis on personality and lifestyle, though the mixture is weighted differently according to the price, and presumably the intended market, of each magazine. Even the most expensive *Radio Times*, featured on its 16 April front cover, a portrait of TV person-ality Angus Deayton, as a trailer for the return of *Have I Got News For You*; though it has to be said that, if personality is also prevalent here, the concern with lifestyle is minimal.

In general terms personality operates alongside genre in setting up the framework of expectations that the audience brings to television. Indeed the two concepts have a connected history, both having been introduced to British television in the 1950s. As we have seen, the genre-orientated *Radio Times* nevertheless found a place for some reference to personalities, like Derek Hart, in its listings for 15 April 1957. Routinely, mention was made of other presen-ters like Cliff Michelmore, Eamonn Andrews and Richard Dimbleby; and some programmes (*Hancock's Half Hour, Meet Jeanne Heal*) carried the names of personalities in their titles. Personality then, like genre, was part of the institutionalisation of BBC television – but it was certainly at the rival network, the commercial ITV, that its full implications were exploited.

Commercial television was introduced to Britain in September 1955. At that time BBCTV was still struggling to establish itself, to emerge from the dominance of radio, and ITV was able to introduce some significant

Fig. 5.2. ITV listings, Monday 15 April 1957, from the TVTimes 12 April 1957. Reproduced by kind permission of TVTimes

innovations to British television. The major change was the introduction of spot advertising, but innovations were also made, for instance, in the style of TV news: 'from the studios of ITN', with named newscasters Christopher Chataway and Robin Day. More generally some cultural historians have made reference to a certain American influence – not because large numbers of American programmes were directly imported (for this was regulated by the 1954 Television Act), but because 'Americanised' cultural values appeared to be promoted by some types of popular programmes. Important here were new forms of light entertainment, influenced by American vaude-ville and by Hollywood film genres, and American formats for quizzes and game shows. Significantly, these styles of programming appeared to be consistent with the values of consumerism, another phenomenon in post-war Britain, to which spot advertising was also directed. This whole commer-cialised value system, represented by ITV, lent itself to promotion by means of an increased emphasis on television 'personalities' (5).

Such a shift of emphasis is evident in the *TVTimes* listings for 15 April 1957 (see figure 5.2). As we have seen, the BBC's schedule for the same day includes over ninety minutes of news and current affairs (*Tonight* and *Panorama*), together with a religious programme for Easter week, as well as its more popular celebrity and comedy programmes (such as *This Is Your Life* and *Hancock's Half Hour*). On the same day, the ITV schedule includes two quiz shows (one of which, *Make Up Your Mind*, features consumer goods and cash prizes), two drama series (including a televised western), a serial thriller (compare this with the BBC's 'cycle of plays' for holy week), a situation comedy and two other comedy shows (alongside forty-five minutes of news and current affairs, including the innovative *What The Papers Say*). At 6.45, *The Patti Page Show* features 'America's lovely singing star', and other programme publicity emphasises 'stars' and 'comperes', or gives promi-nence to well-known names. This difference of emphasis is clearly reflected in the front covers for the two magazines (dated 12 April 1957): for the *Radio Times* chooses to promote its religious plays; whereas the front cover of the *TVTimes* features a big close-up of Rosemary Clooney, the American singer who was to star in *Sunday Night At The London Palladium*.

It is, however, in its feature articles that the *TVTimes* really develops its focus on personalities. For example on page 31 of the 12 April issue we find:

Success is Simple if you . . .

TAKE A PAGE OUT OF PATTI'S NOTEBOOK

Would you like to be a big success? Would you like to be a personality who can sell six million, or more, records? You can easily be. Let Patti Page, blue eyed, blonde American singer with the enchanting voice and the curvaceous figure, tell you how . . .

April 12, 1957   TV TIMES   31

Success is Simple if you ...

TAKE A PAGE OUT OF PATTI'S NOTEBOOK

WOULD you like to be a big success ? Would you like to be a personality who can sell six million, or more, records ? You can so easily be. Let Patti Page, blue-eyed, blonde American singer with the enchanting voice and the curvaceous figure, tell you how.

"All you need," she says, starting slowly and warming up the tempo as she rattles off the items, " is the right voice, the right song, the right conductor, the right engineer, the right record promoter, the right press agent and the right company.

"*The other 98 per cent is just luck !*"

Even then it's still not just a question of singing. You still can't just stand in front of the TV camera and star in the type of show such as Associated-Rediffusion presents Patti in next Friday at 10 o'clock. You have to become a big business boss.

Entourage

"I have a private secretary, a fan club secretary, an accountant, a record promoter, a lawyer, a pianist, a drummer, a musical arranger for records and an organisation for personal appearances.

We now have the second list out of our hair and think that all there is left to do is sing. But no. Now we come to appearance.

The first time Patti rated a biography handout for publicity, her weight was given as 9 st. 4 lb., her measurements : 34-26-36. It wasn't long before she

issued new figures : Weight 8 st. 3lb., measurements, 34½-23-35.

She tells the whole story, quite simply : " I submitted to massage, exercised faithfully, read all the calory charts and brewed every horrible diet dressing they recommended, exhausted myself with long walks and gymnastics, and even read a book on how to think your way to thin.

" *And when I'd worked through that lot, I just starved.*"

So now we know about the organisation and the figure and we think that all there can be left is just to sing. But no. Now we arrive at clothes. You can't just sing ; you've got to dress stylishly.

Costly gowns

In eight weeks of filming her TV show, Patti modelled some £35,000 worth of gowns.

She wore nothing but originals from a famous New York designer, making at least one change in each show. Even with her sizeable income she couldn't afford to buy all the gowns—she borrowed them.

After she had chosen the songs she was to sing, she then had to choose a costume to harmonise with the mood of her melody.

So now we have another item out of the way and the path is clear to stand up and sing. Unless you're going to do it on TV !

Now comes the question of film versus " live " TV. It helps if you have decided views on the subject—as has Miss Page.

"Film for me," she says, wholeheartedly. " It has the advantage of letting you watch your work on the screen.

" Believe me, there's nothing like the feeling you get when you're watching yourself and you ask ' Is that *really* me ?' and your own small, thin voice answers ' Yes, dear, that's you. And don't you think you should have worn your hair differently for that scene ? And that gown could have hung a little better. And that note could have been hit a little harder.' "

But, at least, you can see yourself and

remember all these things for the next time.

So now we know all about the organisation, the appearance, the clothes and the TV technique. And we think that all that's left is to sing. And be a success.

The 'gimmick'

All right, warble your head off. For having worked through the necessities, all you now have to do is get yourself discovered and find a " gimmick."

Patti set about being discovered by singing in a church choir, graduating to radio and singing just as band manager Jack Rael was passing through the town of Tulsa.

He heard her. He liked her. He signed her.

After six months hard work she signed to do her own show and make records.

Records. The very thing to make a singer's name ? Patti made 12 and scarcely caused a ripple in the disc world. Which brings us to the " gimmick."

In her thirteenth record, a tune called *Confess*, Patti dubbed in the harmony with her own voice. The dual voice made the disc an immediate hit. So she followed it up with *With My Eyes Wide Open I'm Dreaming*, on which she dubbed in her voice four times.

Lucky waltz

Now what about that little thing we mentioned early on—luck ? That might come this way.

For the 1950 Christmas records, Mercury (the company for whom she records) came up with a novelty they expected to sweep the country, *Boogie Woogie Santa Claus*. On the " flip " side they tossed in a little number, *Tennessee Waltz*, with Patti doing the vocal.

The boogie number got a few spins with the disc jockeys. Patti's *Tennessee Waltz* sold more than 4,000,000 copies and became the most popular record in two decades.

Warwick Butler

Fig. 5.3. 'Success is Simple ...', from the TVTimes *12 April 1957. Reproduced by kind permission of* TVTimes

Patti Page's most successful record in the 1950s was her version of *Tennessee Waltz*, first released as a B-side in 1950, which sold over four million copies. Following this, her TV show was acquired by ITV, and had been included in its schedules since 1956. By April 1957 then, the British TV audience had over a year's familiarity with *The Patti Page Show*, which is perhaps what accounts for the fact that this feature is tucked away at the back of the *TVTimes* (see figure 5.3). It is essentially a review of her singing career, including portrait photograph and quotations, with an emphasis on the hard work, and the luck, needed to achieve 'success'.

My interest in this somewhat obscure article, about a now forgotten singer, is that it articulates very clearly some key themes in the *TVTimes* of the period. Patti Page is introduced as an American 'personality', but what the article goes on to emphasise is the process through which that status has been achieved. Her natural talent as a singer was discovered, as we might expect, in the parochial context of the church choir, but this was only the start of a process which included her physical transformation (graphic details, including vital statistics, of how the 'curvaceous figure' was developed), her acquisition of a vast wardrobe ('nothing but originals from a famous New York designer') and the development of a business organisation (her 'entourage'). It thus becomes quite clear in the course of this article that Patti Page's 'personality' is a construction, expressed primarily through her physical appearance, which is also the focus for some residual melodramatic doubts about her true identity. Where have we encountered this before?:

> Believe me, there's nothing like the feeling you get when you're watching yourself and you ask 'Is that *really* me?' and your own small, thin voice answers 'Yes dear, that's you. And don't you think you should have worn your hair differently for that scene? And that gown could have hung a little better?' . . .

In Chapter 3, this type of self-questioning was related to Althusser's concept of interpellation, in which the individual adopts a particular form of subjectivity. What is interesting about this *TVTimes* feature is that it functions in a similar way, as a sort of advertisement. The Patti Page success story is constructed as an example to the reader, an effect which is reinforced by the direct address of the headline, the opening paragraph, and by Patti's 'look' in the photograph. What does this look convey? It is not the dreamy off-stage look of the newly glamorous Sarah Davies, the girl in the Cover Girl ad. On the contrary, Patti Page's glamour is direct, friendly and accessible. Her smile is the smile of her own success; but implicitly in the photograph and explicitly in the text, this kind of success is available (with hard work and a little luck) to us all.

As if to confirm the truth of this philosophy, the *TVTimes* of this period is full of similar, British, 'success stories'. Thus in the same issue (on page 11), we find a profile of Phyllis Forrester, 'escort' for the latest Bob Monkhouse show, *Bury Your Hatchet*. Similarly blonde, similarly direct,

Phyllis strikes a pose which accentuates her 'curvaceousness'. Meanwhile the written text proceeds:

> 38, 22, 37 Rock – that's Phyllis Forrester
>
> Bill Haley has been kind to Phyllis Forrester – but he doesn't know it. He's kept her waistline down to a trim 22 inches – but he doesn't know it. She spends half an hour with Haley every morning – but he doesn't know it.
>
> Which is hard luck on Haley, because the silver-blonde Phyllis, fashion model turned escort for *Bury Your Hatchet*, is an easy-on-the-eyeful well worth knowing, with 38-22-37 statistics to prove it.
>
> 'How does Haley come into the proceedings?' I asked her.
>
> 'First thing every morning', says Phyllis, without batting a golden brown eye, 'I have a 30-minute rock 'n roll session to Haley's music, It's the best exercise there is, you know' . . .

However, perhaps it is difficult to represent the life of a game show hostess in quite the same businesslike terms as an international singer. The feature on Phyllis Forrester turns from exercise and diet to her hobbies, which turn out to be pets and photography:

> Photography, in a way, has been a pretty important factor in her life. She was a fashion model working in Switzerland, when a photographer took her picture. And raved over the pink dress she was wearing. And became very friendly. And finally married her.

Lucky Phyllis! . . . Her story clearly echoes the romance genre which we discussed in the previous chapter, and ties this into the now familiar conventions of popular glamour in fashion photography. It will also be worth keeping this example in mind during the next chapter, where we will consider some recent feminist discussions of the construction of femininity in the 1950s. Here, however, despite its anachronistic tone, I think it is important to emphasise that this article, like many others in the *TVTimes* of this period, illustrates a a culture which is also distinctively *modern*. This is the world described by Stuart Ewen, the glamorous consumer society, which was a novel concept in Britain at that time. Historians write of the 1950s as Britain's 'age of affluence', characterised by full employment, and the availability of consumer durables which were to transform domestic life and popular culture. ITV, with its spot advertising, was a publicity machine for this consumer society, but, in the *TVTimes* it also provided accounts of how the good life might be lived. In its features and profiles it illustrated the philosophy, popular in America since the 1930s, of self-improvement, of the enhanced lifestyle, and of the construction of the 'personality' persona. For women in particular, as my examples show, this was a persona to be cultivated through personal appearance – and it is remarkable how stereotyped the desirable image proved to be.

In my next section I shall return to this dominant image of woman in the 1950s – in the form of its apotheosis, Marilyn Monroe. But in the light of the popularity of that image, and indeed all the examples I have considered here, it is worth re-emphasising a further point about its construction, and thus its particular impact on British television culture. For here is an image which is not only modern, but also transatlantic, and even international, in its definition of what a successful personality might be. Contrast this with the distinctively national, and traditionally British, focus of the BBC. On ITV we are very far from the mundane, domestic world of Hancock – here we are presented with a vision of a cosmopolitan consumer culture, which stretches from Los Angeles to Switzerland. And in Phyllis Forrester's lifestyle we catch a glimpse of the emerging youth culture which was to become the international currency of the post-war period.

4 THE FACE OF MARILYN

One of the most interesting, and well-known of Roland Barthes' essays in *Mythologies* is entitled 'The Face of Garbo'. Here, Barthes confronts a major iconic image from the 1930s and subjects it to his familiar method of reading – identifying its connotations and (with some assistance from his knowledge of the period) defining the mythology which these connotations suggest. Barthes' argument is that Garbo's face was an image of divine perfection, 'a sort of Platonic idea of the human creature'; which, in the light of our discussion in the previous chapter, we might relate to the concept of high glamour, prevalent in fashion, as well as film, in the 1930s. Additionally, however, Barthes detects signs of the human, the existential, and even the sexual woman. Thus:

> Garbo's face represents this fragile moment when the cinema is about to draw an existential from an essential beauty, when the archetype leans towards the fascination of mortal faces, when the clarity of the flesh as essence yields its place to a lyricism of woman . . . Viewed as a transition the face of Garbo reconciles two iconographic ages, it assures the passage from awe to charm. (p.57)

For Barthes, the representative image of the new age of 'charm' was provided by Audrey Hepburn. It is interesting that Barthes chose a face from the 1950s, but I think it is strange, in view of his point about the 'lyricism of woman' that he did not refer to Marilyn Monroe. Here then, with apologies to Barthes, I want to make some observations about the face of Marilyn, which I think can be located within the kind of transition he describes. Moreover, Marilyn is *the* iconic image of the 1950s. In theoretical terms, this is a persona which (like Stallone's) speaks to certain aspects of the human condition, not only in its own time, but also, and perhaps particularly, today.

Part of our interest in this persona must be its continued significance, as an art object (Warhol), as a poster, as a postcard etc, in short, as an 'Athena Reproduction' (6). I have suggested that Marilyn is the essential film star: this is basically because I think her persona transcends its time (as Hepburn's and even Garbo's did not) and that she now stands as a symbol for the general phenomenon of stardom.

So can Marilyn's face be read as an iconic image and, if so, what does it represent? This question is not asked innocently. There is an ulterior motive behind this interest in Marilyn's face which is of course that most commentators on her persona, both in the 1950s and since, have chosen to focus on her body. Amid the mountains of paperwork devoted to Monroe, the most important essay from a media studies perspective is Richard Dyer's 'Monroe and Sexuality' in his book *Heavenly Bodies* (1986). Here Dyer mainly deals with Monroe's importance in the 1950s: as signifying a new kind of 'sexual freedom' (a philosophy articulated, in particular, by the magazine *Playboy*); and as a sign which could be interpreted according to popular Freudian ideas about female sexuality. Dyer shows that both these understandings of Monroe were prevalent at the time, and they clearly defined her persona in terms of her physicality. Thus, Monroe = sexuality = the body. I do not at all wish to dispute Dyer's analysis, but I have chosen to look at an image which goes against this trend (see figure 5.4). I want to see if the face can illuminate any other aspects of Monroe's persona, which might allow us to reconsider some of the more conventional interpretations.

And there are, of course, other faces. In choosing this particular image of Monroe's face, I have again, very deliberately, ignored others. This is not, for example, the flirtatious face which *Time* magazine (quoted by Dyer) described, viz: 'the moist, half-closed eyes and moist half-open mouth' (p.57). Nor is this image that Dyer would describe as the typical Monroe pin-up: face and shoulders thrust towards the camera, hands emphasising breasts etc (see Dyer, p.43). Nor is it quite the 'cheesecake' image from Monroe's period as a 'starlet': the coy expression of the sweater girl, or the swimsuit pose (see Dyer, p.30). Here, I have in effect chosen to ignore those images in which Monroe does what she apparently could do so well – that is, act in certain ways for the camera. In this image, Monroe acknowledges the camera's presence, but she does not transform herself into its object. It is as though she has not posed, but simply turned her head, and caught herself being photographed:

> For the still camera, the most photogenic subject is one that freezes well, one that can be ripped out of time, suspended, motionless. The ideal photographic model is one who is able to suggest action while standing still . . . able to maintain a perpetual smile . . .
>
> (Ewen, p.85)

Fig. 5.4. The Face of Marilyn. Uncredited publicity still from Clash by Night *(1951)*

So there are many Marilyns, and mine is a deliberate choice. In starting to interpret its connotations, to arrive, like Barthes, at a mythology, I want to quote what Dyer says about *Monkey Business* (1952):

> The plot of *Monkey Business* concerns a rejuvenation drug. When middle-aged people take it, they become young again, meaning both uncivilised ... and sexy. For the Cary Grant character (Barnaby Fulton), this is realised through his change in response to the Monroe character (Miss Laurel). When earlier she shows him her leg (in order to display her new stockings), he is merely embarrassed; but after he has inadvertently taken the drug, he embarks on a free-wheeling, spontaneous, youthful (= natural) escapade with Miss Laurel – but whereas the joke is that this is him letting his hair down [sic?], she is clearly just getting into it because that's the way she is normally. Tearing along the highway in a sports car he has impulsively (= naturally) bought, she throws her head back, her hair flutters in the breeze, she opens her mouth and giggle-laughs. It is *the* Monroe image, here exactly placed to mean the natural enjoyment of sensation. That this enjoyment includes sexuality is made clear elsewhere in the sequence. (p.38)

Now, as Dyer seems to recognise here, there is often a sense in which Monroe's sexuality is but one aspect of a broader characteristic: the 'natural enjoyment of sensation'. There are other examples: for instance, the way in which 'the walk' in *Niagara* takes Monroe into a party where she ends up swaying and swooning to a contemporary popular record; or in *The Seven Year Itch* where her 'natural enjoyment' is of the sensations produced by an air conditioner. These are, for male characters (and the spectator) sexual moments, but Monroe herself is primarily responding to the pleasures to be derived from contemporary consumer goods. I am interested also in the way in which Dyer emphasises, in *Monkey Business*, the importance of youth. Obviously this is the focus of the plot, but it is also the sign of a certain natural, unconstrained attitude to the pleasures of consumerism. In this reading Monroe = youth = 'the natural enjoyment of (commodified) sensation'. Sexuality is a very important aspect of this, but this is because (as *Playboy* showed) the consumer society is sexy.

In my image of Marilyn Monroe, the film star has become a 'personality'. Here I am using the term in the way it is discussed by Ewen: 'the market-tested gleam of personality' as opposed to the 'idiosyncracies of character'. Did Ewen have in mind Monroe's performance as the Dazzledent toothpaste girl when he wrote these words? In fact the entire plot of *The Seven Year Itch* hinges around Monroe playing herself (with some reflexive irony) as this kind of 'personality' – that is, as a natural, spontaneous and youthful representative of the new consumer culture. *The Seven Year Itch* was released in 1955, the same year as the British public was introduced to ITV. Surely it is not inappropriate to see the Monroe persona – the Marilyn personality – as the prototype for the Phyllis Forresters in the new ITV culture?

5 CASE STUDY: TV TALK SHOWS AND THE 'PERSONALITY EFFECT'

The concept of 'personality' has been associated with television since the 1950s, not only by academic commentators, but also by broadcasters themselves. Thus in the memoirs of prominent broadcasters like Grace Wyndham Goldie (1978) and Geoffrey Cox (1983) there is some discussion of the effects of televising politicians where, for the first time, voters were able to scrutinise their faces and their non-verbal behaviour, in close-up. Cox, a key figure in the development of ITN, argues that the presence of the camera demanded a correspondingly rigorous interview style (which was pioneered at ITN by Robin Day) 'capable of testing and portraying the politician's personality as well as his [sic] policies' (p.49). Here then, a particular kind of personality effect was the product of ritualistic interrogation in the context of the TV news interview, putting 'on record', for public scrutiny, the politician's apparent honesty and sincerity when responding to probing questions.

Other genres of TV programming extended this use of the interview. An innovative series in the late 1950s/early 1960s was the BBC's *Face To Face* with Robert Freeman. In this series, Freeman interviewed celebrities (Gilbert Harding, Tony Hancock, Adam Faith) as well as politicians (Martin Luther King). The focus for the interrogation was psychological as much as political, focusing on the interviewee's personal and emotional life, and supported by a peculiarly intense use of the camera, where the interviewee (never the interviewer) was filmed in extreme close-up, and from unusual angles. In a less intense fashion this interest in the personal and emotional lives of public figures continued in the genre of the 'chat' or talk show. Alongside the kind of probing interview conducted by Robin Day, perhaps it is true to say that the talk show, from the late 60s through to the late 80s, became the major site for extensive televised interviewing; and in Britain, Simon Dee was succeeded by Michael Parkinson, who was himself succeeded by Terry Wogan and Michael Aspel.

In his essay on television's 'personality system', John Langer (1981) gives particular prominence to this kind of talk show interview:

> In the context of the talk-show's carefully orchestrated informality, with its illusion of lounge-room casualness and leisurely pace, the host and guest engage in 'chat'. During the course of this chat, with suitable questions and tactful encouragement from the host, the guest is predictably 'drawn in' to making certain 'personal' disclosures, revealing aspects of what may be generally regarded as the private self, in fact becoming incorporated into television's personality system by disclosing for the purposes of television, one's 'personality'.

... What prevails in the end is not the talk show's diluted hucksterism and commercial 'hype' but its capacity to provide a special setting for personal disclosure where guests appear to be showing us their 'real' selves, where they can discuss how they 'feel' and reflect on their private lives with impunity. If these guests are among the great and powerful or are well known celebrities, which is most frequently the case, this is the place where the cares and burdens of high office or public life can be set aside, where we can see them as they 'really are', which in the end after all, as these programmes set out to illustrate, is just like us, 'ordinary folks'. (pp.360–1)

Thus, according to Langer, a particular kind of personality effect is produced by the talk show interview. In the nicest possible way (for we are all friends in this genre) the interview works in a way which is similar to *Face To Face*, insofar as it is primarily concerned with 'disclosure'. The purpose of the interview is to reveal something of the 'real person' behind the mask of the public figure, and so once again the accent is on honesty and sincerity – being ultimately 'true to oneself'. In the light of our earlier discussion we might observe that this kind of interviewing is entirely under the sway of the melodramatic philosophy of the person. That philosophy encourages a form of interviewing which is closely allied to the practice of confession – a public self-revelation ('What did you really feel when . . .?') in which 'personality' is equivalent to the truth of the 'real person'.

But, in the 1980s, I began to have some doubts about the general applicability of Langer's argument. These doubts began to surface when watching *Wogan* (in 1984, before the programme moved from its one hour Saturday evening slot to its weekday evening slot in the schedule). I have already included in this book two extracts from Wogan's interview, on 10 March 1984, with Bob Monkhouse – and these begin to indicate, to some extent, what was happening. In one extract (this chapter, section 2), there is still a melodramatic focus on 'the real Bob'; but this is immediately distanced by the interviewee's claim that his media personality is a construction (and crucially, so is Terry Wogan's). Elsewhere (see Chapter 2) the interview simply serves as a forum for Monkhouse to tell his funny stories; and I observed that Wogan's interviews frequently shifted into quasi-comedy routines, where he played the 'straight man' for his guests. In such ways, these interviews began to veer away from honest and sincere self-disclosure, towards forms of comedy and verbal *badinage*, encouraging the collaborative display of wit and repartee. Here, the 'truth of the person' was less important than the ability to perform and to participate in verbal games.

That this might be seen as a new trend, and even as a generic shift in the history of the talk show, was confirmed by other developments. For instance, it was confirmed by some of the talk shows reaching Britain from America,

Fig. 5.5. Dame Edna Everage. From The Dame Edna Experience*(1987)*
(London Weekend Television)

particularly by the style of David Letterman (which has been adopted in
Britain by Clive Anderson and Jonathan Ross). It was further confirmed by
the wonderful creation which first appeared on British television screens in
1987, where the talk show was hosted by a theatrical dame, Edna Everage,
played by Australian comedian Barry Humphries (see figure 5.5). In *The
Dame Edna Experience*, this generic transformation of the talk show was
complete. Here indeed 'chat' was reduced to a kind of pantomime, in which
the guests were required to give straight performances, and where the main
source of wit was Dame Edna 'herself'. Furthermore, the rules of the show
allowed for many other traditional conventions (of politeness etc) to be
overturned, so that guests might find themselves reprimanded, criticised, or
even physically humiliated by Dame Edna. Or so it seemed. Certainly, at the
time, some reviewers appeared to be thoroughly bemused:

> The chat show guests, the TV and home audience, never know what will
> come next. Does Barry Humphries? . . . This week, behind a foreground
> of celebrities, Charlton Heston appeared in wheelchair. Dame Edna with
> a cry, 'Chuck, for a minute I thought you'd brought your chariot', sent a

nurse to help him down the stairs. In the process he fell and wasn't seen again. Was his exit real? Or part of the game? Apparently this wasn't the first time Dame Edna has 'aborted' a star interview. So presumably it's just a joke. But it was thoroughly mystifying. Of course Dame Edna isn't what she seems. Anything could be going on under the make-up.

(Chaplin 1987, p.34)

In this, the third show of the 1987 series, the entrance of Charlton Heston was certainly a shock. The set required each guest to descend three flights of stairs to the accompaniment of an on-stage orchestra (Laurie Holloway and the Holocausts). Charlton Heston was in a wheelchair, he explained, because of a tennis accident; on attempting the descent, he fell, and the programme cut to a commercial break (but Heston reappeared, for the full interview, the following week). Were these events, as Patrice Chaplin claimed, 'thoroughly mystifying'? I would suggest that she is writing, as perhaps befits a TV critic, from a position of mock innocence. Arguably, the viewer, by now, knew to expect the unexpected; in any case, Heston's fall was accompanied by audience laughter, and the reaction shots of the other guests (Nana Maskouri and Germaine Greer) gave 'the game' away. *The Dame Edna Experience* was a spoof, a parody of the conventional talk show – just as its 'host', a man dressed as a woman, was a parody of femininity.

To this extent, I think that *The Dame Edna Experience* can be situated within the tradition which David Cardiff (1988) has described as 'mass middlebrow comedy'. In this article he argues that a distinctive type of comedy has developed in British broadcasting, directed towards a lower middle-class (or 'middlebrow') sensibility. This is the kind of irreverent humour associated with The Goons or *Monty Python's Flying Circus*, which makes fun of extremes, particularly upper-class pomposity and (supposed) lower-class ignorance. It is descended, Cardiff suggests, from the theatrical tradition of burlesque: 'a love of spectacle; the mingling of song, dance and comedy; a bland form of topical satire and parody' (p.48). In the context of broadcasting (radio and television, particularly at the BBC) it has made increasing demands on its audience, such that: 'technique is often dazzlingly innovative. It takes time for the public to become accustomed to new conventions, catch-phrases, running gags. The continued allusions to other programmes test the audience's familiarity with the medium' (p.57). Once recruited, however, the audience once again (to repeat a familiar theme of this book) can achieve a certain 'knowingness' – an inside (or 'cultish') knowledge – an awareness of the conventions being parodied or undermined. The audience for *The Dame Edna Experience* may have been initially shocked, but any mystification would have soon been dispelled by the knowingness it encouraged.

It was, however, a particularly clever programme. I think that its clever-ness was derived from the fact that it was not just a parody of the talk show, in the way that *Monty Python*, from a position of critical superiority, made fun of a number of TV genres. Rather, *Dame Edna* can be located within a series of developments which were already taking place within the genre. In the 1980s, conventional talk shows had become less serious as various forms of comedy, and verbal performance, had replaced 'straight' interviewing. The roles of hosts and guests, interviewers and interviewees, had already begun to diverge from the protocols of traditional interviewing – for example, it now became possible for guests to introduce topics and to put questions to their interviewers. In the cause of repartee, it became commonplace for both parties to cast aspersions, or to make snide remarks at the other's expense. *Dame Edna* simply took these developments to their logical conclusion, supported, of course, by our knowledge that she was not what she seemed.

The final significance of the drag act was to reaffirm that none of this was to be taken seriously; or, at its most complex, that we could never know whether any participant on this programme was being serious or not. Apparently straight questions were (occasionally) asked, and apparent 'disclosures' were made, but how could we believe them, in this context? The main point I am making here is that the conditions for the reproduction of the kind of personality effect described by Langer, are now being progres-sively undermined. Even when interviewees are apparently 'being themselves' we can never know whether or not to take them seriously. The talk show has become a game, and 'personality' is now demonstrated by a willingness to play; not by revealing all, with apparent sincerity, in a televised confes-sion.

The Dame Edna Experience may have been an extreme case of the phenomenon I am describing, but it is worth considering, I think, how far these developments have gone. It seems to me that this analysis can be applied to other TV talk shows, such as *Clive Anderson Talks Back*. Can it also be applied to other television genres, to more conventional political interviews for example? It may be that we are beginning to witness the demise of the 'melodramatic project', with its obsessive interest in people 'as they really are'. Or to make this point more carefully: it may be the case that melodrama is still a dominant philosophy, in that melodramatic questions are still asked (particularly in the tabloid press); but it is debatable whether we are able to believe the answers. These days, what anyone says in public, and particularly in the media, may or may not be true: it might be honest, sincere etc, but it might equally be a performance, an act of clever-ness, an exercise in public relations. Even apparent sincerity may be artifi-cial, as Bob Monkhouse has acknowledged. Thus it would seem that Langer's definition of 'personality' has been overtaken by Ewen's: and the 'real person' now has a 'market-tested gleam' which is primarily designed to impress.

FURTHER READING

There is a great deal of work, within the film studies tradition, on the phenomenon of stardom. An extremely valuable collection of essays is contained in Gledhill C. (ed) (1991), but for an earlier summary of this tradition see again Cook P. (ed) (1985) pp.50–3. In addition to the works quoted here, there are further discussions of stars (Lana Turner, Rudolph Valentino) by Richard Dyer in Dyer R. (1992). On the question of 'personality' Stewart Ewen's arguments are summarised in his essay 'Marketing Dreams: The Political Elements of Style' in Tomlinson A. (ed) (1990). See also Susman W.I. (1979). The discussion of Dame Edna in this chapter is based on Tolson (1991), and here I have been influenced by an interesting discussion of 'synthetic personalisation', to be found in Fairclough N. (1989), Chapter 8.

3

SUBTEXTS

6

Ideology

OUR COSMO WORLD

If ever there was a woman who seemed to symbolise the outrageous **heady freedom of beach days**, speed-boats on sparkling water, golden limbs and glorious hedonism – that woman was the young **Brigitte Bardot**. She was the most naturally sexual creature anyone had ever seen and she was the original, the role model all long-haired blondes have been imitating ever since. If you looked just a bit like BB you could, for the past 35 years or so, have found yourself on the arm of a famous sportsman, a film star, a successful businessman. But one of BB's divine attractions was that she seemed to be **the first famously beautiful woman who chose her men**. She didn't *need* them, she wanted them. Unlike her contemporary, Monroe, she was never a victim who had sex with men in order to further her career. And with her wild beauty, her stream of handsome **unsuitable lovers**, her eccentricities, her animal passions, she is a survivor. She's 60 next month, a new husband at her side, and still viewed as a **national treasure** by the French, who adore beautiful and interesting women whatever their age . . .
. . . I once knew a man who knew a man who went to bed with BB. He said she was adorable, patient (no he couldn't get it up at first, he was too scared), terribly tender and did everything she could to please. Doubtless she would approve of Olivia St Claire's loving and useful feature, *How to handle a manhood*, on page 134. Every little sexual pointer could help. Some people seem to know everything – but they don't always pass on vital information. And it's hard to ask. This is why **I never apologise for** *Cosmo*'s **sex articles**. Of *course* there's more to life than sex, but it's such an important, pleasurable part of a good relationship. **Men are often softened and made tender by confident, unselfish sex.**

Editorial, *Cosmopolitan*, August 1994, p.8. (original emphasis)

Cosmopolitan's interest in Brigitte Bardot is not exactly a melodramatic focus on the 'real person'. True, there is some interest in her reclusive lifestyle together with a passing reference to a new husband. There is also a somewhat prurient interest in what she might be like in bed; and it is here, in particular, that I think this editorial article, by Marcelle d'Argy Smith, betrays its primary focus. For the main concern seems to be to try to recruit Bardot's star image, or her more general star quality, to symbolise the values and attitudes which *Cosmopolitan* itself endorses. Prominent among these values and attitudes is a 'philosophy of sex', which I shall consider later. Here though, that 'philosophy' is part of a wider belief system, incorporating youth, beauty and a certain version of women's independence, which Bardot's iconic status apparently confirms. Here's how that belief system has been described by Janice Winship (1987):

> *Cosmo* manifestly subscribes to an ideology of competitiveness and individual success, and to what I call an aspirational feminism. Ardently committed to women 'winning' and with the focus mainly on 'self-assertion', *Cosmo*'s feminism [nevertheless] is limited in what it can achieve generally for women.   (Winship 1987, p.106)

In this chapter, I want to examine the basis for statements like Janice Winship is making. That is to say, I want to do two things: I want to understand why she makes these particular criticisms of *Cosmopolitan*; but I am even more interested in what it means to describe *Cosmo*'s attitudes and beliefs as 'ideological'. Here we have another key concept for media text analysis, which is also used more generally by audiences and readers – what is implied by its use? Clearly the first thing to say is that to define a text in terms of ideology is to take a critical stance. Winship herself is saying that *Cosmo*'s ideology is 'limited' from a feminist perspective. But my main reason for wanting to look closely at Winship's work, is because I think it offers some important suggestions as to the way the analysis of ideology should proceed.

Let us consider some of the connotations of this word. An ideology, we might say, promotes particular ideas (like competitiveness and individualism in *Cosmo*). It is therefore perhaps, a meaning system, and to this extent, virtually synonymous with the concept of 'mythology'. However, ideology also carries with it the further connotation of social and political power. Of course, mythologies are influential, but ideologies are frequently understood to be meaning systems which have achieved social dominance. So we speak of dominant ideology, which imposes itself upon us, obliging ourselves, its potential victims, to find ways of living with, or perhaps 'resisting' this imposition. There is a further implication here, that those who do fall victim to this power are somehow living 'within ideology', whereas we, from our critical perspective, might escape.

There is a version of this argument which particularly troubles me. In my view, a particular problem arises when this critical perspective on ideology is linked to the concept of representation. In my introduction I questioned the relevance of this concept for media text analysis, and it is now possible to be more specific about its limitations. For it is commonly suggested that ideology can be defined as such because it 'misrepresents' (or 'distorts') the truth, or the real situation. One philosophical problem here, which we touched on in our discussion of semiology, arises from the argument that there is not one, but several 'realities', constructed within different sign systems – so on what basis can we claim that our reality is 'true'? But let us leave this question to the philosophers, for there is a more pertinent issue. By reducing the definition of ideology to the problem of (mis)representation, I think we are in danger of radically underestimating its power and influence. In short, this is the easy way out – which Winship, for one, is not about to take.

It is true that some of Winship's work on women's magazines does, at first sight, seem to connect with this conventional perspective. She is dealing, after all, with a form of print journalism which has received a great deal of critical scrutiny, particularly for its promotion of a 'cult of femininity' (Ferguson, 1983). Marjorie Ferguson's book presents a survey of the contents of women's magazines since the war, and she concludes that, although there have been some adjustments to social change, the main cultural themes of domesticity (defining women as housewives and mothers) and personal relationships (where women take primary responsibility) remain. The 'cult of femininity' in these magazines was established in the immediate post-war period, when a mythology of family life was enshrined in the welfare state (Wilson, 1980) and women were targeted as leaders of the new focus on domestic consumption (Winship 1981). Certainly in this period, Winship has argued, it is possible to talk about a 'dominant ideology' of femininity:

> What I want to draw attention to here is the possibility that in the 1950s . . . there *was* a dominant ideology of femininity, and the women's weeklies were contributors to the cultural processes by which hegemonic consent around women's position was strived for, if never finally won . . .
>
> . . . The dominance of the ideology was reflected in the paucity and weakness of alternative and oppositional views on women's position. Betty Friedan's attribution of 'the problem that has no name' to their situation (Friedan, 1965) gives credence to how difficult any dissatisfaction with the housewife role was for women. Within the prevailing terms of the debate, despite their difference from men, women were regarded as equal: within marriage the roles of husband and wife were complementary. It was thus virtually impossible to articulate the view that difference was less a sign of equality than manifestation of subordination. (1992, p.91)

Even in this passage, however, in her description of this 'dominant ideology', Winship is concerned with its complexity. It would therefore be too simple to say that the ideology of women as housewives and mothers 'misrepresented' their real situation. Rather, this *was* their situation, and the main problem was that they were presented with no alternatives. Implicit in Winship's discussion is a systematic account of the way a dominant ideology works. Firstly, it is dogmatic: that is, it strives to present itself as universal, obvious, and hence unquestionable – to reduce its potential critics to silence. Secondly, however, where it recognises the possibility of criticism, the dominant ideology seeks to become *hegemonic*: that is, offering cultural leadership, and establishing a framework within which any debate is contained. The concept of hegemony recognises that dominance is never finally achieved, but rather is the product of a continual process of conflict and renegotiation.

But now consider Winship's most critical observation about this dominant ideology. Not only did it circumscribe the terms of any debate; it also, in the face of potential difficulties, offered its own 'preferred readings'. Hence, gender difference was defined in terms of 'equality' and 'complementarity' rather than men's power and women's subordination. Were these preferred readings in effect 'misreadings' of the true situation? To pick up on another term we will consider in the next section, was the dominant belief in complementarity a form of false consciousness? There are two responses, I think, to this question. One response would be to suggest that the preferred reading here is not so much a misrepresentation, as a *displacement* of the potential problem. That is to say, this strategy is not exactly a 'cover-up'; it acknowledges gender difference, but it projects an ideal solution. The second response would then be to recognise that this solution is only sustainable so long as it has a degree of credibility. We all know that 'happy marriages' exist, for the magazines themselves constantly supply the evidence!

Winship develops this line of argument at some length in her key book *Inside Women's Magazines*. Of course, it is not the case that women's magazines have ever ignored the difficulties experienced by their readers. Quite the contrary, perhaps more than any other print media, these magazines have always been upfront about 'problems'. Thus feature articles and 'problem pages' are full of recognition that the ideal, complementary marriage is difficult to attain, and that some barriers to women's equality remain. The interesting point, however, concerns the way such problems are defined, discussed and dealt with: overwhelmingly, Winship demonstrates, they are discussed in terms of individual difficulties which may be overcome through 'self-help' and personal solutions.

Hence, Winship describes an 'ideological juggling act' in *Woman's Own*, where the identification of marital problems never leads to the questioning of the institution of marriage itself (see, for example, p.85 ff). More generally, there is a continual displacement of common problems into individual stories, reinforcing a prevailing ideology of 'individualism'. But Winship does not simply distance herself from this:

> I am not suggesting that [agony] aunties or magazines more generally are doing a lousy job. On the contrary I'd speculate on how much more lonely and difficult life would be for many women without the support of magazines. What I do take issue with is an ideological commitment to 'the individual', more far reaching than the magazines but with a particular inflection there. The problems this ideology raises are sticky ones. We undoubtedly are individuals. But what we ignore most of the time, or simply do not see, is the scope of the limitations, especially for women, on what individuals are allowed to be . .
>
>   . . . I am caught up in a web of social structures I do not, and cannot, control, and in which only certain paths are open to me, a woman. Feminism insists that for women and men to have the 'freedom' to be individuals . . . those manifold structures, and not just individuals, must be radically changed. (p.81)

This passage is important in several ways. It defines the limitations of the ideology of individualism, which acts as a displacement of structural problems. But also, from my point of view, it makes a most important point about the credibility of ideology. Contrary to what we might have thought about 'dominant ideology', Winship is emphasising that this is not simply 'false consciousness', or a form of misrepresentation. Rather, the power of ideology precisely derives from the fact that it is also, partially, *true*. We *are* individuals, and 'self-help' can be beneficial, particularly in areas such as fitness and diet, as the magazines constantly remind us. Such values can therefore be believed, as well as disbelieved, simultaneously; and ideology works, not because it peddles ignorance, but because it offers credible alternatives, in which we are all, at some level, caught up.

Winship's sensitivity to the complexities of this ideology are related to another point she introduces about her own personal involvement. As she states in her introduction, she herself is a reader of women's magazines. Hence:

> I felt that to simply dismiss women's magazines was also to dismiss the lives of millions of women who read and enjoyed them each week. More than that *I* still enjoyed them, found them useful and escaped with them. And I knew I couldn't be the only feminist who was a 'closet reader'. That didn't mean I wasn't critical of them. I was (and am) but it was just the double edge – my simultaneous attraction and rejection – which seemed to me to be a real nub of feminist concern. (p.xiii)

This again is a crucial statement. The experiential contradiction that Winship acknowledges is what prompts her to begin her own interrogation of women's magazines. Clearly if this interrogation is, in some sense, personal, it is unlikely that it could be simply superior or judgemental. Rather it is more likely that the analysis will focus on particular points of identification and rejection, and will need to be self-reflexive about the pleasures and problems involved. Moreover, the focus of the analysis will be precisely to understand this 'double-edge': how is it that messages and meanings can be criticised and yet simultaneously enjoyed? To put this more emphatically, how can a belief system which can be seen to be limited also be thought of as credible, even 'true'? It is in her attempt to think through these contra-dictions that Winship must embark on a process of critical engagement – from the 'inside' (and the title of her book is significant).

With these points in mind, let us now return to *Cosmopolitan*. While we have taken our tour through Winship's discussion of ideology we have left Marcelle d'Argy Smith smouldering, so to speak, on the back-burner. But now Winship, I think, provides a really interesting perspective on what that editorial contains. Moreover, this is a perspective which leads to a final important point about ideology. Clearly the 'aspirational feminism' in *Cosmopolitan* can now be related to the individualism Winship has described, which is why she feels it is limited, from her own feminist point of view. However in *Cosmopolitan*, such individualism is not restricted to diet, fitness, or even careers – it extends, as we have seen, to sex. 'Good sex' is thus one of the several recipes to be followed; but this gives rise to contra-dictions, not simply between ideals and realities, but rather between conflict-ing versions of the ideal. Where this leaves Marcelle d'Argy Smith is both interesting and controversial.

Indeed, *Cosmopolitan*'s ideology of sex contains all the points about ideol-ogy which we have made, and more. Thus it strives to be dogmatic, partic-ularly in its unquestioning attitude to heterosexuality: '*Cosmo* cannot ask "what makes a woman heterosexual" (in the way that it can ask what makes a woman a lesbian)' (Winship, p.117). On the other hand it also offers some (liberal) recognition to the existence of homosexuality, on the basis that a heterosexual *hegemony* is preserved. More to the point, however, *Cosmopolitan* projects an ideal heterosexuality, to be achieved through 'sexual liberation', that is: the 'notion that "true" individuality is found and fulfilled in the (hetero)sexual quest' (p.112). In this connection, the sexual liberation thesis is particularly critical of what it defines as 'inhibitions', and promotes various forms of 'talking sex therapy' as its solution to sexual problems. Thus: 'so long as a heterosexual couple communicate frankly their different sexualities can be mutually satisfied' (p.113).

As Winship points out, this ideal of sexual liberation can act as a displace-ment for other potential problems in relationships, particularly where the power relations between men and women are involved. On the other hand, it also gives rise to further contradictions in the philosophy of *Cosmopolitan* itself. These become especially apparent in *Cosmo*'s account of *male* sexuality where there is a contradiction between the dogma of 'natural heterosexuality' and the aspirational stress on 'mutual satisfaction'. For as we all know (in ideological terms) male sexuality is 'naturally' about a certain kind of spontaneous 'performance'; to challenge this is, potentially, to threaten the spontaneity and thus the ability to 'perform'. Hence, according to Winship, 'the problem of male impotence' appears in the pages of *Cosmopolitan* as a persistent, and particularly tricky problem, that can only be resolved at the expense of its own aspirational commitments. For 'good sex' to flourish, men must, in d'Argy Smith's phrase, be able to 'get it up'; but here's what Winship has to say about that suggestion:

> To put it in its strongest and most controversial terms, the 'problem' of impotence – not impotence *per se* – is part of the same problem as rape. If the problem of impotence is [male] power having 'failed', rape is a brutal insistence of it. And neither impotence nor rape can be eradicated without an understanding by men as well as women of the need to transform masculinity. (p.114)

Does *Cosmopolitan*, in validating male 'potency', thereby endorse rape? Perhaps not. But Winship's polemical argument does point towards an implicit ideology of 'normal heterosexuality', which is surely questionable from a feminist point of view. Consider, for example, d'Argy Smith's (third-hand) account of Bardot's sexuality, which may be 'confident and unselfish', but also involves her, in an attitude of long-suffering compliance, doing 'everything she could to please'. Marcelle d'Argy Smith's conclusion is straight from the pages of the 'ideal romance', for men (presumably brutes to start with) can be 'softened and made tender' by such behaviour (not literally of course!). For Winship, this is evidence that *Cosmo*'s feminism, when it discusses sexuality, does not go far enough. For me, it represents a challenge to men to rethink, and ultimately to transform, our so-called 'natural' sexual practices.

So let me by way of a conclusion to this review of Winship, make the final point about ideology. It is simply this: that for all its dominance and dogmatism, and for all its ability to project powerfully enticing ideals, ideology is, when examined closely, often curiously unstable. It can be illogical, inconsistent and self-contradictory. It can project ideals which are impossible, not because they are simply 'false' or unattainable, but because they collapse under the weight of their own contradictions. Furthermore, as we have just seen, ideology can also highlight, unintentionally, problems which need to be tackled, and which require radical solutions. In all this, ideology cannot be taken at face value, it cannot be 'taken as read', and it cannot be simply dismissed. It therefore requires close analysis, and careful dissection, to ask the questions and open up the possibilities which ideology would prefer to close down.

2 THEORY OF IDEOLOGY

In the previous section, I have used the work of Janice Winship to try to make some very basic points about ideology. What I have particularly wanted to stress, is the way in which ideological analysis can be thought of as *strategic*. Actually, all theories are strategic, in that they bring certain questions, and methods of analysis, to bear on media texts. But there are two reasons for focusing on Winship's work in particular. The first point to emphasise is ideological analysis involves a systematic form of critical reading. This is, in a sense, an argumentative reading, and it recalls some of the points we made about arguments in Chapter 2. Specifically, the analysis of ideology looks for questionable forms of justification, selectivity of evidence, and contradictory propositions in the texts it is interrogating. The second point, however, indicated by Winship's own personal engagement with her texts, is that this kind of strategy cannot be simply detached (if that is what we mean by 'objective'); rather it involves the reader in an active dialogue with the text, in a process of questioning which might also include self-questioning. This is because the critical analysis of ideology cannot ignore its power to define the reader's own experiences.

But above all, what I hope the previous section has begun to demonstrate is that ideological analysis, as a strategy, can be productive. At its best, it can enable the analyst to see the media text in a new light, not only in terms of its problems and contradictions, but also as regards the unexpected consequences of its arguments. I am making this point most strongly, to emphasise again that ideological analysis is not simply a confirmation of what we already know: as if to recognise it, and give it a name, was all our critical reading might do. 'Ah, a case of individualism' (we might say), 'that's a species of dominant ideology'. Winship's point is that individualism continues to speak with some force, even to us, its critics; it has a level of credibility (perhaps that's why it's 'dominant') and it works, like God, in mysterious ways. Our task, as students of media, is to try to better understand these mysteries, and to reconsider our own involvement in them.

The principal theories of ideology in cultural studies, which have had a major influence on media studies, are derived from Marxism. Predominantly, this includes the works of Karl Marx himself (with his collaborator Frederick Engels) and influential twentieth-century Marxist writers, notably Antonio Gramsci (writing in Italy in the 1920s) and Louis Althusser (writing in France in the 1960s). It is difficult, however, without guidance, to read the original works (with the exception of the 'ISAs essay' by Althusser to which I have previously referred) – this is partly because some of them are intrinsically difficult, but also because the references to ideology, in the classical texts, are dispersed. Marx himself did not write a treatise on ideology, and possibly it is this very fact which has prompted a succession of interpretations and reinterpretations of what this concept might mean. One recent overview (Eagleton, 1991) begins by listing no fewer than sixteen currently available definitions of ideology. In what follows, therefore, I have been extremely selective, concentrating on what I think are the basic issues, where I have been particularly influenced by Stuart Hall's pioneering essays on ideology and the media (Hall, 1977 and 1982).

I want to develop this brief discussion, by looking at two of Marx's own formulations. The first, which is the best known, comes from *The German Ideology* which was written 1845–6 (Marx and Engels, 1970). It is this formulation, in particular, that introduces the concept of a 'dominant ideology':

> The ideas of the ruling class are in every epoch the ruling ideas, ie. the class which is the ruling *material* force of society, is at the same time its ruling *intellectual* force. The class which has the means of material production at its disposal, has control at the same time over the means of mental production, so that thereby, generally speaking the ideas of those who lack the means of mental production are subject to it. The ruling ideas are nothing more than the ideal expression of the dominant material relationships, the dominant relationships grasped as ideas; hence of the relationships which make the one class the ruling one, therefore, the ideas of its dominance. (p.64)

Let us consider this quotation very carefully. It contains two key points, which define ideology in a particular way, and have implications for the kinds of critical analysis which might be possible. The key points are: first, that the dominant ideology consists of the 'ideas of the ruling class', and second, that these ideas are an 'ideal expression of . . . material relationships'. For Marx, of course, the ruling class is the capitalist class and its allies, and his first point suggests that the ruling ideas are in a sense *their* ideas – at least, if the ruling class didn't invent these ideas, it has adopted them as its own. The second point is more obscure, for it is not clear what 'ideal expression' precisely means. What it could mean, however, and what it is often taken to mean, is that the ruling ideas are an idealised version, or again possibly a (mis)representation of the material relationship whereby the capitalist class owns and controls the means of production and the working class does not. Elsewhere in *The German Ideology*, Marx talks metaphorically about the 'camera obscura' effect: you only have to invert the image for the true picture to emerge.

As far as a practice of critical analysis is concerned, much hinges on Marx's conception of the dominance of this ruling ideology – that is, how precisely 'those who lack the means of mental production are *subject* to it'. There are weaker and stronger versions of what 'subjection' could mean. If we assume that these ideas are, essentially, not our own, but the 'ideas of the ruling class', then this might already imply a certain critical distance from them. Moreover, if these ideas are nothing more than 'ideal expressions', then it might be possible to see around them, or even see through them, in some way. I have previously criticised this argument as too simplistic: in fact it reproduces an 'empiricist' account of perception and the formation of knowledge. In this account, ideology is defined as a form of misrecognition; as long as we remain 'in ideology' we cannot see the truth – which, if only the veil were lifted, we could recognise.

Althusser's theory of the interpellation of the subject (see also Chapter 3) can be read in this way, especially because he makes use of empiricist language in his ISAs essay. The criticism sometimes made is that this seems to imply a conception of the subject who needs only to turn his or her head, away from the seductive face of ideology ('This could be you!'), to see things as they 'really are'. Within media studies, such visual metaphors have been particularly powerful in film theory – probably because the cinematic mode of address does precisely engage the point of view of the spectator. In this view, the 'realism' of the cinema appears as an exemplary form of 'ideological misrecognition' which only the avant-garde practices of 'progressive' film makers can disturb.

However, this is not the only way to read Althusser's account, nor is *The German Ideology* the end of the story as far as Marx's theory of ideology is concerned. I want to turn now to another key formulation, which comes from *Capital*, Vol 1, published in 1867. In this passage Marx is explaining how, when we participate in the buying and selling of commodities, we forget how it is that they came to be produced, and in particular the social relations of their production:

> There [in the market-place], the existence of things *qua* commodities, and the value-relation between the products of labour which stamps them as commodities, have absolutely no connexion with their physical properties and with the material relations arising therefrom. There it is a definite social relation between men [sic] that assumes, in their eyes, the fantastic form of a relation between things. In order therefore, to find an analogy, we must have recourse to the mist-enveloped regions of the religious world. In that world the productions of the human being appear as independent beings endowed with life and entering into relation with one another and the human race. So it is in the world of commodities with the products of men's hands. This I call the Fetishism which attaches itself to the products of labour, so soon as they are produced as commodities, and which is therefore inseparable from the production of commodities. (p.72)

To be sure, in this account of the fetishism of commodities, Marx continues to show a certain fondness for visual metaphors. There are, however, some key shifts which represent a revision of his earlier argument. To begin with, the fetishism of commodities, where products appear as things, is not simply an 'idea of the ruling class', or an idea which has a particular class location. In a capitalist society, everybody goes shopping; so everybody, in Marx's sense, participates in this form of fetishism, which thereby becomes all the more believable. However, to take this further, is it appropriate still to talk in this context about 'ideas'? Is fetishism an idea? Marx goes on to discuss, wittily and ironically, a whole series of ideas which are associated with the market-place: such as the equality of individuals (everybody has the right to spend his or her money) and the freedom to choose (which commodities to buy). But these ideas are founded on what seems, in Marx's account, to be akin to a religious faith, and, as we know, religious faith usually entails our involvement in very practical forms of worship.

In fact we shall see later (in Chapter 7) how the concept of fetishism can have a particular relevance for media studies. In Marx's usage, I think this term is gesturing towards the view that ideology is as much unconscious as it is conscious, as much irrational as it is rational. That is to say, if ideology consists of arguments, containing propositions, these do not simply take the forms of ideas which we may or may not find convincing; they also have the force of repeated patterns of behaviour in which we more or less unthinkingly participate. Correspondingly, to pick up on the previous account, it becomes that much more difficult to turn one's face, or to 'see the light'. The notion of ideological misrecognition fails to do justice to our involvement in a highly credible and, it must also be said, pleasurable, ritual such as shopping, which is moreover essential to the way the whole social system works.

It seems to me that Althusser grasps much of the force of this argument in the section of his ISAs essay which precedes his account of the interpellation of the subject. Here, under the heading 'ideology has a material existence', he makes precisely the point that the credibility of ideology is not only to do with 'ideas'; but rather, that ideas are always embedded in rituals – or, in his terms, social practices. In this view, an ideological practice is a complex combination of ways of thinking or saying, and ways of doing or acting. And, as regards critical analysis, this argument would suggest that the interrogation of ideology is not simply a matter of debate, or even disagreement. You cannot simply 'disagree' with ideas which are part and parcel of the way you live your life. As Janice Winship has shown, there are ideologies reproduced in women's magazines which go to the very basis of the way in which we might (or might not) conduct our sexual relationships.

Such arguments about ideology might seem to be leading to the rather pessimistic conclusion that there is, in the end, no escape. Certainly there might be good reason for thinking that sophisticated Marxist accounts, such as those produced by Stuart Hall, are pessimistic on two counts. Firstly, the argument about ideology as social practice, into which we are all interpellated (especially if that interpellation is partly unconscious), makes any idea of individual escape extremely difficult. There is no easy rejection or transcendence of ideology, and it is not possible simply to be 'born again'. Secondly, Hall emphasises that (as part of the 'superstructure') the sphere of ideology plays an essential part in the maintenance of all capitalist societies. This is Gramsci's major contribution: his theory of 'hegemony' stresses that the ruling class does not simply govern by force, but also by ideology, achieving consensus wherever possible. For his part, Hall shows that such a consensus can permit, and indeed foster, the publication of all kinds of opinion and debate (which is why the media are so central), so long as the limits of what can be tolerated are not transgressed.

In that sense, the words I am writing now, and even Marx's own words, are part of Hall's 'ideological effect'. But lest we are tempted to become totally depressed, let me return finally to another of Althusser's arguments. In the opening pages of *Reading Capital* (1970), Althusser traces the way Marx developed his critique of political economy. The economists of Marx's day based their theories precisely on the laws of the market, in their attempts to calculate what counted as a 'fair price' etc. Their assumption was that the market was the lynchpin of the economy, and that the laws of the market (supply and demand, for example) determined the whole economy (an assumption which is shared by many politicians today). Marx, on the other hand, 'broke' with this theory – this was his 'theoretical revolution': he discovered that the driving force of the capitalist economy was not the market, but the relationship between capital and labour at the point of production. However, says Althusser, Marx's 'discovery' was not based on the fact that he, in any simple (empiricist) sense, could 'see' what the classical economists could not see. Rather, Marx developed his theory by working through the discrepancies, contradictions and illogicalities in the classical economists' own arguments.

This is what is meant by 'critique', as opposed to mere criticism (which may be just a matter of opinion). Critique doesn't just criticise, it transforms the terms of the debate (which Althusser terms its 'problematic'). Althusser shows how Marx transformed the problematic of political economy by recognising that the classical economists had produced answers to questions which they hadn't asked, or even thought of. It would be diversionary in this book to enter into these somewhat technical arguments, but, in any case, we have already encountered a similar example of critique in *Inside Women's Magazines*. Winship's reading of *Cosmopolitan* is a critique because it goes beyond the immediate contradictions in its attitudes to sex, to identify an underlying problematic – an ideology of heterosexuality – which is implicated in those contradictions, and is almost certainly beyond the conscious awareness of the majority of *Cosmopolitan*'s contributors. In Winship's view, this problematic needs to be transformed; but, like Marx's critique of capitalism, this points to transformations which can only occur in practice, not in theory.

Metaphorically again, Althusser refers to Marx's method as a practice of 'symptomatic reading'. He suggests that the laws of the market, however obvious they might seem, also carry symptoms or traces of the relations of production in capitalism. These symptoms were what allowed Marx to make his 'discovery'. If we pursue this metaphor, Marx now appears in the guise of a physician, making a diagnosis: the ideology, we might say, carries the signs of its own disease. That is to say, we might be in the ideology and subject to it, but if we read it carefully we might be able to detect its weaknesses and even, like Winship, begin to suggest a possible 'cure'.

3 A SCOTTISH LANDSCAPE

Living in a place which is also a centre for international tourism can give rise to some strange experiences. There is, perhaps, something flattering in the fact that the streets where you do your shopping, or the countryside just up the road, are classified as 'sights' which the tourists travel for miles to see. It is also amusing, and occasionally disconcerting, to find tourists taking photographs of buildings and views which to you, as a local inhabitant, are entirely familiar. You find yourself, for a second or two, drawn into surveying your own patch through alien eyes – 'Now what did they see in this? Does this really make an interesting picture?' Presumably inhabitants of places like London, Bath and York, as well as Edinburgh, share these experiences – but there is something far more weird about living in Scotland. In Scotland we have to cope with another level of tourist expectations which are derived from all the publicity they've read and all the Hollywood films they've seen, which together have constructed a veritable iconography of 'Scottishness'. You know the sort of thing: kilts, bagpipes, castles, lochs, Scottie dogs etc, etc. Scotland, we might be tempted to say, has become a 'genre'.

Actually, what I want to explore in this section is whether these phenomena can be more usefully and critically understood in terms of the concept of ideology. That is to say, it may be that these conventional images of Scotland are locatable within a more general set of beliefs and attitudes, which have a certain dominance in our culture, but which are also, perhaps, unstable and contradictory. For these purposes I want to consider, not some of the more extremely kitsch products of the tourist industry (plastic Loch Ness monsters and so on) which are readily available in Edinburgh; but rather a relatively inoffensive, and even tasteful postcard (see figure 6.1). In generic terms, this postcard conforms to the conventions of landscape

Fig. 6.1. 'Scotland'. Postcard by permission of Roberto Matassa

photography – it presents a 'view', according to the conventions of perspective we discussed in Chapter 3. In semiological terms, we might say that it also offers a mythology of nature (as 'natural', and perhaps 'peaceful', but also undoubtedly 'majestic'). It is an image that is pleasant to look at, and it presents what would seem to be a favourable image of Scotland. If you received this postcard from a friend you might be attracted enough to want to go there.

So what could possibly be ideological about this, and why should we subject it to a detailed critical reading? Let us clear one possibility out of the way from the start. It might be possible to advance the argument that this postcard misrepresents Scotland – the 'Scotland is not really like that' argument. But if we are to make this argument I think we need to distinguish between two different versions of it. The crude version which, needless to say, I want us to avoid, might argue along the following lines: we know this is in fact a picture of Glencoe; we also know that Glencoe contains (in addition to the occasional hotel and ski centre) the main trunk road from Glasgow to Fort William; therefore at any time of the day we might expect to see buses and lorries, not to mention the ubiquitous tourist caravans, trundling past. This picture makes the A82 look like a peaceful country lane – it therefore gives a false impression (an 'idealised expression'?) of the

'reality' of Glencoe; and thus, from our position of knowing what it is 'really
like', we can reject this position as 'ideological'. I hope I have now said
enough to establish that sophisticated theories of ideology need have nothing
to do with such crudely empiricist arguments!

But perhaps there is a more interesting version of the 'Scotland is not really
like that' position. Here, the object of our attention would not be what is
missing from the image, but rather the way the caption has been used.
Perhaps the caption is intended as a simple denotation to identify the place
for the tourist who might send the postcard home. Unfortunately, however,
it also involves connotations that are highly contentious: for it suggests that
this photographic landscape can be seen as somehow representative of
Scotland. Thus, whatever Glencoe is 'really like', what is at issue here is a
rhetorical strategy (which is another instance of metonymy) whereby this part
of Scotland comes to stand for the whole. As Colin McArthur (1986) has
commented, there is something very strange about the fact that 'a country
five-sixths of whose population live in cities and are oriented towards industrial production . . . should be constructed . . . exclusively in rural highland
terms'. He goes on to suggest that this 'is a complex issue of the construction of national identity and the reasons why such constructions were and
are necessary' (pp.117–9).

Here, we are back to the point about an iconography of Scottishness,
which this postcard, however tastefully, reproduces. McArthur has argued
that this iconography is 'ideological', not because it presents a totally false
view of Scotland, but because it reproduces a dominant set of beliefs and
attitudes which have imposed themselves on Scotland, and have constructed
Scotland, and its people, in that image. Prominent among these beliefs is the
view that the heart, or spirit of Scotland, lies in the Highlands. Thus, the
Highland landscape, with its mountains, glens and lochs, is said to contain
a timeless majesty which has infected its inhabitants. Today, these alleged
qualities find their expression in the pride with which the Scots identify with
their culture, as demonstrated by the wearing of the kilt, and the traditional
music and country dancing. And of course this is not simply false – it is true,
Scots really do behave like this! For confirmation you only have to attend a
hogmanay, a wedding ceilidh, or (for the benefit of the tourists) the
Edinburgh military tattoo.

But there is now some considerable scholarship (especially Chapman, 1978
and Womack, 1989) which demonstrates that these beliefs about Scotland
have their origins in particular cultural developments during the second half
of the eighteenth century. This was, of course, the period of the industrial
and agricultural revolution which established, in Britain, the capitalist system
which Marx subsequently analysed. As far as Scotland was concerned, this
was also a period in which the Scottish highlands were transformed, both
politically (a military occupation followed the defeat of the Jacobites in

1745), and economically (according to the prevalent theory of 'improvement', increasingly larger estates were established to maximise income from such activities as forestry and sheep farming). The consequences of all this are well known (at least in Scotland): namely the destruction of the clan system and the eviction, often forcible, of thousands of tenants from their crofts (the Highland 'clearances'). But such was the power of the dominant economic theory, supported by the then prevalent philosophies of 'Enlightenment' (Adam Smith was the key figure in Scotland), that even those who perceived and regretted the human suffering and dislocation, could conceive of no real alternative to what was happening.

Instead, as Womack demonstrates, their regret was aestheticised. By the late eighteenth century, in several European countries, the belief in progress which was characteristic of the Enlightenment was beginning to encounter a degree of disillusionment and doubt. Romanticism, as a philosophical and artistic movement, developed a form of criticism essentially moral in its emphasis. Again, I would stress the distinction here between 'criticism' and 'critique', for Romanticism failed to disturb the problematic on which it was founded. On the contrary, it remained wedded to the Enlightenment philosophy which it opposed: that is to say, it accepted the inevitability of progress and historical change, but it also found virtues in what was being replaced – particularly moral virtues like simplicity, honesty and strength of character. As far as the landscape was concerned, what had previously appealed to the eye as 'picturesque' (exhibiting a certain harmony between the natural and the cultivated), was now displaced by an interest in the 'sublime' (the wild and untamed landscape of the imagination). In English literature, the poetry of William Wordsworth provides the best known examples.

In these circumstances, the Scottish Highlands provided an exemplary location. Here there were, in living memory, the traditional moral virtues of clan loyalty and subsistence farming; and here there was a landscape which still presented evidence of its intractability and resistance to progress. Crucially, however, here was a region of Scotland whose political independence had been destroyed and which was therefore in no position to oppose the cultural forces which might be brought to it from the outside. For those who argue that this construction of the Highlands is ideological, it is precisely this conjunction between the ideas of Romanticism and Scotland's political and economic dependence (on the union with England) that is the deciding factor. Thus Womack, with a rhetorical flourish, concludes:

> It would be perverse to deny that the myth [of the Romantic Highlands] has had a crudely ideological function, or that it has served to legitimate the depressing course of Highland history within the UK over the last two centuries – the cultural patronage, the frivolity and neglect, the impoverishment of communities and the misuse of the land. This story is by no

> means over, and any discourse about the Highlands which continues, today, to naturalise a 'traditional Highland way of life', to make a trans-historical idyll out of pre-clearance Strathnaver or to hymn the moral savour of the golden wine of the Gaihealtachd, risks complicity with the same techniques of power. (pp.175–6)

It is possible to over-generalise this rhetoric. For instance I think it is stretching the point to imply that this 'cultural patronage' places the Scots in a position which is equivalent to that of the indigenous peoples of other colonised territories. For Scotland (even in the Highlands) has not become a third-world country: indeed the central contradiction as far as Scotland is concerned may well be between its cultural and political subservience and its relative economic prosperity. Thus it is the ideological dimension, in particular, which has become the main focus for contemporary critical analysis. Here, as Colin McArthur and others have shown, it is still possible to detect a form of cultural imperialism which is expressed in terms of a series of oppositions between the 'core' (the heartland of the capitalist economy) and its 'periphery' (the dispersed colonial territories). Sometimes this is known as the 'grand dichotomy' (Goody, 1977), for it produces a whole series of conceptual distinctions, such as:

Core	Periphery
city	country
culture	nature
cultivation	wilderness
civilisation	barbarism
democracy	dictatorship
modernity	tradition
individuality	community
reason	emotion
parent	child

Of course, one needs only to add the fundamental opposition, between 'us' and 'them' to make the point that this dichotomy comes from a perspective which is very much rooted in the 'core'.

Thus, when I look at a Scottish landscape, I may be looking at a real place, but I am also looking through eyes which have been taught to focus on a particular field of vision. Within this field, I am encouraged to see the Highlands of Scotland as fundamentally different from the industrial heartlands of the South, and so I will try to ignore whatever may remind me of them, such as the presence of buses and cars. More particularly, I have been taught to view the Highlands as somehow timeless and traditional, and expressive of a spirituality which I cannot find in the city. All of this is, of course, based on the fact that I am not from the Highlands myself, but rather that I am a visitor passing through, and so I can look on the peripheral landscape with the contemplative and condescending eye of one who has been transported from the core.

In the centre of my postcard is a little white Highland cottage. It looks like a holiday home, but let's assume there might be someone living there – what would he or she, the 'native', make of all this? Rush out to entertain us with kilt and bagpipes? Hopefully not. More likely, I guess, the native will develop a more acute sense of the sort of ambivalence which I experience, sometimes, in touristified Edinburgh. That is to say, it is (possibly) flattering to have someone taking pictures of your house, but it is unsettling to see one's own place through alien eyes. It is even more disturbing to realise that your place, and you yourself, are the destination for a multi-million pound leisure industry which demands that you remain, for all time, just as you are. For, of course, such demands are impossible: just the few pounds of tourists' money which come your way will change your 'traditional' way of life, and the buses which bring the tourists cannot be kept out of view forever. Such are the experiential instabilities and economic contradictions that lie just out of sight, and beyond the frame, of the idealised Scottish landscape.

4   THE QUEEN AT CHRISTMAS

The processes of cultural divergence and subordination discussed in the previous section raise fundamental questions, at least in the minds of many Scots, about what it means to be 'British'. On one level, as regards the nation state, Scots are recruited to a cultural formation in which they are invited to occupy at best an exotic, but many would argue a subservient, role. At another level, this Scottish experience is illustrative of a wider point, that 'Britain'/the 'UK' (or however this entity is named) is in fact a composite of diverse core and peripheral identities. And as far as the British media are concerned, it is particularly instructive to look at the way different peripheral cultures achieve distinctive forms of visibility within national media networks.

For instance, as Britain's longest running TV soap opera testifies, there remains a peculiar national fascination for a certain image of 'The North' (1). I do not have the space here to explore the many permutations of 'northern-ness' in the British media – these have been usefully surveyed elsewhere (2) – but there is one fundamental point which can be made. As Rob Shields (1991) points out, there is some considerable debate in the British context about where the geographical boundaries of The North might be. This is because the region has a symbolic as well as a real presence in British culture – so there is disagreement about the 'true' North, particularly with respect to its southern fringes. However, there is much less controversy about the northern boundary of The North – namely, that this region, as a cultural space, does not include Scotland. Which is of course to say that the definitions of 'North' and 'South' in Britain refer specifically to England. Scotland remains outside these debates (with its own internal division between Highlands and Lowlands).

The general point to which these esoteric observations are leading is that the cultural/symbolic geography of Britain is in fact defined by England. It is England which occupies the position of the core, particularly southern England, and particularly the area around London known appropriately as the 'Home Counties'. Correspondingly it is 'Englishness' that is hegemonic in the discussion and definition of British cultural identities. What 'Englishness' might be is, again, a topic of some debate, but it would certainly include two different though connected images. The first image is that of the pastoral English landscape, the village green, the church and the pub, with the ubiquitous game of cricket. The second image is that of the formal State occasion, uniting the national architecture of parliament and church (of England) with the monarchy. These two images were connected in recent memory, in the TV coverage of royal weddings, which would frequently cut from central London to to the local pub on the Spencers' or Fergusons' country estates. However, whether such coverage will be possible in future is a matter of some debate.

For this 'Englishness', it would seem, is currently under threat. Its internal hegemony is threatened, to some extent, by the kinds of debates about the constitution of the nation state which are current in Scotland and elsewhere. Its external face is also threatened by a new international order in which Britain is no longer a colonial power, and (as a section of the Conservative Party would claim) its powers of national sovereignty are under review. More generally there is, particularly in Europe, a reconstruction of nationalisms – not an end to nationalism by any means, but a radical questioning of superstates (the old Soviet Union, Yugoslavia, Czechoslovakia) of which Britain remains a (possibly anachronistic) example. But rather than speculate on its political future, I think it is more appropriate in this context to analyse the current instabilities of this national culture as it appears in the British media. As good an example as any was provided by the Queen's Christmas broadcast in 1994.

The importance of the royal Christmas broadcast, particularly as a form of cultural legitimation for the BBC, has been emphasised by Paddy Scannell (1988). His main argument is that broadcasting not only has the power to organise daily and weekly schedules, as we have previously discussed, but it has also constructed an annual calendar which revolves around coverage of religious festivals, annual State occasions and major sports events. In addition, programme planners have recognised the importance of the seasons and extended holiday periods. Perhaps the highlight of these annual offer-ings has been Christmas, which still attracts special attention in terms of publicity and critical review (the critical review of Christmas 1994 was in fact far from favourable). But here is Scannell's account of the way the royal broadcast fits into these proceedings:

> From the very beginning Christmas was always the most important date in the broadcast year. It was the supreme family festival, an invocation of the spirit of Dickens, a celebration of 'home, hearth and happiness'. It was no coincidence that Reith had worked hard for years to persuade the King to speak, from his home and as head of his family, to the nation and empire of families listening in their homes on this particular day. The royal broadcast (the first was in 1932) quickly became part of the ritual of the British Christmas, and is a classic illustration of that process whereby tradition is reinvented. It set the crowning seal on the role of broadcast-ing in bonding the nation together, giving it a particular form and content: the family audience, the royal family and the nation as family. (p.19)

Scannell's discussion here condenses a number of important points. The royal Christmas broadcast has been one key mechanism through which broad-casting has sought to unite the British nation. Here, at 3pm every Christmas day, is an invitation to enter an 'imagined community' of listeners and viewers, simultaneously receiving the sovereign's words. At the same time, the broadcast has helped to secure the legitimacy of the monarchy, particu-larly as Scannell puts it, through that sense of 'tradition' which it evokes. The fact that this tradition is only sixty years old merely makes it consistent with the modernity of most of the supposedly 'ancient' royal traditions (see Cannadine, 1983). However, what unites the legitimacy of the monarchy with broadcasting is precisely the notion of the family, as the head of the royal family speaks to a nation of families on this supremely family-centred occasion. Perhaps it is worth reminding ourselves that this occasion – the Dickensian Christmas – is yet another 'invented tradition', introduced in the same period (mid-nineteenth century) as the modern traditions of monarchy were first conceived (see Open University, 1981).

To what extent is it appropriate to apply the concept of ideology to this occasion? It is certainly possible to focus on the content of the speech itself, to criticise its relevance and challenge its assertions. For example the Queen's message of 1994 focused (as befits the 'spirit of Christmas') on the possibil-ities for peace around the world; but it was surely not her fault that as we were watching footage of her own State visit to Russia, that country's army was invading its own southern province of Chechnya. Thus, in keeping with the theory of ideology which I have oulined in this chapter, I think we are on stronger ground if we pay attention, not to areas of misrepresentation, but rather, in Althusser's terms, to what this occasion sets out to achieve, as a social ritual. At this level, what the Queen is saying is but one feature of an ideological practice which seeks to interpellate the viewer, to an imagined national community with the sovereign at its head. Consider for instance, the way the theme of prospects for peace is developed, and anchored, in the following passage from the Queen's speech of 1994:

> Next year we shall commemorate the fiftieth anniversary of the end of the Second World War. The celebrations will no doubt be spectacular and I hope we all enjoy them. But we can also each in our own way ensure that they leave a lasting mark in history. If we resolve to be considerate and to help our neighbours, to make friends with people of different races and religions and, as the Lord said, to look to our own faults before we criticise others, we will be keeping faith with those who landed in Normandy and fought so doggedly for their belief in freedom, peace and human decency.

Out of context, it might be questionable how far the D-Day landings (whatever their necessity as an international strike against Nazism) truly embodied the Christian virtues of neighbourliness and humility to which the Queen refers. But the issue of logical consistency is surely beside the point. For the ideological strategy of this speech was to mobilise a popular memory of World War II as the nation's (England's?) 'finest hour'. Christian virtues were thus yolked to a memory of national greatness, in which the Queen herself was doubly implicated. First, in her symbolic role, she would preside over these commemorations (and she was shown, in this broadcast, taking the salute from D-Day veterans on the Normandy beaches). Second however, at another point in her speech, the Queen spoke of her own personal memories of those years. She has her memories and we have ours, and so to that extent we are united.

This unity was reinforced by the televised structure of the broadcast and by its mode of address. Thus the Queen spoke to us, her subjects, directly (she is never interviewed). From time to time the broadcast cut to news footage, with the speech continuing as voice-over, which provided literal illustration to support its argumentative structure. But it was here, in the structure of this broadcast, that I began to detect a certain ideological instability. For in 1994, the speech itself was 'framed' by two extended pieces of montage, set to music. In the first, introductory piece, we were simply presented with shots of the march past of the D-Day veterans (at Aramanche, June 1994), to the tune I recognise as 'Colonel Bogey' (which reminds me of the patriotic war film *Bridge On The River Kwai*). However, the second montage, which provided the conclusion to the broadcast, used both this footage and other news film of the Queen being (one might say) 'regal', edited to two (sung) verses of the national anthem. *Two* verses of 'God Save The Queen'; wasn't this perhaps a little excessive?

Here the Queen was shown at formal ceremonies, inspecting troops, waving to crowds and meeting 'her people'. The Queen Mother and Prince Philip appeared in some shots, but no other members of the royal family. The montage concluded with a particularly spectacular superimposition, of the royal standard over a shot of fireworks (which, as a previous shot had shown, were being fired over the Royal Yacht *Britannia*). These shots, and the music, reminded me of another genre with which I am familiar, namely the (presidential-style) party political broadcast. Here then (and without the usual warning) we had a ten-minute PPB on behalf of the monarchy – which is to say that the Christmas broadcast was now an exercise in public relations. Perhaps it was ever thus . . .

But the excessiveness of this monarchical sentiment was surely symptomatic of some fundamental questions. Question 1: why were there no shots, in this broadcast, of the extended royal family? Answer: because the younger generation had spent most of the previous year publicly tearing itself apart - which as a multi-media circus, involving the collaboration of the publishing industry and the national press as well as broadcasting and broadcasters, was perhaps the most significant media phenomenon of the year (3). Question 2: why were the younger royals behaving in this way? Answer: because they seem themselves to have subscribed to a public relations strategy entirely founded on the melodramatic philosophy of 'the person' (4). Question 3: what has been the effect of this public relations strategy? The results of opinion polls began to appear in the second week of January 1995 (5), but in its own inimitable fashion the *Sun* jumped the gun. Opposite yet another royal story in which Charles (on holiday in Klosters) delivered 'an icy snub to Fergie', it asked (4 January 1995): 'Why don't we watch the Queen's speech anymore?', and, alongside its evidence of a spectacular decline in ratings, the *Sun* produced its answer in suitable graphic form (see figure 6.2).

Instability, inconsistency, contradiction. It would be unwise and unnecessary to speculate here on the future of the British constitution. What is more relevant is the way a key tradition in British broadcasting now appears (at ITV at least) to be under review, destabilised it would seem, by the force of contradictory tendencies in the media and public relations industries. Again, there is no necessary connection between these and other political and economic tendencies mentioned earlier, but clearly, on a variety of fronts, at least some elements of the national (English) ideology are simultaneously called into question. Who knows? Perhaps, at such moments, the hegemony of this national culture is threatened. The moral authority, if not the political power, of the core of this national culture appears to be compromised. But then, despite Scannell's arguments, it is debatable whether the Queen's Christmas broadcast has ever been a truly *national* event – for of course it is hogmanay, and not Christmas, which is the main family festival in Scotland.

Why don't we watch the Queen's speech any more?

THE Queen's speech used to be as much a part of Christmas Day as turkey and presents.

But one of Britain's great institutions is dying a death, with more people switching off every year.

In 1987, 27.9million people watched the Queen on TV.

But last year that figure dropped to just 15.7million—2.4million fewer than the previous Christmas and the third year running that the Queen's ratings have dropped.

Scandals

Experts believe it is because people have lost their respect for the Royals in the wake of numerous scandals.

Royal author Brian Hoey says: "It doesn't surprise me that viewing figures have dropped—it's because of the growing disillusionment of ordinary people towards the Royal Family.

"It appears to be a knock-on effect of the astonishing behaviour of some of the younger members of the Royal Family.

"We had the Princess of Wales's Squidgy tapes, Charles's Camillagate tape and topless photos of the Duchess of York with her financial adviser John Bryan sucking her toes.

By HILARY DOUGLAS

"For generations the Royal Family has been the emotional focal point of the British people.

"In the light of recent events that image has been sadly dented and no longer are they seen as the cosy, comfortable family they once were.

"It deeply saddens me to say it but the magic and mystique of monarchy has worn off to a great extent—never to return.

"If the Queen's Christmas message were a commercial programme its producer—and its presenter—would be called in front of the programme controller to explain the drop in ratings.

"In fact ITV has already suggested moving the Queen to a non-prime-time spot—which would have been unthinkable even five years ago."

Stephen Hasler, chairman of the Republican Society, says: "The Queen is at the head of a family which now has no example to offer the people of Britain.

"The magic and mystery has disappeared in the face of the countless revelations about the private lives of the younger Royals.

"No amount of the Queen talking about her world visits in her speech can overcome the damage.

"The Royals are no longer the ideal family to which we can all aspire. It has been damaged and is effectively gone forever."

Fig. 6.2. Feature article, the Sun, 4 January 1995. By permission of News Group Newspapers Ltd

5 │ CASE STUDY: 'BLACK AND WHITE IN COLOUR'

In any case, it is also possible to argue that the national culture which has promoted a particular version of 'Englishness' is today being reconstructed in other, less hysterical ways. In the final section of this chapter, I want to raise some questions about the impact on post-war Britain of the cultures of diverse, but particularly black, ethnic groups. I want to explore the possibility that what it means to be British, and even perhaps 'English', can no longer today have the focus which it might have had half a century ago. In this context the popular memory mobilised by the sight of the veterans of D-Day (and I did not see a single black soldier) has to be regarded as anachronistic. There is another more contemporary, more diverse, national culture that the Queen's speech simply failed to address. In suggesting that black groups and communities have made a significant impact on British culture, I am largely following the arguments of Paul Gilroy in his important book *There Ain't No Black In The Union Jack* (1987). However I will supplement his arguments with my own examples and what is perhaps a contentious 'postscript'.

Gilroy argues that black people in Britain have been obliged to confront a particular form of dominant ideology which he defines as the 'new racism'. This racism is articulated to the concepts of national culture and identity (Britishness/Englishness) which we have previously outlined, insofar as 'the politics of race in this country is fired by conceptions of national belonging and homogeneity which not only blur the distinction between "race" and nation, but rely on that very ambiguity for their effect' (p.45). Thus the new racism speaks of an 'Island Race' etc; it projects a form of 'ethnic absolutism' ('England for the English') – except that, in this ideology, the term 'ethnic' is usually reserved for people of colour. Whites, being hegemonic, avoid defining themselves in this way. Thus argues Gilroy:

> The new racism is primarily concerned with mechanisms of inclusion and exclusion. It specifies who may legitimately belong to the national community and simultaneously advances reasons for the segregation and banishment of those whose 'origin, sentiment or citizenship' assigns them elsewhere. [West Indians and Asians] for different reasons . . . are judged to be incompatible with authentic forms of Englishness. (p.45–6)

Or, if black people are to be accepted, then they must, in this ideology, be prepared to renounce any other cultural allegiances. Such is the implicit message of a Conservative election poster analysed by Gilroy (pp.58–9), and it was explicitly reinforced, in characteristic style, by the infamous 'cricket test' proposed by former Conservative minister, Norman Tebbit (6).

It is important to recognise that Gilroy's 'new racism', with its equation between race and nation is, of course, founded on an old racism which dates at least from the eighteenth century. A useful account of the old racism is provided by Jordan and Weedon (1995). This racism was founded on the exploitation of colonised territories and the enslavement of subjugated peoples. It defined black people as, in essence, inferior, and even subhuman – definitions which received a particular emphasis from the ideas of the Enlightenment, which we have previously touched upon. Thus, while western, white societies were to be characterised as progressive, rational and civilised; black peoples were seen as primitive, irrational and barbaric. Such distinctions, in this extreme version of the grand dichotomy, have supported the popular (white) view of blacks as somehow closer to nature, to animal instinct, and thus to uncontrolled sexuality. In turn, such views have been used to legitimate a whole panoply of dominant institutions, ranging from slavery and apartheid, to a particular fascination for 'the black exotic' in

modern(ist) western art. I will not extend these points here: Jordan and
Weedon engage critically with a host of relevant examples.

Instead, I want to focus on the black experience of racism in contemporary Britain. My exploration (which is admittedly second-hand, for I am
white) is of the power of such ideologies to shape the experiences of those
defined (as inferior) by them; at the same time acknowledging that such
definitions have provoked responses in various forms of negotiation and
resistance. If I have any insight into the black experience of racism, then it
has been substantially provided by a documentary film which was made in
1964, and subsequently shown by the BBC in 1992 during its series 'Black
and White in Colour'. This film, directed by Philip Donnellan, misleadingly
entitled *The Colony*, features a number of West Indian immigrants to
Birmingham recounting and analysing their experiences of living in Britain
(see figure 6.3). Stylistically, the film is entirely a montage of images and
voices (interspersed with music from a gospel/folk group) where some statements are delivered direct to camera, others are recorded in group discussion, and others are used as voices over sometimes contradictory imagery
(remember the points about 'dialectical montage' made in Chapter 2). There
is no presentation and no commentary, save for a somewhat incongruous
opening about mixed race adoption (7). It is a film in the tradition of social
impressionism pioneered by Denis Mitchell (Corner, 1991b) and it provides
a frank and moving account of the initial contact, in Britain, between blacks
and whites.

> [*v/o shot of black male factory worker*]
>
> Sometimes we think we shouldn't blame the people, because it's we who
> have come to your country in trouble. On the other hand we think, well
> if they in the first place had not come to our country and had spread their
> false propaganda we would never have come to their's. But then, if we
> had not come we would be none the wiser. We would still have the good
> image of England, thinking they are what they are not.
>
> [*cut to shot of white female shop assistant*]
>
> And the English would be as ignorant of us.

One of the most interesting and useful aspects of *The Colony* is the way it
provides an oral history, from the migrants' perspective, of West Indian
immigration to Britain. This is particularly useful in view of Gilroy's argument
that one effect of racist ideology is to repress the historical process by which
subordinate ethnic identities are formed. Overwhelmingly, the stories told in
this oral history are of immense disappointment and disillusionment. Some
disappointment seems almost inevitable, as people arrived from the Caribbean
with an image of England's 'green and pleasant land', only to find themselves

Fig. 6.3. Stills from The Colony, *Philip Donnellan, BBC, 1964*

working (if they were lucky) as factory workers in Birmingham. At the beginning of the film there is a montage of shots of Birmingham's civic buildings (including the statue of Queen Victoria) juxtaposed against voices telling of the 'false propaganda' that was exported to the West Indies by the British. ('When I was at school . . . we were taught to sing this "Land of Hope and Glory, Mother of the Free" . . . and to recite, what the hell was it? "Children of the Empire, you are brothers all . . ." and you want to know something? We believed it, you know, in all sincerity . . .') But the shattering of these imperialist illusions was accompanied by another kind of realisation, that something was rotten at the core of this so-called 'civilisation':

[*Man in bedsit; speech to camera*]

When a civilised, developed society like this introduces such argument then something must be wrong. You see, the Englishman is a very funny creature. He likes his change of scenery; he likes the variety in life. As a matter of fact in England you have a country of variety – the changes of the season – and it is part of, it has entered into the people themselves. Yet the Englishman, or the white man for that matter, doesn't want the variety of the human species. He likes to see white only. He can't admit that the same variety that makes the world possible and beautiful in all other aspects is the same thing that applies to the human race.

What develops in this oral testimony is a shift from the narrative of personal experience to the analysis of specific insights and problems. In particular, a major problem is the strange behaviour of white people, as the immigrant comes face to face with ethnic absolutism. Why, asks one woman, when she spoke one day to a white co-worker about her ethnic origins, did her workmate advise her to be silent? Why, asks another man, despite the fact that you work with white people, and converse with them at work, does this never extend to any kind of social contact outside the workplace? But then, there is the most insidious effect of all, which is told, with great clarity, in words which echo precisely the Althusserian theory of interpellation:

[*Spoken in the context of a group discussion*]

On first coming here we were all sort of, we all had our little insularities. What I've noticed nowadays is that the West Indian is no longer considering himself a Jamaican, Trinidadian, Barbadian, Antiguan – we are all – we are subtly, but inexorably considering ourselves as – we are all coloured people. Nowadays you pass one pavement; over on the other pavement a chap waves to you. You don't know him; you are positive he don't know you, yet he waves to you. Why? Because you have one thing in common, one thing which makes him now realise that we can wave to each other and expect to be waved (at) in return. I do not like that . . .

I have not come across a clearer illustration of this most fundamental point: that 'black' is not a pre-given or essential category, but on the contrary that it is a constructed identity.

Before West Indians came to Britain, as far as their cultural identity was concerned, 'blackness' was not an issue. It only became an issue in the conditions imposed by the ideology of ethnic absolutism. Thus, 'white' constructs 'black' as its opposite, as its 'other'; and this 'black' is then internalised, problematically and reluctantly, through the process of mutual recognition (hailing) which Althusser calls interpellation. In my next chapter I shall explore some further consequences of this important point.

But, of course, this is certainly not the end of the story. It is equally important to recognise that, just as the dominant ideology contains its own contradictions (and even the Queen is now exhorting us to 'make friends with people of different races'), so it is also responded to by those who become its subjects. In this respect Althusser's discussion of interpellation is too deterministic – there has to be room for further development and transformation. *The Colony* was made in 1964; in that same year the Bluebeat record label was established in London (an initial success was *Madness* by Prince Buster) and Millie Small's *My Boy Lollipop* made it into the mainstream UK chart. The relevance of these coincidences is, in Gilroy's argument, that a key response to the new racism can be traced in the organic development of relations between 'black' and 'white' forms of popular music and subculture (see also, Hebdige 1979). Central to this is the recognition that 'black' transcends its parochial British construction, and relates to an international diaspora of cultural influences. For instance, black people in Britain have made use of a variety of cultural resources imported from the USA and Africa, as well as an increasingly international Jamaican popular culture.

Some of the contributors to *The Colony* speak of the possibility that younger generations might find ways of breaking the mould of ethnic absolutism. In fact, the most telling example in Gilroy's book was produced twenty years later, in 1984, by a reggae DJ, comedian, and regular performer on the Channel 4 series, *Black on Black*. According to Gilroy, Smiley Culture's record *Cockney Translation* 'transcended the "schizophrenic" elements which composed the contradictory unity that provided the basic framework for a potential black Britishness' (p.195). It did this by establishing a series of humorous equivalences between London's black patois and cockney rhyming slang – again, through a kind of linguistic montage in which the implied cultural whole was greater than the sum of its parts:

> Say cockney fire shooter. We bus' gun
> Cockney say tea leaf. We just say sticks man
> You know dem have a wedge while we have corn
> Say cockney say 'Be first my son'. We just say Gwaan!

> Cockney say grass. We say outformer man . . .
> Cockney say Old Bill. We say dutty Babylon . . .

As Gilroy comments:

> Neither of the two languages available to black Londoners appears
> adequate for the expression of their complex cultural experience by itself
> . . . The ease with which [Smiley Culture] moves from one idiom to the
> other is counterposed to the barrier which racism has erected between the
> two language groups and which is signified in the separate, parallel
> positions occupied by these two inner city voices. The record contains a
> veiled but none the less visible statement that the rising generation of
> blacks, gathering in the darkened dance-halls, were gradually finding a
> means to acknowledge their relationship to England and Englishness. They
> were beginning to discover a means to position themselves relative to this
> society and to create a sense of belonging which could transcend 'racial',
> ethnic, local and class-based particularities and redefine England/Britain
> as a truly plural community. (p.196)

Gilroy suggests that Smiley Culture can be characterised, in Gramsci's terms,
as an organic intellectual. That is to say, his record articulates, in a popular
style, a critique of the frameworks imposed by the dominant (hegemonic)
ideology. Gilroy's optimism stems, I think, from the observation that Smiley
Culture is neither denying, nor celebrating, but rather interrogating the limits
of the cultural identities which have been imposed, but also creatively developed by blacks living in Britain. At the same time, he argues that 'it is impossible to theorise black culture in Britain without developing a new perspective
on British culture as a whole' (p.156, his emphasis). This is because the
forging of new identities, through the activities of organic intellectuals like
Smiley Culture, are transforming the grounds of what 'Britishness' might
mean, of its mythologies and connotations, at least for the working-class
youth of Britain's inner cities.

This is not of course, to deny the continued power of the new racism, with
its spokespeople in the British establishment. But the essential point, which
will serve as a necessary conclusion to this chapter, is that, whatever their
power to define and restrict, dominant ideologies are always open to decon-
struction, to challenge and to critique. Ideology is then, a process of struggle – initiated, inevitably by those who are subjected to its power, for whom
it is most immediately and experientially problematic; but also assisted, as I
hope this chapter has shown, by the analysis of ideological problematics and
practices developed in media studies. In its analysis of ideology, media studies
is necessarily critically engaged. Which takes us right back to Janice
Winship's account of the feminist commitment in her critique of women's
magazines.

A speculative postscript

Sometimes, I think, the dominant culture itself can establish interesting, and perhaps unintended, possibilities. Consider the following exchange, which occurred on the popular British TV programme *Blind Date*, in autumn 1994:

CILLA:	To be fair to Justina, I mean that's what *Blind Date* is all about. You came on and you told the truth.
JUSTINA:	I certainly did.
CILLA:	You did, and he got on your nerves, more than once.
JUSTINA:	Yes he did. He just wasn't the guy for me at all. And I needed to sort of come across like that and tell everyone.
CILLA:	Yes you did. Oh but are you upset by what Justina said?
IAN:	Absolutely gutted.
JUSTINA:	You must have guessed though.
IAN:	No, not really. I mean we went out on a date. There was no romance at all [J: Nothing]. But I thoroughly enjoyed the date.
CILLA:	Yes but I mean weren't you insulted? I mean she said you were weedy.
IAN:	I was weedy [*turns to studio audience*] Am I weedy? [**audience:** No!] Thank you.
JUSTINA:	[*turns to audience*] You didn't see his body [*audience groans*].
CILLA:	[*laughs*] I would quit while I was ahead if I were you Justina. Justina I mean, why were you so insulting?
JUSTINA:	Erm, he's a lovely guy, for some other girl.
IAN:	Can I have my say after this?
CILLA:	Yes [*audience: protracted applause*].
JUSTINA:	But if you'd come up to me in a club or something I would have sort of like turned around and walked off [*audience: groans*].
CILLA:	So Ian now you've asked for your go. It's your go. What have you got to say?
IAN:	Justina is a very very [*inaudible audience interjection*] powerful girl. Definitely without a shadow of a doubt speaks her mind. And er, I like that in a woman. [CILLA: you masochist] But not this woman [*audience cheers – protracted applause*]. But I'm not taking anything away from Justina here – I thoroughly enjoyed my time and I'm very glad that she picked me . . .

Such are the irresistible banalities of *Blind Date*. We can only speculate at the real reasons for Justina's hostility – Ian's alleged 'weediness' seems hardly fair – but he remains chivalrous to the end. What is very interesting however, in all shows of this type, is the part played by the (off-camera, but audibly participating) studio audience. Clearly and emphatically, the audience is on Ian's side; and even Cilla, while she maintains the veneer of non-serious banter through which most of the exchanges are handled (and they are punctuated throughout by audience laughter), can scarcely conceal her own apparent sympathies. The point is that this kind of 'people show' operates in terms of a popular 'commonsense', which includes a set of moral criteria (notions of human decency, fairness and so on). In these terms, Justina's harsh criticisms of Ian seem to have overstepped the mark.

It may or may not be relevant that she is white and he is black. *Blind Date*, however, is interesting in this respect. As Jordan and Weedon (1995) point out, the format for this show is international, and there are American and Australian versions. Individuals get to choose their partners (on the basis of pre-scripted answers to pre-scripted questions) from behind a screen, whence they are sent to more or less exotic locations. Justina and Ian have been to a health farm, and here they are the following week recounting their experiences. But Jordan and Weedon claim that such racial mixing could not occur on the American version of the show, where an informal apartheid predetermines the selection of participants.

Inter-racial dating is a regular feature of *Blind Date*, and it is clearly an assumption of the programme that more permanent relationships might be formed. Can any conclusions be drawn from this as far as the currency of racism in British popular culture is concerned? Any grounds for optimism would need to be heavily qualified: for this is certainly not a progressive transformation of British culture in the sense proposed by Gilroy (an unreconstructed heterosexism is the programme's dominant ideology). Nor do I believe that there has ever been a programme where a white participant is given a choice between three black people, whereas the reverse is routinely the case. The acceptability of blacks on *Blind Date* is thus conditional on their willingness to play a game whose rules have been established by the dominant, white culture. But with all these reservations (and possibly more) can it be suggested that here, in the dominant culture (and not confined, as Gilroy's example, to the 'darkened dance-hall'), we have a format of which one consequence (which may be unintended) is to raise awareness of the possibility, and even the acceptability, of inter-racial relationships? At any rate, it is now possible for a black person, like Ian, to be included in the moral consensus which lies at the heart of this kind of 'people show'.

FURTHER READING

There has not been space in this book to do justice to the huge amount of work on ideology in media and cultural studies. There are several introductions to ideology, ranging from the highly accessible (such as Cormack M.

(1992), Chapters 1–3; and Storey J. (1993), Chapter 5; to the more detailed and complex books by Larrain J. (1983), Chapters 1 and 3; and Eagleton T. (1991). The latter book, in particular, must be read selectively, for though there are useful discussions of the work of Marx (p70 ff) and Althusser (p.136 ff), and Chapter 2 is generally helpful, there are also shows of sophistry and polemic (Chapters 1 and 7) which the reader would do best to avoid. My thinking on ideology in this chapter has been strongly influenced by the work of Stuart Hall, and especially by the essay 'Culture, the Media and the Ideological Effect' in Curran J. (ed) (1977). My experience is that students find this essay heavy going, but the last few pages, where Hall discusses ideology and the media, certainly repay the effort.

There is also a vast body of literature on questions of national and ethnic identities. For a summary of theoretical discussions of national identity see Tomlinson J. (1991). For further discussions of 'Britishness/Englishness' see Chambers I., 'Narratives of Nationalism' and Donald J., 'How English Is It?', in Donald J *et al.* (eds) (1984); and see Schwarz B, 'Conservatism, Nationalism and Imperialism', in Donald J. and Hall S. (eds) (1986). For further discussion of the historical role of the BBC in promoting versions of the national culture see MacKenzie J., ' "In touch with the infinite": the BBC and the Empire 1923–53', in MacKenzie J. (ed) (1986).

The ideological functions of the British monarchy are discussed by Rosalind Brunt in 'A Divine Gift to Inspire? Popular cultural representation, nationhood and the British monarchy', in Strinati D. and Wagg S. (eds) (1992), but the key essay remains Cannadine D. (1983) (extracts also in Donald J. and Hall S. (eds) 1986).

For an extensive sociological discussion of racism, which includes a consideration of racism as ideology, see Miles R. (1989). An introduction to the relationship between European and non-European cultures is provided by Stuart Hall in 'The West and the Rest: Discourse and Power' in Hall S. and Gieben B. (1992), Chapter 6 (this also raises theoretical questions which are discussed in my next chapter). Racism in western media is discussed by Stuart Hall in 'The Whites of their Eyes: Racist Ideologies and the Media', in Alvarado M. and Thompson J. O. (1990); and (in relation to post-colonialism) by Stuart Hall, 'Cultural Identity and Diaspora', in Rutherford J. (ed) (1990).

7

Discourse

1 | ON STEREOTYPES

In his (1988) essay about the dominance of 'white' as an ethnic category in film, Richard Dyer discusses an experimental video in which white people are invited to talk about their identities. This is his account of the opening vox pop sequence:

> Asked how they would define themselves, the white interviewees refer easily to gender, age, nationality or looks but never to ethnicity. Asked if they think of themselves as white, most say that they don't, though one or two speak of being 'proud' or 'comfortable' to be white. In an attempt to get some white people to explore what being white means, the video assembles a group to talk about it and it is here that the problem of white people's inability to see whiteness appears intractable. Sub-categories of whiteness (Irishness, Jewishness, Britishness) take over, so that the particularity of whiteness itself begins to disappear; then gradually, it seems almost inexorably, the participants settle in to talking with confidence about what they know: *stereotypes of black people.* (p.46, my emphasis)

The previous chapter examined the way in which ideologies (of gender, nationality and race) define dominant and subordinate identities. Indeed we have seen that the very visibility of 'black' in our culture, is the effect of an ethnic absolutism which privileges 'white'. To this extent, Dyer's remarks about white people's 'inability to see whiteness' are not surprising. But what I think is particularly interesting is the way in which Dyer develops this discussion to focus on what, in the end, it is possible for these white people to talk about. For if 'whiteness' cannot be put into words, clearly 'blackness' can – but not only blackness, for Irishness, Jewishness and Britishness are equally possible topics. What is it that allows us to speak about some things, in certain ways, and not others? It would seem that particular languages are available which enable us to 'talk with confidence about what we know'.

Dyer also suggests that one thing which it is possible to speak about with confidence is stereotypes. Previously (in Chapter 2) we examined one form of this confident speaking, in the oral narratives or anecdotes commonly exchanged in chat shows. In such narratives, talk about stereotypes may be a deeply rooted and perhaps very general feature of the structures of common speech. But it is also intriguing that some phenomena seem to be more easily stereotyped than others, and that there may be some categories, like 'white' for which no stereotypes exist at all. If we consider the identities referred to in Dyer's discussion, as well as stereotypes of black people, I think we might have very little difficulty in recalling stereotypes of 'Irishness' and 'Jewishness'; but what about the stereotypical Brit? Stereotypes of 'Britishness' may not be so readily available (unless, that is, we happen to be Irish!).

Here's how Dyer begins to develop this point:

> There is no doubt that part of the strength and resilience of stereotypes of non-dominant groups resides in their variation and flexibility – stereotypes are seldom found in pure form and this is part of the process by which they are naturalised, kept alive. Yet the strength of white representation, as I've suggested, is the *apparent absence altogether of the typical*, the sense that being white is coterminous with the endless plenitude of human diversity. (p.47, my emphasis)

Once again then, Dyer is relating his discussion of the prevalence of stereotypes to issues of cultural dominance and subordination. These, as we have seen, can be analysed in terms of ideology. It is thus the dogmatism of the dominant ideology that imposes its stereotypes on those it identifies as subordinate or deviant. Stereotypes might then be defined as a narrow and restrictive (but also resilient) set of meanings or concepts produced within an ideology – as racism, for example, has produced stereotypes of blacks. But I am equally intrigued here by Dyer's suggestion that, for an ideology to operate in this fashion, it must be possible to construct some sense of the 'typical'; that is to say, it must be possible to typify. I shall return to this point in a moment, for I think it opens up a further dimension to our critical analysis of media texts.

However, even if we compare what we have said so far, with other classic discussions of stereotypes, we can see that there are some important theoretical differences. Here I am thinking in particular of Walter Lippmann's (1922) account, where stereotyping is seen as a general and universal human activity. Lippmann's approach is, broadly, a variant of cognitive psychology, in which stereotypes are a feature of the way human beings generally perceive and organise their experiences. At times, there is not much difference between the way Lippmann talks about stereotypes and the way Saussure discusses signs, for both are part of the elementary process by which arbitrary meanings are imposed on the world. And it is worth noting how a particular kind of political conclusion follows from this argument: for if stereotypes are arbitrary, then we need to remind ourselves that they are provisional, however authoritative they might appear. Lippmann's discussion is thus a liberal critique of some of the more dogmatic excesses of the human sciences of his day, with their 'loose talk about collective minds, national souls and race psychology' (p.139).

But, if Dyer is correct, stereotyping cannot be regarded as a general feature of human communication. On the contrary, it is a specific procedure developed in those particular forms of communication that involve the exercise of power. Another interesting approach to this question is provided by Isaac Julien and Kobena Mercer (1988), in their introduction to the issue of *Screen* in which Dyer's essay appears. Again, with reference to race, they are discussing the problem of political 'marginality'. With so few films being made by black people, with so few chances open to black people to enter the public sphere, whatever can be defined as an instance of 'black culture' is all too often taken to be 'typical' of black people as a whole. (It occurs to me that my own use of *The Colony* in the last chapter might be an instance of this.) Thus, argue Julien and Mercer:

> . . . the restricted economy of ethnic enunciation is a political problem for at least two important reasons. First, individual subjectivity is denied because the black subject is positioned as a mouthpiece, a ventriloquist for an entire social category which is seen to be 'typified' by its representative. Acknowledgement of the *diversity* of black experiences and subject-positions is thereby foreclosed. Thus, secondly, where minority subjects are framed and contained by the monologic terms of 'majority discourse', the fixity of boundary relations between centre and margin, between universal and particular, returns the speaking subject to the ideologically appointed place of the stereotype – that 'all black people are the same'. (p.5, original emphasis)

Once again this is an argument about cultural power, but it is adding a further dimension to the distinction between 'core' and 'periphery' which we considered in the previous chapter. Hitherto, in the analysis of ideology, we have looked at the way in which dominant meaning systems have established oppositional categories, which they have imposed (through interpellation) on their 'subjects'. These subjects (women, national and ethnic groups) have had to struggle, with and against, these problematic meaning systems, to construct what Gilroy calls their own 'expressive cultures'. This kind of critical perspective is implied in the arguments of Julien and Mercer, but they are also, I think, raising critical questions about the strategy which an expressive culture might adopt. Thus, it is not enough for blacks (or anyone else) to criticise and contest the dominant meaning system, it is also necessary to consider the form of that contestation, and to choose the grounds for the contest, to avoid incorporation by the very categories one is seeking to transcend. It is here, at the level of strategy, that the question of 'typification' is most problematic.

The further dimension, that Julien and Mercer are introducing, points towards another set of considerations in media text analysis. Stereotypes are now not just meanings or concepts which are imposed on people, for they also establish places, or positions from which people may speak. To speak as a 'black' is now, if you are not very careful, to speak as a 'typical black' – 'typical' that is, in the eyes of the people you are speaking to. This is a place or position you occupy as you are speaking, and it is established for you by the dominant culture. This is because the dominant culture is now working, not only through meaning systems, but also through established ways of speaking (or writing, or visualising). For this reason, in media studies, the term 'signification' (which refers, as we have seen, to the construction of meanings) is frequently extended in the concept of signifying *practice*. This extended definition carries the further implications that, as one speaks, one is also engaged in a practice of speaking, and that media texts can be studied for the way they mobilise particular signifying practices.

In the next section, we will return to these theoretical points, but for now, let us stay with the question of stereotypes. For what we are now saying about stereotypes is that it is not just a question of what it is or is not possible to speak about (Dyer's video example); it is also that, having been, as it were, 'stereotyped', a person has, in a very real and practical sense, been *positioned*. Thus whatever might be said in response to the stereotype, by way of argument or critique, is still likely to appear as 'typical' ('they *would* say that, wouldn't they?'). In this way, a person has not only been interpellated, that person has also been 'typified'; and this is another effect of the dominant culture – blacks can easily be typified in this way, whereas whites, it would seem, cannot. But this is because stereotypes are not, in fact, universal; on the contrary they are the product of particular signifying practices which are mobilised in (among other places) media texts.

Consider, for example, documentary films. There are certainly several variants in the documentary genre, which do not all engage in 'typification' to the same extent. For instance, a common form of documentary in contemporary British television focuses on 'human interest', and is more concerned with people as (exemplary or eccentric) individuals than as representatives of social groups. Equally popular however, and prestigious in institutional terms, are documentaries which take an 'anthropological' interest in people from other cultures, which are sometimes defined in this genre as 'disappearing worlds'. Again, like any format, this is not static, and developments have certainly occurred in areas such as the relationship between film makers and their 'subjects', and in the form and function of interviews. But I hope I may be forgiven for choosing an example here which is designed to advance the general point, that forms of 'typification' are the product of particular signifying practices.

My example comes from a television programme, now (thankfully) discontinued, which was shown on Channel 4 in 1987. *Odyssey*, presented by writer and naturalist Andrew Mitchell, seems to have been designed as a kind of *National Geographic* magazine for TV. Thus, even before the programme starts, a continuity announcer sets the scene: 'Travel now, from the Sahara to the Arctic, via South America and China, and you don't even have to leave the house'. Mitchell, speaking to camera, in a library suitably decorated with houseplants, tells us that this edition will feature 'frogs in the Central American rainforest; birdlife in the remote Arctic island of Spitzbergen; and a journey through the backroads of rural China . . . First though we're going in search of the legendary camel caravans of the Sahara', travelling with a film crew, 'to the remotest corners of the desert'.

The stars of this film are the Tuareg people, 'still to be found' with their camel caravans in the southern regions of the Sahara. We are given some impressions of their nomadic existence, which is described as ancient, but also threatened by modern economic conditions. The status of the Tuareg is particularly enhanced by their environment – a harsh environment to which they have adapted, but which (in this film at least) is also shown to have a certain Romantic beauty. The Tuareg survive by trading in the settlements through which they pass, like Faschi, which is built around an oasis. But consider now the way we are introduced to the people of Faschi, and how they are positioned by the signifying practices used in this film:

[*long shot of group/cut to close-ups of children's faces*]

v/o: At dawn Faschi turns out to be a forlorn, sandblown place. Some 200 people live here, Tupus, settled people of mysterious origin, distinct from the nomadic Tuareg.

[*Cut to landscape of salt pits*]

v/o: On the outskirts are the legendary salt pits, a patchwork of sun-scorched flats. Here then is the true reason for the survival of this old oasis.

[*cut to long shot of man working in salt pit*]

v/o: Natural salt is coaxed from the earth by flooding the pits, then from the natural process of evaporation, the salt crystallises white from the earth-stained water. One wonders how may Europeans can ever have stood here in the remotest spot on earth.

Given the initial promise of armchair travel, reinforced here by the combination of voice-over and camerawork, it takes a huge effort of will to recall that, of course, this place is not at all 'remote' to the Tupus themselves. Rather, a sense of remoteness has been constructed through the signifying practices used in the film, and this is the basic premise for our interest and fascination. It remains even in the brief moments when the Tupus themselves get to speak:

> [*shots of men climbing palm trees/close-ups of women's hands and arms working to pack dates*]
>
> V/O: Dates are the other source of wealth in the oasis. Around October, men climb the trees and knock down the bunches. The women strip the bunches and pack the dates into baskets. Dates are known as the bread of the desert. Together with camels' milk they are the staple food of the Tuareg and a basic food for the people here.
>
> [*woman in close-up speaks to camera*]
>
> SUBTITLES: We're packing this year's dates. It's been a good harvest this year. There are four of us in my family. This is our food.

Up to a point, I think we can say that this kind of anthropological documentary is operating in terms of a familiar western ideology. This is again, a version of the 'grand dichotomy', in which the other culture is seen (from the perspective of our armchair) to be primitive and exotic. However, in this film, the 'grand dichotomy' is supported by a theory, more or less explicitly articulated in the commentary. This theory owes much to the popular legacy of Charles Darwin, and it is founded on notions of adaptation and survival. Hence, the almost obsessive interest in how people live in this (to us) inhospitable environment (and the more inhospitable the environment, the better, in this kind of film). Hence also the visual fascination with resources and people working, and the anthropological interest in the sexual division of labour. But there is also another kind of visual fascination, and it is illustrated by the close-ups of the children's faces as we are introduced to the Tupus.

In this kind of film, people are defined by their culture, or 'way of life'. These ways of life are classified (as 'nomadic' for instance, or 'settled') and there is sometimes an implicit evolutionary perspective (thus it might be thought that a 'settled' way of life is more 'civilised'). Within such cultures (as portrayed in anthropological documentaries) everyone is essentially the same, since everyone lives the same kind of life (indeed these are the cultures of 'peoples' such as Tuaregs, or Tupus). So we do not get to see eccentric or deviant members of these cultures, nor is there any 'human interest' in them as individuals. On the contrary the people who appear in such films appear as 'types', as typical of their cultures. They even speak as types ('this is what we are doing/this is what we always do'), and their typification is guaranteed visually by the close-up shot of the face, a distinctive physiognomy, which confirms a particular ethnic or racial origin.

It should not be assumed that these filmic conventions are only applied to people from far-away countries. It is possible to adapt the anthropological perspective to look at distinctive ways of life in our own society, as is illustrated to some extent by the British documentary film *Housing Problems*. In that film, as we have seen, although individuals are introduced by name, they are also positioned as 'typical' slum dwellers, delivering their testimony to camera. They are positioned, partly by the way they talk (in distinctive cockney accents), but more particularly by the way the camera establishes a visual distance between 'them' (as participants) and 'us' (as spectators – see Higson, 1986). This is to say again, that the positioning is achieved through a signifying practice which makes use of specific techniques, of interviewing, camerawork and editing. It is the use of these techniques, as much as what is said in its arguments, which produces the overall effect of the film.

If I was to define the signifying practice I have been describing here, I would want to call it *ethnography*. A literal definition of this word might be 'writing about peoples'. I am not suggesting that this is its only definition – for ethnography is also a methodology which is commonly used in media audience research. Nor am I suggesting that this is the only way in which stereotypes are produced, for one would still want to use this term to refer to the inhabitants of particular narrative structures. However, I shall return to this discussion of ethnography as a signifying practice which produces its own distinctive forms of typification. For, if we recall Dyer's discussion, and ask what it is that stereotypes of 'blackness' have in common with 'Jewishness' and 'Irishness' (but with more difficulty 'Britishness') we would have to conclude that these groups are all definable as 'other cultures', in terms of 'ethnicity', within which their representatives usually appear as 'typical'.

2   THEORY OF DISCOURSE

Another term, which is interchangeable with 'signifying practice', but which is now more commonly used in media studies, is the concept of discourse (1). This is the final, and most challenging, concept that I shall introduce in this book, for it defines the most radical approach to media text analysis. It might be altogether too simple to present this as a progressive narrative whereby media text analysis has become increasingly sophisticated. However, there is a sense in which, if semiology led the field in the 1960s – early 1970s, and ideology theory dominated the later 1970s – early 1980s, discourse theory (of a particular kind) has now overtaken both as the leading critical paradigm. But I want to argue here that this is not simply a matter of reject-ing previous approaches (otherwise there would be no point to the earlier chapters in this book). Rather, these advances in the field of media text analysis should be understood as adding further considerations to be taken into account.

In general terms, if semiology provides a way of analysing meanings, and ideology provides a way of talking about the relationship between meanings and social structures, what discourse theory has achieved is a way of rethink-ing that relationship. At the heart of the matter is the question of social power. As we have seen, ideology theory talks about the imposition of dominant meaning systems, and is interested in the way people are recruited to, and possibly resist, those dominant systems. But the power that estab-lishes the dominance of these systems is, in ideology theory, an external social power: it might, in simple Marxist accounts, be the ruling class that has this power; in more complex versions, dominant ideologies are reproduced by the social system. In discourse theory, however, power is not external but inter-nal to meaning systems; meaning systems themselves are powerful. This is because meaning systems are now seen, not simply as systems (structured like language), but also as signifying practices. And it is not simply that meanings are embedded within social practices (as they are in Althusser's theory of ideology); meaning and practice are now indistinguishable. Meaning *is* practice, in discourse theory.

The particular theory of discourse I am introducing here derives from the work of Michel Foucault. The introduction of Foucault to media studies runs a similar risk to the introduction of Marx, for neither wrote specifically on the media, nor were they interested, particularly, in popular culture. In fact, the bulk of Foucault's work is concerned with the history of sciences and social institutions, which he sees as part of a distinctively modern approach to the government of populations. It may be stretching a point to suggest that the media is a social institution which can be located within this perspec-tive, but I think some of our conclusions about genre, as a way of regulat-ing media consumption, do begin to point in this direction. There is, however, a more specific example in Foucault's work, which connects with one of our previous discussions and which will provide a way in to defining more precisely what the theory of discourse entails.

Recall Janice Winship's analysis of the ideology of sex and sexuality featured in the pages of *Cosmopolitan*. Winship shows that within its overall 'aspirational feminism', *Cosmopolitan* reproduces a (contradictory) ideology of sexual liberation, based on a notion of 'true individuality' to be achieved by the loss of 'inhibition' – particularly the so-called 'problem of male impotence'. Moreover, like other women's magazines, *Cosmopolitan* is generally obsessed with sex, both in terms of the amount of space it devotes to sexual technique and the discussion of sexual problems. But this can be seen as one instance of a more general phenomenon, discussed by Foucault in *The History of Sexuality* (Vol 1). Here, he is interested in the fact that, despite the alleged 'Victorian' repression of sex, western societies, since the eighteenth century, appear to have been continuously preoccupied with sexuality and sexual 'problems'. Sex has become a subject for scientific and social investigation; but, more generally, it has also become a popular cultural obsession. In fact, in the following passage, Foucault might well be referring to *Cosmopolitan*:

> From the singular imperialism that compels everyone to transform their sexuality into a perpetual discourse, to the manifold mechanisms which, in the areas of economy, pedagogy, medicine and justice, incite, extract, distribute and institutionalize the sexual discourse, an immense verbosity is what our civilization has required and organized. Surely no other type of society has ever accumulated – and in such a relatively short span of time – a similar quantity of discourses concerned with sex. It may well be that we talk about sex more than anything else; we set our minds to the task; we convince ourselves that we have never said enough on the subject . . . It is possible that where sex is concerned, the most long-winded, the most impatient of societies is our own. (p.33)

Foucault's explanation of this phenomenon is interesting. Whereas ideology theory would regard all this talk about sex as a massive distraction, or displacement of social contradictions, Foucault argues that it performs some important and useful 'governmental' functions. Sexual orientation can be used to classify individuals; alleged sexual 'perversions' can justify forms of 'treatment'; but, more generally, the pursuit of sexual fulfilment is a major way in which people 'discipline' themselves. In our culture, happiness is defined by sexual goals, which in turn require appropriate forms of living (for example, as heterosexual couples). In Foucault's general perspective, this is one way in which social populations are 'policed'. Perhaps it would not have occurred to us, in our innocent reading of women's magazines, that this is their ultimate social function. But Foucault's arguments not only raise interesting questions about the institutional functions of the media, they also invite us to look more closely at the particular forms in which all this talk about sex (this 'perpetual discourse') occurs.

For instance, at its most precise, Foucault's theory of discourse focuses on the operations of specific discursive techniques. In *The History of Sexuality*, he discusses the technique of the confession, suggesting that a particular ritual in the Catholic Church can be seen as a prototype, in modern western societies, for a whole range of common discursive events. As far as the media are concerned, we have previously touched on some of these events – for instance, the confessional style of some forms of interviewing, or the problem pages in women's magazines. Foucault's argument is that we have, in a sense, become 'confessional' societies, insofar as it is generally regarded as positive and beneficial to disclose problematic personal experiences to significant (and sympathetic) 'others'. But here is Foucault's precise description of the confessional technique:

> The confession is a ritual of discourse in which the speaking subject is also the subject of the statement; it is also a ritual that unfolds within a power relationship, for one does not confess without the presence (or virtual presence) of a partner who is not simply the interlocutor but the authority who requires the confession, prescribes and appreciates it, and intervenes in order to judge, punish, forgive, console and reconcile; a ritual in which the truth is corroborated by the obstacles and resistances it has had to surmount in order to be formulated; and finally, a ritual in which the expression alone, independently of its external consequences, produces intrinsic modifications in the person who articulates it: it exonerates, redeems and purifies him [sic], it unburdens him of his wrongs, liberates him and promises him salvation. For centuries, the truth of sex was, at least for the most part, caught up in this discursive form. (pp.61–2)

For Foucault, the 'governmental' function of the discourse of sex is practically supported by the ritual of the confession. This is because the confession works as a technique that involves simultaneously the production of specific forms of statement, and the reproduction of particular relations of power. Let us consider these two features in more detail. The confessional statement exhibits certain characteristics: initially there is some hestitation, some uncertainty, for there are 'obstacles to be surmounted'; subsequently perhaps, as a narrative, the discourse may pour forth, and even be accompanied by floods of tears. In all this, the confessee occupies a position, as the subject of the narrative, but also as subjected to the reactions and responses of the confessor. The confess*ee* is thus dependent on the presence, or 'virtual presence' of the confess*or*, and to this extent is subject to his or her power.

Note also that, for Foucault, the confession always works this way, 'independently of its external consequences'. That is to say, in this theory of discourse, the concept of technique is used to describe particular mechanisms which produce their own intrinsic effects, whatever their particular location, and whoever the participants might be. It is the case that we cannot ignore external factors, as we shall see in a moment, but at the core of this approach we are concerned with technical operations in the same way (to use a common analogy) as an engineer might be concerned with the inner workings of a machine. A discursive technique is a machine for the production of certain kinds of statement, which positions its participants in relations of power, and produces, routinely and consistently, its own intrinsic effects. Such is the consistency of the confession, or the interview, or the letter to the problem page – whatever the particular discursive technique might be.

In a wider context, however, the concept of 'discourse' refers to the deployment of these particular techniques within discursive fields or formations. For instance, Foucault is here considering the use of the confession within the discursive field of sex and sexuality (whereas it might equally be located within the field of criminal justice). So discourse theory is not only concerned with the analysis of techniques (the production of statements and power relations); it relates these to wider institutional practices and their associated 'bodies of knowledge'. Typically, we might expect to find that the positions established within specific discursive techniques will correlate to institutional roles and social statuses (the roles of psychiatrist and patient, of police officer and criminal, for example). These roles and statuses are themselves supported by conceptual frameworks that define institutional purposes. Many western institutions, of the sort Foucault has analysed (asylums, hospitals and prisons) have derived some legitimacy from the claim that their particular knowledges are 'scientific'. Foucault, however, would prefer that we treat such claims with a degree of scepticism; or at least that we recognise that institutional knowledge is always, simultaneously, bound up with the exercise of social power.

Perhaps the clearest example, in Foucault's work, of such a 'discursive formation' is that given in his book on medical discourse, *The Birth of the Clinic*. In this account, modern medical discourse is the product of a number of institutional developments in the late eighteenth–early nineteenth centuries. Many of these developments were of a very practical sort, ranging from standardised techniques for physical examination and treatment, to mundane procedures for record-keeping and timetabling, which were now gathered together under the one roof of the general hospital. Such techniques reproduced professionalised power relations, between doctors and patients, nurses and ancillary workers; but they also encouraged the production of new forms of medical knowledge. In these great institutions, with their systematic methods of recording, it was now possible to begin to classify a range of medical conditions, producing newly observable categories of disease. Here, advances in medical science are seen to be contingent on the operation of mundane techniques and institutional routines.

But now consider the most radical implication of this perspective. What was effectively produced in the 'birth of the clinic', in the new medical institutions, was a distinctive understanding of the human body. Medical science made its own discoveries (such as the circulation of the blood) and again, these were contingent on new forms of examination and surgical intervention. In a more general sense, however, in this period, the human body became an object for a new kind of medical gaze. When, in these terms, a doctor is examining a patient, he or she is now operating through a field of medical concepts, and in terms of an established set of routines, which allow the body to be 'seen' in very specific ways. Such practices are, of course, policed by the medical profession itself – and woe betide a doctor who confuses the medical with any other kind of bodily gaze. The radical conclusion to be drawn from this is that a discourse, through its techniques and its concepts, and through its power relations, constitutes its own objects – that is, its own particular version of reality. This is, to some extent, reproducing the arguments of classical semiology; but it is also showing, in very practical, institutional and historical ways, how 'realities' have been constructed.

I suppose it might be generally accepted that the medical gaze, after an intensive period of training, might have its own specialised ways of looking at its objects. Clearly there are also practical instruments, such as microscopes, which support the medical profession in this respect. But what is more challenging to explore, is the proposition that Foucault has established a theoretical framework that might be applied to popular cultural, as well as scientific, 'ways of seeing'. For, if we were to apply this framework to the analysis of media texts, we would not only be interested in programmes, like *Cardiac Arrest*, where the medical gaze is (perversely and satirically) dramatised. Rather, we would also be examining the possibility that the media too, as series of institutional spaces, are mobilising discursive practices which constitute their own objects, within their own specific fields of vision. It is in this light, for example, that we might begin to define the 'cultural type' as the object for an 'ethnographic gaze' which, in its anthropological documentaries, the media institution reproduces. Are there any other instances of this kind of phenomenon?

3 | THE MALE GAZE

How do classic Hollywood films introduce their female stars? Consider the following account of Marilyn Monroe's entrance in *The Seven Year Itch* (1955):

> Her first appearance . . . is a classic instance of woman as spectacle caught in a shot from the male protagonist's point of view. It opens on Richard (Tom Ewell), on his hands and knees looking for something, bottom sticking up, a milk bottle between his legs – the male body shown, as is routine in sex comedies, as ludicrously grotesque; he hears the door bell and opens the door to his flat; as the door opens light floods in on him; he looks and there is a cut to the hall doorway, where the curvy shape of a woman is visible through the frosted glass. The woman's shape is placed exactly within the frame of the door window, the doorway is at the end of the hall, exactly in the centre of the frame; a set of enclosing rectangles create a strong sense of perspective, and emphasise the direction of Richard's/our

gaze. The colouring of the screen is pinky-white and light emanates from behind the doorway where the woman is. All we see of her is her silhouette, defining her proportions, but she also looks translucent. The film cuts back to Richard, his jaw open in awe, bathed in stellar light. (pp.63–4)

Richard Dyer offers this account of Monroe's entrance as a final (ultimate?) example of the power of 'white' in film. However it will also serve to remind us of a scenario which is common in Hollywood cinema. The first appearance of the female film star, particularly if she is a 'sex goddess', is capable of bringing the narrative flow, briefly, to a stop. For a moment or two she is constructed as an object for erotic contemplation. Other well known instances include the first appearance of Rita Hayworth in *Gilda* (1946), where, in response to her husband's call ('Are you decent?'), she tosses back her head and turns to face the camera, posing in a way which is reminiscent of a glamour photograph. Or consider a second example, which is almost identical to the scenario described by Dyer, where in *The Postman Always Rings Twice* (1946), Lana Turner first appears, bare-legged and statuesque, in a doorway. Interestingly, as if again to prove Dyer's point, she is dressed, head to foot, in white (see figure 7.1)

It is worth stressing that there is a particular technique at work in all these examples. In every case, the scenario hinges on the introduction of the female star to the principal male character. The story-line has followed the male protagonist to this point, where the woman first appears within his field of vision. Technically, as Dyer points out, this field is established through the use of point of view, where the camera is positioned with the male protagonist, and gives the spectator his perspective. At its most intense, the actor is not included in the shot, so the spectator now seems to be looking through his eyes. And it is at this precise moment that, for a second, the narrative stops. Narrative is interrupted by spectacle in this scenario where the spectator is positioned with the male protagonist in an intense gaze at the woman.

The Postman Always Rings Twice is particularly clear, and manipulative, in this respect. John Garfield, sitting at the bar of the café where he has just been given a job, has his attention distracted by an object rolling across the floor. The camera, following his point of view, tilts down to focus on the object, which turns out to be a tube of lipstick. As the object stops rolling, the camera then tilts up again, finally offering a shot of Lana Turner's legs. From this we cut to the shot of her entire body, framed by the doorway. Garfield then gets up, retrieves the lipstick, and hands it to Turner. Meanwhile we are given close-ups of her face, but not of his, and as he approaches, shots of Turner admiring her own image in a compact mirror. After Garfield hands her the lipstick she applies it, poses again, turns and closes the door. A smell of burning reminds Garfield of the hamburger to which he should have been attending.

Fig. 7.1. Lana Turner as Cora in The Postman Always Rings Twice *(1946).*
© *1946 Turner Entertainment Co. All Rights Reserved*

I know of no better illustration of the mechanisms first described by Laura
Mulvey in her very influential essay 'Visual Pleasure and Narrative Cinema'
(1975). Mulvey argues that the construction of 'dominant specularity' in
Hollywood cinema also routinely privileges the male gaze. That is to say, not

only is a male character the protagonist in the narrative structure, but also the camerawork is organised around his point of view. Thus, the spectator is placed in a position of visual, as well as emotional, identification. Furthermore, the gaze which is then on offer is erotically coded so that the spectator's general pleasure in looking (which Mulvey calls 'scopophilia') is structured in particular ways. The principal forms of erotic looking offered by Hollywood cinema are voyeurism (where the spectator is teased by a partial or oblique view of the object) and fetishism (where the object is fully on display). In the movement from the point-of-view shot of Turner's legs to the long shot of her body in the doorway, *The Postman Always Rings Twice* constructs a shift from voyeurism to fetishism. The shot of Turner in the doorway is a classic fetishistic image – but this might require some further explanation.

The term 'fetish' can be commonly understood to refer to an object of worship. Perhaps it also has further connotations, suggesting that this form of worship is primitive (idolatrous) and that the object, as well as fascinating, is also dangerous. Such definitions and connotations do seem to apply particularly well to the way women are presented in many Hollywood films – where the term 'sex goddess' is precisely appropriate, and where, in classic *film noir*, she is required to play the *'femme fatale'*. However, as an object of worship, the fetish must assume a particular visual form: it must be enticing, attracting our continuous attention; but simultaneously, in order not to become too threatening, it must be also held at a distance. There is thus, in both voyeurism and fetishism, an intense ambivalence, a desire to see but not be seen, a desire to look but not to touch. One way of distancing the fetish is to put it on a pedestal; another way is to frame it, so that it now appears as an icon. This is why (like Monroe in Dyer's example) Lana Turner stands framed by a doorway in this shot.

As is well known, Mulvey's explanation for these ambivalences makes extensive use of psychoanalytic theory. These are *male* ambivalences, she argues, and they have their roots in the construction of male desires. In psychoanalytic theory, the achievement of genital masculinity is contingent on the (unconscious) experience of the Oedipus complex, where the boy is offered the possibility of identification with the father on the condition that he renounce his sexual desire for the mother. This is, however, an offer he cannot refuse, for it is accompanied by the threat of castration. Henceforth, the body of the woman will remind him of this threat – it will be desired, but it will also appear threatening. It is therefore to allay such threats, that the body of the woman is symbolically transformed, in voyeuristic imagery which excites, and fetishistic imagery in which the threat, while on view, is contained.

In my experience, many students, particularly men, have problems accepting this theory. Certainly, there are criticisms that might be made of its speculative and ahistorical focus, and of its highly metaphorical nature. But let us also acknowledge its strong points. Psychoanalysis offers an explanation of why it is that men, and not women, are obsessed by the kinds of imagery we are describing; and it is able to extend this explanation to account for the manifestly irrational structures of censorship in our culture. It is a theoretical account which can be very readily applied to the structure of the discursive formation which we define as 'pornography' – where voyeuristic and fetishistic images of women are routinely available, and images of the erect penis are systematically censored. In psychoanalytic terms, this is because the phallus is the focus for masculine identification. Hence it is the subject of this discursive formation, and it cannot, except with difficulty, be objectified. Psychoanalysis would therefore argue that pornographic discourse is *phallocentric* – and just as whites, in an ethnocentric culture, cannot speak of whiteness; so, in phallocentrism, it is this ultimate symbol of masculinity that cannot be displayed.

But perhaps it is stretching the bounds of credibility to argue that the images of women in classic Hollywood films are pornographic. I would rather put this another way and suggest that we are dealing here with a phallocentric discursive formation whose products take a variety of generic forms. At the basis of this formation are the techniques we have described, in particular the techniques which establish visual point of view. Such techniques involve relations of power between subjects and objects, those who gaze and those who pose. However, in this discursive formation, these positions are mapped on to gender, so, as John Berger famously put it, it is the man who looks and the woman who turns herself into 'an object of (his) vision' (1972, p.47). But Berger was, of course, principally describing the characteristics of the nude in classical western art, and we (with the assistance of Mulvey) have been analysing Hollywood films. I think we have to conclude that, as this discourse has been institutionalised, so its genres have proliferated, ranging from fine art, through glamour photography and film, to some ('soft') forms of pornography.

It is thus a key effect of this discursive formation that it constructs the body of the woman as a particular kind of object. Again, this is an illustration of Foucault's radical argument, that discursive practices constitute their own objects, and it can be usefully compared and contrasted with the formation of the medical gaze. There, as we have seen, the medical discourse defines the body as an object for examination and treatment; here the woman's body has become an object of erotic fascination (2). However, to speak of 'objectification' is only to establish a starting point for a whole series of further questions which concern the various permutations of 'the look' within phallocentric discourse. For although the discursive mechanism of the male gaze routinely produces its effects, it is surely too simple to assume that, in every instance, its object is reduced to passivity.

Berger goes on to suggest that the woman who is its object, also internalises the male gaze. 'Women watch themselves being looked at . . . (which) determines . . . the relation of women to themselves' (p.47). Of course, as many feminist writers have argued, this internalisation of 'the look' can be commercially exploited in ways which are negative and self-destructive for women. It can also, however, become the basis for potentially critical forms of self-consciousness, which are apparent in the particular ways in which the object, in such a discourse, occupies her position of objectification. For instance, all sorts of further possibilities are suggested by Lana Turner, as she responds to John Garfield's scrutiny. First she returns his look; then she looks at herself; then she applies the lipstick in a performance which, though for him, is also in a sense for her. In watching herself being looked at, Turner is both inside and outside her position; and insofar as she is aware of herself performing as an object, her performance becomes a form of 'masquerade' (3). In other words, as we shall go on to explore, even within a highly coded discursive practice, there is a certain room for manoeuvre. But, in any case, as she shuts the door behind her, we know that she has his fate in her hands.

4   SPECTACULAR ETHNOGRAPHY

There is a certain visual style, or rhetoric, which is commonly reproduced in the ethnographic film. Often, such films begin with a high-angle shot of a landscape, perhaps from an aeroplane, or slowly panning across a vast expanse of desert, bush or jungle. Then, as if by chance, we will spot a clearing. Zooming in over the treetops we will begin to recognise a few signs of human settlement – huts perhaps, or an encampment. Or alternatively, a nomadic group (like the Tuareg) will emerge through the desert's heat haze. We have arrived – for of course, this is a kind of visual journey; and at once, even before the other culture becomes clearly visible, the film is constructing our position as a visitor, a tourist, and an ethnographic voyeur.

And when the other culture does come into view, it is offered, to the western consumer, as a visual spectacle. In saying that this amounts to a rhetoric, I am emphasising that the camerawork and the editing have their own persuasive effects, over and above (but usually in collusion with) what the voice-over is saying. Thus at the same time as the other culture is being classified, verbally, by its name, geographical location, and place along the Darwinian chain of human evolution, so the camera is positioning the spectator within a particular kind of ethnographic gaze. In many films, the wide shot of the landscape is superceded by a series of alternating long shots and close-ups. The long shots show the group *in situ*, in the context of its 'daily life'. In these shots, people and livestock come and go, disappearing and reappearing, seemingly absorbed in their customary routines. Then, in the close-ups, we are presented with details of their activities and fragments of people's bodies. As we have previously noted, there is a particular emphasis here on shots of people working, often practising unfamiliar skills. There are also the ubiquitous big close-ups of faces, some staring into the camera. Ultimately the big close-up shot is pulled out to re-establish the total context, so that the whole process can begin once again.

If you possess a video recording of this sort of film, it is worth momentarily turning down the sound, so as to observe more clearly what the visual rhetoric is doing. Essentially, in an ethnographic film, very little happens; it is the absolute antithesis of the Hollywood action movie. Indeed, rather than offering a narrative sequence of events, propelled by some form of conflict or disruption, the ethnographic film is largely static, with its focus on a (more or less) stable way of life. Accordingly, such films are slow, and the shots are allowed to linger. Possibly this is to reinforce our sense of the slow pace of so-called 'primitive' cultures, but its effect is to construct a visual spectacle which is even-paced, rhythmic and almost hypnotic. Returning to the sound, we find that this visual rhythm is accompanied by an aural montage of natural sounds, animal cries and unintelligible human speech. We might be totally disorientated, were it not for the authoritative explanations offered by the voice-over.

In such ways, ethnographic films construct a relationship between the familiar and the strange. On one side there is the basic reassurance that derives from our location in the comfort of our own domestic space. Then there is the familiar ethnocentric ideology, the grand dichotomy, which it is the function of the voice-over to reproduce. The very fact that this is a voice-over, from an invisible source (an anthropologist, or narrator) reinforces its authority. Additionally, in many modern films, further reassurance is provided by the recruitment of an individual member of the other culture, who is introduced by name, to act as a privileged informant. The anthropological commentary is then supported by interviews with the informant, who is thereby humanised, particularly if it can be demonstrated that he (for it is usually he) is a member of a family. The universality of sex, and systems of kinship, provides a further point of contact, not only with human cultures, but also, as Coward (1984) has shown, with the world of nature (and there are similarities worth exploring between the genres of ethnography and natural history on TV).

But, for all these elements of familiarity, there remains the spectacle of the other. The spectacle is a constructed effect of the visual rhetoric whereby we are placed, on one hand, at a visual distance, and yet positioned, on the other, in an intense and intrusive practice of visual scrutiny. A particularly clear example of this was produced in 1988 for the *Disappearing World* series on Granada Television. Leslie Woodhead's film of the Wodaabe people of northern Africa (Niger and Nigeria) made standard use of the voice-over, to locate this nomadic culture in its semi-desert environment. It also recruited a privileged informant, Gorjo ('friend of the whites') with his wife and eight children. Gorjo expounded the Wodaabe philosophy of why a nomadic way of life is preferable to a settled existence; and it was his family ceremony (the naming of a new child) that became the highlight of the film. But then, it also became clear that this human context was but the pre-text for the film's main purpose, which was to offer to the western viewer a highly original, and even disturbing visual spectacle.

That such a spectacle was the main emphasis, was evident in the publicity for the programme, which circulated through various newspapers in July 1988. Here for example, is the populist version, from Linda Grant's review in the *Evening Standard* (22 July 1988):

> Somewhere near the Nigerian border, the tribesmen of the Wodaabe are getting ready for a big night out. They lie on the ground gazing at their reflections in hand-mirrors, lovingly painting their faces. Gorgeous Gorjo in his dreadlocks, sequins and feathers bears an uncanny resemblence to Boy George . . .
>
> Then the big moment arrives. The painted men start to trip the light fantastic, or rather the Yake, a dance where they seek to make contact with special powers which will make them irresistible to women. They, in turn, titter a bit and then select the most beautiful tribesmen for their own, going off with them into the bush for a bit of Wodaabe whoopee.

Clearly, in this highly ethnocentric account, part of the novelty value of Woodhead's film was its depiction of a situation in which western sex-roles are reversed. In Wodaabe culture, defined through a particular ideology of beauty, it is men who objectify themselves to attract the attention of women (see figure 7.2). Their objectification involves the sculpting of hairstyles, the intricate application of make-up (whitening and lengthening the face, which now appears almost as a mask) and the wearing of symbolic costumes (wide-brimmed hats, feathers and skirts). These preparations, and the subsequent ritual dance, provide an opportunity for the usual intensity of close-up, both on the activity of making-up and the spectacle of the mask-like faces. But Grant's reference to Boy George also indicates a further level of ethnocentric fascination: for this is not only interesting in terms of role reversal; it also, to western eyes, looks like a form of transvestism.

Leslie Woodhead himself, in an article for the *Guardian* was not above making these connections:

> The occasion was a Wodaabe dance in an area of scorched semi-desert in Northern Nigeria where the Sahara merges with the drought-ravaged Sahel. To complete the circle of narcissism, I was filming the young men's make-up session for television. Finding ourselves surrounded by Boy George look-alikes when we'd come to make a film about some of the

Fig. 7.2. Still from Disappearing World, *Leslie Woodhead (1988). By permission of Granada Television Ltd*

world's poorest nomads was odd enough. Odder still was to discover the Wodaabe obsession with male beauty which scatters the shrivelled bush with gorgeous dandies . . .

The Yake dance was the climax of our filming, a weird spectacular which demonstrates the extremes of Wodaabe display. With make-up flashing in the gloom, the young men flare the whites of their eyes and bare their teeth in an ecstasy of self-advertisement.

Looking at this film, I cannot avoid making some connections between this kind of ethnographic visibility, and the classical western representations of women that have been offered to the male gaze. In both contexts, an ongoing textual stucture (there a narrative, here an argument) is interrupted or transformed by the potential for visual spectacle. The spectacle itself becomes a troubled fascination: it is intensely, obsessively, interesting, but it also evokes an anxiety (there to do with sexual, here to do with cultural, difference). In this respect, the representation of the other culture in the moment of its ceremonial display, provides the visual equivalent of the fetishised objectification of women. Both strategies are instances of discursive practice, where the objectification of the other is achieved through a structured gaze which is predicated on relations of power.

But in this respect, the Wodaabe are doubly interesting. In their ceremonial they almost seem to be challenging the basic categories on which such power relations are founded. For here are black men putting on 'white face', in gestures which seem deliberately exaggerated; and here also are men performing objectification in ways that westerners typically associate with women. Once again, we seem to be in the territory of the masquerade, that allows for and even encourages the possibility of transvestism. The fact that black men seem (to us) to be masquerading as white women, in a situation that is also conventionally heterosexual, might strike us as perverse and even potentially disturbing. But this is a reading that can only be produced in a context where the ceremonial dance is being served up as a spectacle for the western/phallocentric viewer. And its potential disturbance is contained within this discursive context, where the spectacle is held at a distance by the ethnographic gaze.

However there is another film about the Wodaabe, made by the German director, Werner Herzog. This film, *Herdsmen of the Sun*, was broadcast as part of a BBC2 series of anthropological films entitled 'Under The Sun' (1991). To some extent, Herzog's film is also conventionally ethnographic, depicting the nomadic existence of the Wodaabe and explaining aspects of their ritual and ceremony. Visually, Herzog is particularly fond of extended slow pans across static scenes of encampment set against the flat and bare semi-desert. His film goes further than Woodhead's in revealing that the recent history of drought in the Sahel has amounted to a severe threat to the Wodaabe economy, and we are shown the destitution with which some Wodaabe, now deprived of their herds, are faced. Nevertheless I do not think that ethnography, or even current affairs journalism, are the real motives behind Herzog's film. For what stays in the memory are four highly strange and contradictory sequences where shots of the Wodaabe way of life are set to western operatic music.

In one sense, this looks like a fairly pernicious form of exploitation. Whereas, in the conventional ethnographic film, shots of a camp being struck might be contextualised by some attempt to explain, say, the sexual division of labour – here they are accompanied by Maria Callas singing Handel's Largo. The result is a kind of aesthetic romanticisation, where the other culture is offered as an object for meditative contemplation. In these terms it is not difficult to interpret say, a slow pan of a tribesman with a camel crossing a modern road bridge, as some sort of statement about the continuity between ancient and modern cultures. But what of the opening sequence where the Wodaabe men, dressed in their finery, baring their teeth and rolling their eyes, now appear to be singing, not their own tribal song, but the Callas version (on a scratchy 78) of *Ave Maria*? What is achieved

Fig. 7.3. Still from Herdsmen Of The Sun, *Werner Herzog (1991). Les Films d'ici, Paris*

here by the representation of tribal people as enthusiastic drag queens (4) (see figure 7.3)?

I have to confess to being entirely perplexed by this discursive strategy, which I suspect might be Herzog's intention. On one hand it is impossible to ignore the symbolic violence done to the other culture by taking its rituals out of any context which might be meaningful to the people involved. This is ethnocentrism gone mad – pushed to an extreme which becomes uncomfortable to watch. And yet, on the other hand, what this strategy achieves is a polysemic fluidity which raises questions about some of the fixed positions conventionally reproduced within western discourses. Thus, in Herzog's film, not only are the boundaries between races and genders semiotically transgressed; but also the grand dichotomy itself, the distinction between 'primitive' and 'civilised' cultures, appears to be disturbed. Here a 'subordinate' culture mimics the 'dominant', in a camp parody of its claim to universality. As a strategy then, it is certainly exploitative; but it is an exploitation which has turned its (made-up, mask-like) face against the exploiter. It is an illustration of what can be achieved by the manipulation of discursive techniques, against the grain of their normal use within a discursive formation.

5 CASE STUDY: LOOKING AT MEN ... AND BOYS

'I am seated in the living room of a council house in the centre of a large English city' (writes Valerie Walkerdine, 1986). 'I am there to make an audio-recording as part of a study of six-year-old girls and their education. While I am there, the family watches a film, *Rocky II* (1979), on the video. I sit, in my armchair, watching them watching television. How do I make sense of this situation? (p.173).

Walkerdine makes sense of her situation in the Cole's living room in three very interesting ways. First, she attempts to explicate the meaning, and the pleasures, of *Rocky II* as a popular narrative film. In so doing she offers a critique of the intellectual dismissal of such films as 'escapist fantasies': certainly they are fantasies; but crucially they relate to the critical ways in which people make sense of their lives. This is demonstrated in the second part of Walkerdine's discussion, where she argues that lives are partly lived through fantasy and, that far from being opposites, 'fantasy' and 'reality' converge. In this sense it is possible to understand Mr Cole's enjoyment of *Rocky* as a mediated confirmation of aspects of his own identity. But then, third, Walkerdine points out that her own identity as a researcher is implicated in this situation. Towards the end of her essay she asks some important questions about what is involved in watching other people watching videos, or indeed watching other people at all. She wonders whether some forms of sociological research might, in fact, be versions of the ethnographic voyeurism discussed in the previous section.

However, interesting though it certainly is, it seems to me that Walkerdine's account of the pleasures of watching Rocky films misses, or at least minimises, some other critical issues. In particular, one critical point not fully developed concerns the nature of the spectacle constructed by this film. Walkerdine points out that one of the advantages of watching a video is that the film can be paused and replayed for repeated visual satisfaction. But it is interesting to note which sections of *Rocky II* particularly fascinate the male members of the Cole family. Following is part of Walkerdine's transcript, where scenes from the video are set alongside the family's conversation (Note: 'F'= Mr Cole; 'M'= Mrs Cole; 'R'= Robert, their son).

Walkerdine's transcript

F: Hey watch this Rob.

R: Does he kill him?

F: Watch.

F pauses video or winds back to the closing round because M is handing out the tea and cakes.

R: Mum hurry up.

F: You ready?

M: What

F: We've yet to see the end of this.

Rocky fighting championship round, pitched against huge black opponent. Things aren' looking good. Rocky is taking a beating. The crowd is going wild, cheering, shouting. Rocky is in his corner with his trainer, Chris, who is warning him.

ROCKY: I know what I'm doing.

CHRIS: Listen. You're getting killed out there.

ROCKY: It's my life.

Both fighters are in their corner with coaches. They are both badly beaten.

The commentator favours Rocky's opponent. He says 'All he has to do is stay awake to steal the title'.

There is talking in the background. M asks R to get something for her (her slippers?). R is put out.

R: Dad, stop it for a minute.

F: Ohh, June.

M: Well I wasn't to know. I thought you'd stopped it just for me.

F: No we didn't stop it just for you. He's been trying to watch it.

The video is stopped again and wound back to the fifteenth round.

Walkerdine reveals that Mr Cole particularly enjoys the fight in *Rocky II*, indeed he wants 'to have [it] on continuous and instant replay for ever, to live and triumph in that moment' (pp.176–7). In the transcript it is clear that Rob, the son, is also included in these pleasures. Walkerdine suggests that the focus for Mr Cole's identification is that he too, as a working-class labour activist, is metaphorically a 'fighter'. As we have previously discussed, Stallone, as Rocky and as Rambo, became in the 1980s something of an iconic representative for popular male aspirations. But what is it that makes *men* especially fascinated with the spectacle of the fight? What makes them want to watch it over and over again?

By round fifteen of the world title fight which is the climax of *Rocky II*, both fighters, Rocky and Apollo Creed, are exhausted. They have beaten the hell out of each other (see figure 7.4). Rocky in particular has been on the floor twice previously, almost 'out for the count', and his face is such a mess of blood and bruises that he can hardly see. It is a miracle that he is able to resurrect himself in the final round for a series of knockout blows that leaves

Fig. 7.4. Sylvester Stallone as Rocky in Rocky II *(1979). Rocky © 1976 United Artists Corporation. All rights reserved. Still photo courtesy of MGM/UA*

both fighters sprawled on the canvas. Meanwhile, as regards its technique, the film enables the spectator to experience every moment. We hear the sickening thud of each punch as it lands on the face or body. Visually, some sequences of slow motion are used to almost freeze the spectacle, and we can see the blood and sweat flying as each successive punch is landed. When Rocky is almost knocked out, the film offers us his point of view, as he desperately tries to get Apollo back into focus. In short, as Walkerdine points out, this is not a realistic portrayal of boxing: it is a gladiatorial contest staged as a visual spectacle for the (male) spectator.

It is not difficult to make sense of this kind of event in terms of the psycho-analytic theory developed by Mulvey and subsequent writers. For if, in phallocentric discourse, the female body is offered as an erotic spectacle, that possibility must be denied when the male body is displayed. Or, to be more precise, there is in this discourse an equally obsessive (homoerotic) interest in men's bodies, but this is censored and disavowed. The male body is there-fore displayed in spectacular fashion, but at the same time it is beaten and humiliated. There is a strong element of sado-masochism: sadism in the pleasures of punishment; masochism in the identification with the victim. And just as the fine art tradition of the female nude provides prototypes for the mediated objectification of women, so there are artistic precedents for Rocky – in the sadistic martyrdom of St Sebastian, and of course, the iconic representation of the tortured body of Christ as a spectacle on the cross.

Steve Neale (1983) has pointed to the fact that gladiatorial contests, in which men's bodies are ritualistically beaten or destroyed, are a regular feature of Hollywood films, from epics and westerns to contemporary action movies. The epic in particular, with its 'classical' iconography, offers the display of male flesh; and in *Spartacus* (1960), a frequently discussed example, this is explicitly the object of a perverse and corrupt (because Roman) erotic gaze. The contemporary western, from Leone and Peckinpah to *Young Guns* (1988), regularly relishes the spectacle of the shoot-out, with slow motion intensifying the spillage of blood and guts, and bodies flying everywhere. Such use of slow motion, while it provides the narrative climax, also constructs the spectacular in a way similar to that described by Mulvey, in that it suspends narrative continuity. Furthermore, in contemporary action movies the spectacular male body is frequently the subject of video montage sequences (for example, when Rocky is training) which both condense, but also transcend, the flow of the story.

Richard Dyer (1982) has suggested that there is an element of hysteria about much of this. In a discussion of the male pin-up, he points out that the male body is rarely, if ever, displayed to the spectator as a passive object. Male models do not pose like female models, for men's bodies must carry connotations of power and activity (what Berger calls 'presence'), or alter-natively a god-like spirituality. Male pin-ups often look up or out of the frame, their minds presumably on 'higher things'. In phallocentrism, men's bodies are only sexualised with difficulty and the models often look somewhat ridiculous. Hysteria can of course mean hysterically funny, as well as 'over the top'; or perhaps, in the case of the Chippendales, there is a mixture of both.

However, it is the second sense of hysteria which prevails in *Rocky II*. As we have seen, Stallone's body is an example of the new 'musculinity', described by Yvonne Tasker. One current form of fascination with men's bodies is the particular interest in body-building where muscularity, signifying male power, is carried to excess. Male bodies have now become spectacular on the basis that they are (literally) 'larger than life', and this carries implications, which are not explored by Walkerdine, of the possibility of contradictory forms of masculine identification. Built bodies may be spectacular but in ideological terms they are also 'unnatural', and thus, in a sense, unreal. The new musculinity is for most men an impossibility – though, it might have, as Tasker argues, some interesting implications for women. At least there are, in contemporary body culture, a variety of new forms of female masquerade, ranging from the use of plastic surgery to the cultivation of hard bodies for women. And possibly, the sight of Linda Hamilton, in *Terminator 2* working out, flexing her muscles and carrying guns does begin to disturb some of the certainties of the phallocentric gaze (5).

Perhaps also today there is a greater variety of spectacular masculinities. I am now about to enter speculative territory, so let me try to clarify the issues at stake. In phallocentric discourse, as defined by Mulvey, there is a pre-occupation with the phallus as the key signifier of sexual difference, on its absence in women and its presence in men. Thus, as we have seen, the absence is managed by objectification, and the presence is either obsessively censored or hysterically displaced. Equally there is the fascination, in our culture, for the transcendence of phallocentric categories – particularly with men in drag appearing as women, and with women masquerading for, and as, men. Such transgressions have generated a vast range of roles and identities, which the mass media in all its forms has continually explored. It is a range that extends from the manufactured glamour of the *femme fatale*, to the phallic 'she-man' or 'butch-femme' (see Straayer 1990). There is, it seems to me, no clearer example of the exploitation of these possibilities, than the career of Madonna, which might be seen as a 'grand tour' through the permutations of phallocentrism. It is therefore perhaps not surprising that, more than any other contemporary artist, Madonna has been a focus not only for popular interest, but also for a steady stream of academic commentary and speculation (6).

But I do not want to conclude this book by making further contributions to the Madonna industry in media studies. Rather, I want to move on to look at another contemporary pop act which might (and I offer this tentatively) be the basis for a more interesting discussion. In 1994, the Brit Award for the best video (Britain's pop music 'Oscars') went to Take That for *Pray*. It is difficult (for me) to see wherein lies the particular artistic merit of this production. It looks entirely conventional, as a visual montage which punctuates the phrases of an inoffensive, somewhat soulful song. The visual montage was shot (Gary Barlow tells us, in the video collection *Everything Changes*) in Acapulco, and it consists of various shots (some colour, some monochrome) of members of the band posing on a beach, intercut with more intriguing settings (a fountain, a temple-like interior) which have vaguely classical connotations. Videos like this have been around since the early 1980s (remember the 'New Romantics'?), but perhaps the key development with Take That is simply the emphasis given to displays of the male body, statuesque or choreographed, and in various degrees of semi-nudity.

Take That is a pre-fab band – its members recruited as much for their looks and dancing ability as for any musical talent (Gary appears to be the only real musician in this band). In an era when pop music is synthesised and pre-recorded, the accent has shifted to video, and to dance in performance. Again, Madonna is the major international star, but Take That, in a more modest way, demonstrates that this is a genre that can foreground men's as well as women's bodies. And Take That has a following that is, apparently, gay as well as straight, male as well as female. In *Pray*, the semi-nudity shifts from poses reminiscent of classical statues, to the narcissistic, auto-erotic, stroking of bare chests and shoulders. In this video there is no suggestion of sexual interactivity: it's the boys, separately, doing it for themselves.

In fact *Everything Changes*, the latest video collection, reinforces the impression that we are here in a culture of the boys. And what nice boys they are! The music promos are interspersed with individual interviews – a sort of 'at home' with each of the five band members, but where 'home' can incorporate a favourite Indian restaurant or football club. The talk is endlessly about families and pets, and mates in the local community; and it is significant that this is the northern working-class community, centred around Manchester, which since before the days of *Coronation Street*, has long been associated with a certain human authenticity (7). Alternatively in *Everything Changes*, the band occupies a studio, swapping in-jokes and innuendoes in a way which reminds me of the early Beatles. These nice, northern boys are each others' mates, so their sexuality is both displayed, and yet made innocent and harmless. In group situations they touch each other's bodies (a lot) but we know, all the time, that they are just 'larking around'.

It seems to me that the male body displayed in Take That videos is identical to that captured in the photograph by Frances Angela, which adorns the front cover of an important collection of essays on men and masculinity (Chapman and Rutherford (eds) 1988) (see figure 7.5). It is also an image

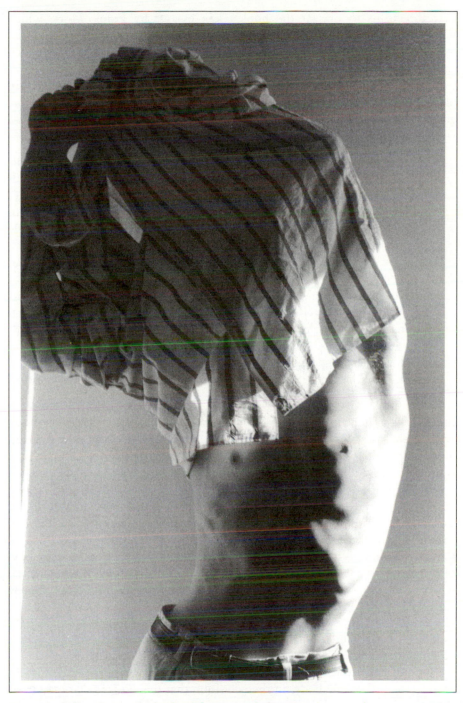

Fig. 7.5. The new male body? Photograph by permission of Frances Angela

that directs us to one of the book's key essays, by Frank Mort, which discusses a new (in the 1980s) masculine style constructed through advertising and fashion. Mort argues that 'young men are being sold images which rupture traditional icons of masculinity. They are stimulated to look at themselves – and other men – as objects of consumer desire. They are getting pleasures previously branded as taboo or feminine' (p.194). Here's how Mort goes on to discuss the mid-1980s British advertising campaign for Levi 501s, which involved the male model, Nick Kamen:

> Two features are especially worth noting. First the fracturing and sexualisation of the male body, condensed around the display of the commodity – the jeans. Cut close-up focus on bum, torso, crutch and thighs follows standard techniques of the sexual display of women in advertising over the last forty years. But now the target is men. More to the point, male sexuality is conjured up *through the commodity*, whether jeans, hair-gel, aftershave or whatever. Though Kamen stripped to his boxer shorts and white socks ... it was the display of the body *through the product* that was sexy. Belt, button-flies, jeaned thighs, bottoms sliding into baths was what made the ads erotic, less the flesh beneath. And so the sexual meanings in play are less to do with macho images of strength and virility (though these are certainly still present) than with the fetishised and narcissistic display – a visual erotica. These are bodies to be looked at (by oneself and other men?) through fashion codes and the culture of style. (p.201)

For Mort's argument it is essential that these new images of the male body are stylish. For my argument it is equally important that the new men on display are *young* – that they are not in fact men, but boys. Ultimately, I want to suggest that patriarchal masculinity has been displaced rather than subverted in these new forms of male consumerism – but then, putting this in a wider context, I am not sure just how 'new' much of this really is. Certainly a youthful male body has been on display since the 1950s in a variety of genres of popular culture. For instance, for all his hysterical phallic gyrating, wasn't Elvis Presley once, in his more moody moments, a 'sexy boy' of this kind? Or take a look, if you can, at *A Streetcar Named Desire* (1951), where following a domestic disturbance, Marlon Brando (as Stanley Kowalski) stands in a wet, ripped T-shirt calling for his wife Stella to return. Here the spectator is given Stella's point of view, and is permitted to gaze as she runs her hands down his muscular back, but only on the basis that he is here reduced to tears, and thus now appears as a big baby.

My (tentative) conclusion then is that phallocentric discourse can allow an erotic gaze at the male body on the condition that this body is divorced from patriarchal power. In becoming an object, the man becomes a boy, and the homoeroticism, as in Take That videos, is contained by youthful innocence.

Such an argument would also extend to the recent heterosexual interest in 'toy-boys', and to the so-called 'female gaze' which is on offer in films such as *Thelma and Louise* (1991). Immensely enjoyable though this film certainly is, in its satirical portrayal of patriarchal masculinity, and its fantasy of a femininity which is transformed on the road, it seems to me that the hetero-sexuality (whatever the lesbian subtext might be) remains problematic. For when Thelma (Geena Davies) has her first satisfactory heterosexual experi-ence with JD (Brad Pitt) – an experience which incorporates her point of view of his jeans-clad bum, and a performance to camera by Pitt stripped to the waist/flies open – in the manner of Levi's advertising – we know that this is only possible because he is again, a boy. Patriarchal men are boring, but they catch up with you in the end.

An afterword

Or do they? One of the focal points for critical discussion of *Thelma and Louise* has been the film's ambiguous conclusion. Confronted by the overwhelming power of the police (forces of law/patriachy) our heroines decide that they have reached the point of no return – so they kiss and drive their Thunderbird over the edge of the precipice into the final freeze-frame. It is an image of ultimate escape, an ecstasy of flight which is also, of course, in realist terms, suicidal. So by some feminist critics this ending has been seen (pardon the pun) as a cop-out. The film is unable to pursue the conse-quences of its transgressive logic. That is to say, by positioning women as protagonists of an action-adventure, the film constructs their point of view, and it allows them to perform 'masculinity' (a masquerade which includes the use of guns, in gangster-style hold-ups); but in Hollywood cinema such female subversion of phallocentrism cannot have a future, and its narrative pleasures must ultimately self-destruct.

However, in this context it might be helpful to place *Thelma and Louise* in a broader generic tradition. Certainly it is (in 1980s terms) an action-adventure, and a 'road-movie', of sorts; but I have been struck by the similar-ities between this film and the melodramatic western, as discussed by Laura Mulvey in her article on *Duel In The Sun* (Mulvey, 1981). Here Mulvey describes a genre, or sub-genre, which differs from the classical western, insofar as its problematic is not to test but ultimately to uphold patriarchal law; rather it is to explore and to subvert patriarchal conventions from a female point of view. In *Duel In The Sun* the heroine has a choice of relation-ships with representatives of conventional (patriarchal) and unconventional (delinquent) masculinity. In choosing the latter, she is given the space to express her own 'masculinity', as a sort of tomboy, which includes the use of guns. The melodrama reaches a farcical conclusion where, following a final shoot-out, the ill-fated lovers die in each others arms. Again the transgressive possibilities are self-destructive; but Mulvey uses this example to illustrate the instabilities of phallocentric identities which, even in the sway of its dominant regime, Hollywood cannot entirely repress.

The key point here, as with *Thelma and Louise*, is that, at least for the duration of the narrative, other identifications and other pleasures are achieved. At the very least, the masquerade denaturalises the conventions of the genre. Here is a recent commentary on *Thelma and Louise* by Sharon Willis (1993):

> If our readings take the film's conclusion, or its heroines' destination, to decide its meaning, then we repress the partiality and disruption that make its journey so compelling. Such are the readings that pronounce the film dangerous and wrong-headed because it invites women to take on whole-sale the tired old cliches of Hollywood masculinity and male bonding that prevail in the history [of] westerns, road movies and action films. For women to embrace and celebrate feminine versions of these cliches . . . such readings argue, advances nothing and merely inverts the current gender imbalance in representation. But this argument skips over the process by which the film parades the take over of these cliches, a process that foregrounds the posturing involved. And this posturing has at least two effects. It remobilizes for women viewers the pleasures of fantasmatic identifications with embodied agents of travel, speed, force and aggression . . . At the same time the spectacle of women acting like men works to disrupt the apparent naturalness of certain postures when performed by a male body. (pp.124–5)

In the first chapter of this book I suggested that it has been a key aim of media studies to question the 'naturalisation' to which mythologies aspire. Here, in the final chapter I have tried to show that there are several ways in which media texts themselves do this, particularly in the masquerades which are possible in the discourse of phallocentrism. This is Mulvey's argument about *Duel In The Sun* and it is Willis' argument about *Thelma and Louise*: that the transgressive pleasures of the text are not simply compromised by its narrative closure. However, this is not the end of the argument, for there is a further twist to the story of 'Thelma and Louise'. And lest we are tempted to get carried away by the pleasurable possibilities we can identify in such texts, I think we must conclude with a salutory reminder.

Throughout 1994, different scenarios from *Thelma and Louise* were adapted in a series of adverts on British television for Peugeot cars. The Thunderbird was replaced by the Peugeot 106, designed and targeted, presumably, at the female consumer. In the latest ad (at the time of writing) our heroines have been recruited into the Hollywood film industry. It turns out that they have been employed as stand-ins on the set of *Thelma and Louise*, where shooting of the final scene is in progress. When the director threatens to 'bring on the real actresses' our heroines decide that they cannot part with the 106, so they drive it at great speed away from the set and towards the precipice . . . but of course this is only a back-drop, which the car bursts through.

In the course of this book we have looked at several similar examples, which would seem to be at the cutting edge of contemporary mass-mediated culture. What conclusions can we finally draw? We can make the point again about intertextuality which is a prevalent feature of this culture. We might object that the subversive pleasures we have derived from the film are here being commercially exploited – but then, we are reminded that the film itself was a commercial product in the first place. So we are constructed, once more, as knowing consumers, on at least two levels. Firstly, the ad exploits our knowledge of the film; but secondly, this ad reflexively deconstructs its own production process. It is, after all, just a set. So in my search for a fitting conclusion to this survey of our mediated culture perhaps I can use this as an exemplary case. For we now surely know that, in the end, this is only the media; and that our mediated pleasures and identities are based on seductive fabrications.

FURTHER READING

A relatively accessible overview of his theory, by Foucault himself, is 'The Subject and Power', published as an Afterword to Dreyfus H. and Rabinow P. (1982). Another accessible summary of Foucault's work as a whole is provided by Sarup M. (1993), Chapter 3. However, in my view, the most authoritative account of Foucault's theory of discourse is given by Cousins M. and Hussain A. (1984), Chapter 4.

In the 1980s the concept of the 'male gaze' has been thoroughly integrated into film studies in a series of essays (mainly published in the journal *Screen*) which are now usefully gathered together in *Screen* (ed) (1992). For a critical summary of this (and other) work see Stacey J. (1994), Chapters 1 and 2. The possibility of a 'female gaze' is explored in Gamman L. and Marshment M. (eds) (1988); and there are further discussions of 'masquerade' in Doane M. A. (1982). For further discussion of 'camp' see Dyer R. (1992); and for a salutory corrective to the critical acclaim for Madonna see Bordo S. (1993).

A useful recent collection of essays on ethnographic film is Crawford P. and Turton D. (eds) (1992); and a critical perspective on ethnography as discourse is provided by James Clifford's essay 'On Ethnographic Authority' in Clifford J. (1988). A very interesting account of ethnography as a sociological 'genre', which focuses on its textual features, is Atkinson P. (1990).

Notes

Introduction

1. These figures apply to media consumption in Britain and are taken from O'Sullivan T. *et al.* (1994b), Ch 1.

2. See, in particular, Hobson D. (1982), and Brunsdon C. (1983), '*Crossroads*: Notes on Soap Opera', in Kaplan E.A. (ed) (1983).

3. For a summary of auteurism as an approach to film studies see Lapsley R. and Westlake M. (1988), Ch 4; and Cook P. (ed) (1985) p.114 ff.

Chapter 1

1. Williamson J. (1986), p.223–7.

2. See Glasgow University Media Group (1982 and 1985).

3. Masterman L. (1985), p.170.

Chapter 2

1. For discussions of montage editing in early Soviet cinema see Bordwell D. and Thompson K. (1986), p.359–62; and Monaco J. (1977) pp.322 ff.

2. For further discussion of Eisenstein's editing techniques see Bordwell D. and Thompson K. (1986) p.224–7.

Chapter 3

1. I wrote this sentence before advertising appeared in Britain, in 1994, for the new National Lottery. Apparently the Lord Kitchener/'Voice of God' approach is still alive and well – for TV adverts and posters for the Lottery featured a celestial finger pointing towards a man standing at the window of his apartment building, with the slogan 'It could be you!'.

2. One of the most important books in the development of media studies, by John Ellis (1982), takes this approach. It remains, nevertheless, particularly in relation to this chapter, highly recommended reading.

3. See Lapsley R. and Westlake M. (1988) Ch 5; and Cook P. (ed) (1985) p.242 ff.

4. Cook P. (ed) (1985) p.243–4.

5. See Bordwell D. and Thompson K. (1986) p.210 ff.

6. Bartle, Bogle, Hegarty was the agency responsible, in the 1980s for the highly acclaimed British advertising for Levi 501 jeans. These ads have attracted academic as well as popular attention from for instance, Dick Hebdige (1988, Ch7) and Frank Mort (1988). For further discussion of Mort's argument see pp.214.

7. See also Jhally S. (1990), p.122 ff.

Chapter 4

1. For a definition of soap opera as a genre see Geraghty C. 'The Continuous Serial – A Definition' in Dyer R. (ed) (1981). For discussion of the significance of this genre for women see: Hobson D. (1982); Brunsdon C. (1983); Modleski T. (1984) Chapter 4; Kuhn A. (1984).

2. Two collections containing essays on various TV genres are Bennett T. *et al.* (eds) (1981), and Strinati D. and Wagg S. (1992). For further discussion of situation comedy see Neale S. and Krutnik F. (1990) Chapter 9.

3. An excellent collection of essays on TV genres from a historical perspective is by Corner J. (ed) (1991), *Popular Television in Britain*, London: BFI.

4. For a detailed summary of work on genre in relation to classical Hollywood cinema, see Cook P. (ed) (1985) p.58 ff.

5. As a further indication of the diversity of sources of profit for Time-Warner, perhaps I could add that, when I approached the London office of Warner Bros for permission to reproduce the advert for *The Fugitive*, I received a letter by return requesting a fee of $1000! When I phoned to check I was told that the rules are made in Burbank, not London, so my only option was a transatlantic negotiation. At this point, I'm afraid, my patience ran out.

Chapter 5

1. Sellers R. (1994), *Harrison Ford: A Biography*, Warner Paperback.

2. See Jonathan Rutherford, 'Who's That Man?', in Chapman R. and Rutherford J. (eds) (1988).

3. One conventional theory of different types of sign distinguishes not simply between 'arbitrary' and 'motivated' signs (de Saussure), but between the 'icon', the 'index' and the 'symbol' (C.S. Pierce). In this theory the icon is equivalent to the motivated sign, the symbol is equivalent to the arbitrary sign, and the index is a sign which has a physical or material connection with what it signifies – for example, 'there's no smoke without fire'. For further discussion, see O'Sullivan T. *et al.* (1994a).

4. The historical development of a conversational style in British broadcasting is discussed as a distinctive 'communicative ethos' by Paddy Scannell, 'Public Service Broadcasting and Modern Public Life', in Scannell P. *et al.* (eds) (1992).

5. For a discussion of the general impact of American popular culture in post-war Britain see Hebdige D. (1988) Chapter 3. Aspects of popular culture and the development of British TV in the 1950s are surveyed by John Corner in Corner J. (1991a); but in considering the importance, in this context, of the *TVTimes*, I have been particularly influenced by a paper which I think remains unpublished: Keith Bartlett's, 'British Television in the 1950s: ITV and the Cult of Personality' (International Television Studies Conference, 1986).

6. Athena Reproductions is a chain of high-street shops specialising in posters, postcards etc, with a flavour of 'popular art'. It had flourished in Britain since the 1970s, but as coincidence would have it, as I wrote this reference (in 1995) the company (temporarily) went out of business.

Chapter 6

1. I refer, of course, to *Coronation Street*. For a discussion of the cultural origins of this TV programme, which sets it in the context of a particular version of 'northern-ness', see Richard Dyer's Introduction in *Coronation Street* (1981).

2. Shields R. (1991), Chapter 5.

3. In 1994, the publication of books by Andrew Morton (a journalist) about Princess Diana, and by Jonathan Dimbleby (a broadcaster) about Prince Charles, was accompanied on each occasion by extended TV documentaries, as well as by the inevitable press comment and speculation.

4. That this represented something of a revolution in the British monarchy's approach to public relations was argued by Edward Pilkington, in 'Changing the Guard', the *Guardian*, 31 October 1994 (Section 2, pp.8–9).

5. See the *Guardian*, 9 January 1995.

6. In 1990, former cabinet minister Norman Tebbit was quoted in the *Los Angeles Times* proclaiming that 'too many Asian immigrants failed "the cricket test" by cheering for the country they had come from, not the one they now lived in . . . It's an interesting test. Are you still harking back to where you came from or where you are?' (the *Guardian*, 20 April 1990). The next day the *Guardian* reported that members of both the Asian and West Indian communities were 'outraged' by his remarks.

7. Pauline Henriques who introduces this film, is one of the subjects interviewed by Jim Pines, in Pines J (ed) (1992), p.32.

Chapter 7

1. In the literature on media and cultural studies, there are probably as many variations in the use of this word, as Terry Eagleton has discovered for 'ideology' (see p.161). In particular, 'discourse' is a term used in linguistics to refer to the analysis of verbal utterances which are larger than sentences. It is also used loosely and interchangeably with 'ideology' to describe organised

systems of thought, or cultural perspectives (particularly by Marxists who persistently fail to understand Foucault's use of this word). Here, influenced by the interpretation of Foucault made by Mark Cousins and Athar Hussain (1984), I have attempted to use this term very specifically to define, not a general feature of media texts, but a way of understanding aspects of their operation which involve the use of specific practices and techniques. Here then, 'discourse' means something quite different from 'ideology'; or rather, the two terms refer to quite distinct critical approaches to text analysis.

2. The question of the difference between the medical and the erotic gaze is interestingly raised in a film I have seen recently. In *Disclosure* (1995) Tom Sanders (Michael Douglas) accuses his boss Meredith Johnson (Demi Moore) of sexual harassment. Under legal interrogation Sanders is asked why, if he was resisting her advances, did he have an erection. He replies that this was a 'natural' response – a classic illustration of the ideology of male sexuality that Winship discusses! To this the lawyer representing Johnson retorts that it would be very odd if her doctor too had this type of 'natural' response . . .

3. This concept is now established in film studies, following an influential article by Mary Ann Doane (1992). In Doane's discussion masquerade refers to two possibilities: first, that the female spectator might identify with the male position and second that, as Doane herself puts it, femininity might be 'flaunted' or performed to excess. It is the latter possibility that is realised by Lana Turner in *The Postman Always Rings Twice*.

4. The effect is not unlike the scenes in another recent 'cult' film, *The Adventures of Priscilla: Queen of the Desert* (1993), where operatic arias are mimed by Guy Pearce dressed as a drag queen, sitting on a massively fetishised high-heeled shoe, as the bus (Priscilla) carries our transvestite heroes on their journey into the Australian outback.

5. See Tasker Y. (1993), Chapter 7.

6. See for instance: Scwichtenberg C. (ed) (1993); Lloyd F. (ed) (1993); Frank L. and Smith P. (eds) (1993) for recent examples of this trend.

7. See again, Shields R. (1991), Chapter 6.

References

Aitken I. (1992). *Film and Reform: John Grierson and the Documentary Film Movement*. London: Routledge.

Allen R. (ed) (1992). *Channels of Discourse Reassembled*. New York: Routledge.

Althusser L. (1971). "Ideology and Ideological State Apparatuses". In *Lenin and Philosophy and other Essays*. London: New Left Books.

Althusser L. and Balibar E. (1970). *Reading Capital*. London: New Left Books.

Alvarado M. and Thompson J.O. (1990). *The Media Reader*. London: BFI.

Atkinson P. (1990). *The Ethnographic Imagination*. London: Routledge.

Barthes R. (1957/1973). *Mythologies*. London: Paladin.

Barthes R. (1977). *Image-Music-Text*. Edited by Stephen Heath, London: Fontana.

Beniger J. (1987). Personalization of Mass Media and the Growth of Pseudo-Community. *Communication Research*, **14**, 3.

Bennett T. *et al.* (eds) (1981). *Popular Television and Film*. London: BFI.

Bennett T. and Woollacott J. (1987). *Bond and Beyond: The Political Career of a Popular Hero*. London: Macmillan.

Berger J. (1972). *Ways of Seeing*. London: Penguin.

Bode S. (1993). "Clocking The Future", *Sight and Sound*, **3** (8).

Bordo S. (1993). "Material Girl: The Effacements of Postmodern Culture". In Schwichtenberg C. (ed), *The Madonna Connection: Representational Politics, Subcultural Identity and Cultural Theory*. Boulder: Westfield Press.

Bordwell D. and Thompson K. (1986). *Film Art: An Introduction*, Second Edition, New York: Alfred A. Knopf.

Brand G. and Scannell P. (1991). "Talk, Identity and Performance: *The Tony Blackburn Show*". In Scannell P. (ed), *Broadcast Talk*, London: Sage.

Brookes R. (1992). "Fashion Photography: The Double-Page Spread", in Ash J. and Wilson E. (eds), *Chic Thrills. A Fashion Reader*. London: Pandora.

Brundon C. (1983). *Crossroads*: Notes on Soap Opera. In Kaplan E.A. (ed) *Regarding Television*. Frederick, MD: University Publications of America.

Buscombe E. (1970). "The Idea of Genre in The American Cinema", *Screen*, **11**, (2).

Cannadine D. (1983), "The Context, Performance and Meaning of Ritual: The British Monarch and the 'Invention of Tradition' c1820–1977". In Hobsbawm E. and Ranger T. (eds), *The Invention of Tradition*, Cambridge University Press.

Cardiff D. (1988). "Mass-middlebrow laughter: The origins of BBC comedy", *Media, Culture and Society*, **10** (1).

Chaplin P. (1987) *The Listener* October 8 p. 34.

Chapman M. (1978). *The Gaelic Vision in Scottish Culture*. London: Croom Helm.

Chapman R. and Rutherford J. (eds) (1988). *Male Order: Unwrapping Masculinity*. London: Lawrence & Wishart.

Chatman S. (1978). *Story and Discourse: Narrative Structure in Fiction and Film*. Ithaca, NY: Cornell University Press.

Clifford J. (1988). *The Predicament of Culture*. Cambridge Mass.: Harvard University Press.

Collins J. (1993). "Genericity in the Nineties: Eclectic Irony and the New Sincerity". In Collins J. *et al.* (eds), *Film Theory Goes To The Movies*. New York: Routledge.

Connell I. (1980). "Television News and the Social Contract". In Hall S. *et al.* (eds) (1980).

Connell I. (1992). "Personalities in the Popular Media". In Dahlgren P. and Sparks C. (eds), *Journalism and Popular Culture*. London: Sage.

Cook P. (ed) (1985). *The Cinema Book*, London: BFI.

Cordova R. de (1985). "The Emergence of the Star System in America", in Gledhill C. (ed) (1991).

Cormack M. (1992). *Ideology*, London: Batsford.

Corner J. (1991a). "General Introduction: Television and British Society in the 1950s". In Corner J. (ed) *Popular Television in Britain*. London: BFI.

Corner J. (1991b). "Documentary Voices". In Corner J. (ed), *Popular Television in Britain*. London: BFI.

Corner J. and Hawthorn J. (eds) (1994). *Communication Studies: An Introductory Reader*. London: Edward Arnold.

Cousins M. and Hussain A. (1984). *Michel Foucault*. London: Macmillan.

Coward R. (1984). *Female Desire*. London: Paladin.

Cox G. (1983). *See It Happen*. London: The Bodley Head.

Craik J. (1994). *The Face of Fashion*. London: Routledge.

Crawford P. and Turton D. (eds) (1992). *Film As Ethnography*. Manchester University Press.

Curran J. *et al* (eds) (1977). *Mass Communication*. London: Edward Arnold.

Curran J. and Porter V. (eds) (1983). *British Cinema History*. London: Wiedenfeld & Nicolson.

Devlin P. (1979). *The Vogue Book of Fashion Photography*. New York: Conde Nast.

Doane M.A. (1982). "Film and the Masquerade. Theorizing the Female Spectator". *Screen* **23** (3–4). Reprinted in *Screen* (ed) (1992).

Doane, M.A. (1992). *Femmes Fatales*. New York: Routledge.

Donald J. *et al.* (eds) (1984). *Formations of Nation and People*. London: Routledge.

Donald J. and Hall S. (eds) (1986). *Politics and Ideology: A Reader*. Milton Keynes, Open University Press.

Dreyfus H. and Rabinow P. (1982). *Michel Foucault: Beyond Structuralism and Hermeneutics*. Brighton: Harvester.

Dyer G. (1982). *Advertising as Communication*. London: Methuen.

Dyer R. (ed) (1981). *Coronation Street*. London: BFI.

Dyer R. (1982). "Don't look now: The Male Pin Up". *Screen* **23** (3–4). Reprinted in *Screen* (ed) (1992).

Dyer R. (ed) (1986). *Heavenly Bodies: Film Stars and Society*. London: BFI.

Dyer R. (1988). "White", *Screen* **29** (4).

Dyer R. (1991). "A Star Is Born and the Construction of Authenticity", in Gledhill C. (ed), (1991).

Dyer R. (1992). *Only Entertainment*. London: Routledge.

Dyer R. (1994). "Don't Look Now: The Male Pin Up". In *Screen* (ed) (1992).

Eagleton T. (1991). *Ideology: An Introduction*. London: Verso.

Ellis J. (1982). *Visible Fictions*. London: Routledge.

Ewen S. (1988). *All Consuming Images*. New York: Basic Books.

Fairclough N. (1989). *Language and Power*. Harlow: Longman.

Ferguson M. (1983). *Forever Feminine: Women's Magazines and the Cult of Femininity*. London: Heinemann.

Feuer J. (1992). "Genre Study and Television". In Allen R. (ed) (1992).

Fiske J. (1982). *Introduction to Communication Studies*. London: Methuen.

Fiske J. (1987). *Television Culture*. London: Methuen.

Foucault M. (1973). *The Birth of the Clinic*. London: Tavistock.

Foucault M. (1978). *The History of Sexuality*. **1**, London: Allen Lane.

Frank L. and Smith P. (eds) (1993). *Madonnarama*. Pittsburgh: Cleiss Press.

Frye N. (1970). *Anatomy of Criticism*. New York: Atheneum.

Gaines J. and Herzog C. (1990). *Fabrications: Costume and the Female Body*. New York: Routledge.

Gamman L. and Marshment M. (eds) (1988). *The Female Gaze*. London: The Women's Press.

Giddens A. (1990). *The Consequences of Modernity*. Cambridge: Polity Press.

Gilroy P. (1987). *There Ain't No Black In The Union Jack*. London: Routledge.

Glasgow University Media Group (1982). *Really Bad News*. London: Writers and Readers.

Glasgow University Media Group (1985). *War and Peace News*. Milton Keynes: Open University Press.

Gledhill C. (1991). "Signs of Melodrama". In Gledhill C (ed), *Stardom. Industry of Desire*. London: Routledge.

Goddard P. (1991). "Hancock's Half Hour: A Watershed in British Television Comedy". In Corner J. (ed) (1992).

Goldman R. (1992). *Reading Ads Socially*. London: Routledge.

Goody J. (1977). *The Domestication of the Savage Mind*. Cambridge University Press.

Hall S. (1977). "Culture, the Media and the Ideological Effect", in Curran J. *et al* (eds) (1977).

Hall S. (1982). "The Rediscovery of Ideology: the Return of the Repressed in Media Studies". In Gurevitch M. *et al.* (eds) *Culture, Society and the Media*. London: Methuen.

Hall S. *et al.* (eds) (1980). *Culture, Media, Language*. London: Hutchinson.

Hall S. and Gieben B. (eds) (1992). *Formations of Modernity*. Cambridge: Polity Press/Open University.

Hall-Duncan N. (1979). *The History of Fashion Photography*. New York: Alpine Books.

Hartley J. (1982). *Understanding News*. London: Methuen.

Heath S. (1976). "Narrative Space", *Screen*, **17** (3). Reprinted in Heath S., *Questions of Cinema*. London: Macmillan (1981).

Hebdige D. (1979). *Subculture: The Meaning of Style*. London: Methuen.

Hebdige D. (1988). *Hiding In The Light*. London: Routledge.

Herzog C. (1990). "'Powder Puff' Promotion: The Fashion Show-in-the-Film", in Gaines J. and Herzog C. (1990).

Herzog C. and Gaines J. (1991). "'Puffed Sleeves Before Tea-time': Joan Crawford, Adrian and women audiences". In Gledhill C. (ed) (1991).

Higson A. (1986), "'Britain's outstanding contribution to the film': The documentary-realist tradition", in Barr C. (ed), *All Our Yesterdays*. London: BFI.

Hiley M. (1983). *Seeing Through Photographs*. London: Gordon Fraser.

Hobson D. (1982). *Crossroads: The Drama of a Soap Opera*. London: Methuen.

Horton D. and Wohl R. (1956). "Mass Communication and Para-Social Interaction", extracts reprinted in Corner J. and Hawthorn J. (eds) (1994).

Jhally S. (1990). *The Codes of Advertising*. London: Routledge.

Jordan G. and Weedon C. (1995). *Cultural Politics*. Oxford: Blackwell.

Julien I. and Mercer K. (1988). "Introduction: De Margin and De Centre", *Screen* **29** (4).

Kaplan E. A. (ed) (1983). *Regarding Television*. Fredericksburg: University Publications of America.

Kosloff S. (1992). "Narrative Theory and Television", in Allen R. (ed) (1992).

Kuhn A. (1984). 'Women's Genres: Melodrama, Soap Opera and Theory', *Screen* 25(1). Reprinted in *Screen* ed. (1992).

Kumar K. (1977). "Holding the Middle Ground: the BBC, the Public and the Professional Broadcaster", in Curran J. *et al.* (eds) (1977).

Langer J. (1981). "Television's 'Personality System", *Media, Culture and Society* 3 (4).

Lapsley R. and Westlake M. (1988). *Film Theory: An Introduction*. Manchester University Press.

Larrain J. (1983). *Marxism and Ideology*. London: Macmillan.

Leiss W., Kline S. and Jhally S. (1990). *Social Communication in Advertising*, 2nd Edition, New York: Routledge.

Levinson S. (1983). *Pragmatics*. Cambridge University Press.

Lippmann W. (1922/1994). "Stereotypes", in Corner J. and Hawthorn J. (eds) (1994).

Lloyd F. (ed) (1993). *Deconstructing Madonna*. London: Batsford.

McArthur C. (1986). "The Dialectic of National Identity: The Glasgow Empire Exhibition of 1938", in Bennett T. *et al* (eds), *Popular Culture and Social Relations*. Milton Keynes: Open University Press.

MacCabe C. (1974). "Realism in the Cinema: Notes on Some Brechtian Theses", *Screen* 15 (2). Extracts reprinted in Bennett T. *et al.* (eds) (1981).

McCroskey J. (1978). *An Introduction to Rhetorical Communication*, 3rd Edition, Englewood Cliffs: Prentice Hall.

MacKenzie J. (ed) (1986). *Imperialism and Popular Culture*. Manchester University Press.

McLuhan M. (1964). *Understanding Media*. London: Routledge.

Marx K. and Engels F. (1970). *The German Ideology*, Part 1 (ed C.J. Arthur), London: Lawrence and Wishart.

Marx K. (1887/1970). *Capital*, Vol 1, London: Lawrence and Wishart.

Masterman L. (ed) (1984). *Television Mythologies*. London: Comedia.

Masterman L. (1985). *Teaching The Media*. London: Comedia.

Miles R. (1989). *Racism*. London: Routledge.

Modleski T. (1984). *Loving with a Vengeance: Mass Produced Fantasies For Women*. New York: Methuen.

Modleski T. (ed) (1986). *Studies In Entertainment*. Bloomington: Indiana University Press.

Monaco J. (1981). *How to Read a Film*. Revised Edition, New York: Oxford University Press.

Montgomery M. (1986). "DJ Talk", *Media, Culture and Society* 8 (4).

Moores S. (1995). "Media, Modernity and Lived Experience", *Journal of Communication Inquiry* 19 (1).

Morley D. (1978). *The Nationwide Audience*. London: BFI.

Mort F. (1988). "Boys Own", in Chapman R. and Rutherford J. (eds) (1988).

Mulvey L. (1975). "Visual Pleasure and Narrative Cinema", *Screen* 16 (3). Extracts reprinted in Bennett T. *et al.* (eds) (1981). Also reprinted in *Screen* (ed) (1992).

Mulvey L. (1981). "Afterthoughts on 'Visual Pleasure and Narrative Cinema' inspired by *Duel in the Sun*", *Framework*, Summer 1981.

Neale S. (1980). *Genre*. London BFI; extracts reprinted in Bennett T. *et al.* (eds) (1981).

Neale S. (1983). "Masculinity as Spectacle". *Screen* 31 (1).

Neale S. (1990). "Questions of Genre". *Screen* 31 (1).

Neale S. and Krutnik F. (1990). *Popular Film and Television Comedy*. London: Routledge.

Open University (1981). "Popular Culture Themes and Issues 1", U203 *Popular Culture*, Block 1 Units 1/2, Milton Keynes: Open University Press.

Orwell G. (1937/1962). "Down The Mine", in *Inside The Whale and Other Essays*. London: Penguin.

O'Sullivan T. *et al.* (1994a). *Key Concepts in Communication*, Second Edition, London: Routledge.

O'Sullivan T. *et al.* (1994b). *Studying The Media: An Introduction*. London: Edward Arnold.

Palmer J. (1991). *Potboilers: Methods, Concepts and Case Studies in Popular Fiction*. London: Routledge.

Paterson R. (1980). "Planning the Family: The Art of the Television Schedule", *Screen Education* No 35.

Philips D. (1990). "Mills and Boon. The Marketing of Moonshine", in Tomlinson A. (ed) (1990).

Pines J. (1992). *Black And White In Colour*. London: BFI.

Propp V. (1970). *The Morphology of the Folk Tale*. Austin: University of Texas Press.

Radway J. (1984). *Reading The Romance: Women, Patriarchy and Popular Literature*. London; Verso.

Rutherford J. (ed) (1990). *Identity*. London: Lawrence and Wishart.

Rutherford J. (1992). *Men's Silences: Predicaments in Masculinity*. London: Routledge.

Ryall T. (1970). "The Notion of Genre", *Screen* **11** (2).

Sarup M. (1993). *An Introductory Guide to Post-Structuralism and Postmodernism*. Hemel Hempstead: Harvester Wheatsheaf.

Saussure, F. de (1916/1974), *Course In General Linguistics*. London: Fontana.

Scannell P. (1988). "Radio Times: The Temporal Arrangements of Broadcasting in the Modern World". In Drummond P. and Paterson R. (eds), *Television and its Audience: International Research Perspectives*. London: BFI.

Scannell P. (1992). "Public Service Broadcasting and Modern Public Life". In Scannell P. *et al.* (eds) (1992), *Culture and Power*, London: Sage.

Schatz T. (1993). "The New Hollywood". In Collins J. *et al.* (eds), (1993).

Schwichtenberg C. (ed) (1993). *The Madonna Connection: Representational Politics, Subcultural Identity and Cultural Theory*. Boulder, CO: Westview Press.

Screen (ed) (1992), *The Sexual Subject: A Screen Reader in Sexuality*. London: Routledge.

Shields R. (1991). *Places On The Margin*. London: Routledge.

Smith J. (1988). "Photographic and illustrative fashion representation". In Ash J. and Wright L. (eds), *Components of Dress*. London: Comedia.

Stacey J. (1994). *Star Gazing: Hollywood Cinema and the Female Spectator*. London: Routledge.

Storey J. (1993). *An Introductory Guide to Cultural Theory and Popular Culture*. Hemel Hempstead: Harvester Wheatsheaf.

Straayer C. (1990). "The She-man: postmodern bi-sexed performance in film and video", *Screen* **31** (3).

Strinati D. and Wagg S. (1992). *Come On Down? Popular Media Culture in Post-War Britain*. London: Routledge.

Susman W.I. (1979). "'Personality' and the making of twentieth century culture". In Higham J. and Conkin P. (eds), *New Directions in American Intellectual History*. Baltimore: Johns Hopkins University Press.

Tasker Y. (1993). *Spectacular Bodies*. London: Routledge.

Todorov T. (1976). "The Origin of Genres", *New Literary History* **8** (1).

Tolson A. (1985). "Anecdotal Television", *Screen* **26** (2).

Tolson A. (1991). "Televised Chat and the Synthetic Personality". In Scannell P (ed) *Broadcast Talk*. London: Sage.

Tomlinson A. (1990). *Consumption, Identity and Style: Marketing Meanings and the Packaging of Pleasures*. London: Routledge.

Tomlinson J. (1991). *Cultural Imperialism*. London: Pinter.

Walkerdine V. (1986). "Video Replay: Families, Films and Fantasy". In Burgin V. *et al.* (eds), *Formations of Fantasy*. London: Methuen. Reprinted in Alvarado M. and Thompson J.O. (1990).

Williams R. (1976). *Keywords*. London: Fontana.

Williams R. (1977). *Marxism and Literature*. Oxford University Press.

Williamson J. (1978). *Decoding Advertisements: Ideology and Meaning in Advertising*. London: Marion Boyars.

Williamson J. (1986). *Consuming Passions*. London: Marion Boyars.

Willis S. (1993). "Hardware and Hardbodies, What do Women Want?: A Reading of *Thelma and Louise*". In Collins J. *et al.* (eds) (1993).

Wilson E. (1980). *Only Halfway To Paradise. Women in Post War Britain*. London: Tavistock.

Winship J. (1981). "Woman becomes an 'individual' – femininity and consumption in women's magazines 1954–69". *Stencilled Occasional Paper 65*, Centre for Contemporary Cultural Studies, University of Birmingham.

Winship J. (1987). *Inside Women's Magazines*. London: Pandora.

Winship J. (1992). "The impossibility of Best: Enterprise meets domesticity in the practical women's magazines of the 1980s". In Strinati D. and Wagg S. (eds), (1992).

Womack P. (1989). *Improvement and Romance: Constructing the Myth of the Highlands*. Basingstoke: Macmillan.

Wyndham Goldie G. (1978). *Facing the Nation: Television and Politics 1936–1976*. London: The Bodley Head.

Index

Adventures of Priscilla: Queen of the Desert, The 221
advertising ix, 3, 6–13, 16, 28–32, 57, 70–9, 214, 216
  formats 72–8
Advertising Standards Authority 13, 79
Aitken, Ian 52
Allen, Robert 52
Allen, Woody 65
Aliens 109
Althusser, Louis 56–7, 59, 70, 139, 160, 162–5, 172, 192
Alvarado, Manuel 184
American dream 121, 133
anchorage 29–30
Anderson, Clive 147, 149
Andrews, Eamonn 135
Angela, Frances 212–3
Anstey, Edgar 44, 47
Aristotle 30, 93
argument 29–33, 44–7, 51, 55, 72, 160, 173, 204
Arnold, Matthew xiii
Aspel, Michael 145
Athena Reproductions 142, 220
Atkinson, Paul 217
Auden W.H. 51
Auf Wiedersehn Pet 135

Bacall, Lauren 129
Bardot, Bridget 153–4, 159
Barr, Charles 52
Barthes, Roland 5–7, 10, 13, 26, 28–9, 38, 51, 141
Bartle, Bogle, Hegarty 71, 219
Bartlett, Keith 220
Battleship Potemkin 37–8

The Beatles 212
Bella 9
Benetton advertising 78–9
Beniger, L? 61
Bennett, Tony 119, 219
Benson & Hedges 13
Berger, John xvii, 35, 200–1, 210
Bergman, Ingrid 12
Bias 18, 21, 26
Black, Cilla 130, 182–3
Black On Black 180
Blackburn, Tony 60–2
Bladerunner 106
Blazing Saddles 92
Blind Date 182–3
Blockbusters 107, 121
Bode, Steven 107
Bogart, Humphrey 12
Bordo, Susan 217
Bordwell, David 218–9
Boy George 203
Brand, Graham 60
Brando, Marlon 205
bricolage 35
British Broadcasting corporation (BBC) 18–19, 23, 58, 62, 96, 135, 137, 141, 145, 148, 171, 177
British Documentary Film Movement 43–51, 67
British Petroleum advert 76–7
Britten, Benjamin 47
Broadcast 100
broadcasting 58–65, 126, 130–1
  and interpellation 58–62
  regime of 62–5, 130
Brooks, Mel 92
Brooks, Rosetta 112, 114

Brunsdon, Charlotte   218–9
Brylcreem advert   74–5
Buscombe, Edward   91

Cahiers du Cinema   66
Calamity Jane   92, 108
Callas, Maria   205
Cannadine, David   172
Cardiac Arrest   97–100, 104, 196
Cardiff, David   148
Carnegie, Dale   133
Carson, Johnny, 130
Casablanca   12, 17, 42
Casualty   98–9
celebrities   133–5, 145
Chambers, Iain   184
Channel   4   189
Chaplin, Patrice   148
Chapman, Malcolm   167
Chapman, Rowena   212, 219
character(s)   41, 43, 51, 55, 65, 87,
     93, 125, 133
Chataway, Christopher   127
Chatman, Seymour   41
Chippendales, The   211
cinema   65–70, 95–6, 106, 109–11
   action cinema   107, 120–2, 124,
      215–6
   classic narrative cinema   42, 65–70,
      108, 219
   dominant specularity   65–70, 198
Clifford, James   217
Clooney, Rosemary   137
Coalface   44, 47–9
codes   15–16, 61
Colony, The   172–180, 187
Collins, Jim   108–9
comedy:
   drama   99, 135
   'mass middlebrow'   148
   situation comedy   97, 100, 104
communicative intentionality   84
community:
   imaginary   61–2
   imagined   172–3
   mediated x-xi
   pseudo   61
Connell, Ian   65, 124
connotation   6–7, 9, 17–24, 76, 154,
     167, 199
consumers   57, 74, 77–8, 96, 201
   'knowing' consumers xii, 7, 10, 12,
      16, 78

consumer society   116, 133, 137,
     140–1, 144, 214
continuity editing   49, 68–9
Cook, Pam   80, 119, 150, 218–9
Cordova, Richard de   121–2, 124
core/periphery   169–171, 187
Cormack, Mike   184
Corner, John   100, 219–20
Coronation Street   170, 212, 220
Cosmopolitan   153–4, 158–9, 164,
     192–3
Coulson, Andy   124–5
Cousins, Mark   217, 221
Cover Girl International advert   53,
     74, 139
Coward, Rosalind xvii, 57, 202
Cox, Geoffrey   145
Craik, Jennifer   115
Crawford, Peter   217
critique   164, 168
Curran, James   52, 184
Curtis, Tony   92

Daily Star, The   124
Daily Telegraph, The   99
Dalrymple, Theodore   99
Dame Edna Experience, The   147–9
Darwin, Charles   190, 201
Davies, Geena   215
Day, Barry   71–2
Day, Robin   130, 137, 145
Dean, Letitia, 135
Deayton, Angus   135
Dee, Simon   145
denotation   5, 17
Devlin, Polly   114
Die Hard   108
Dimbleby, Jonathan   220
Dimbleby, Richard   135
Disappearing World   202
Disclosure   221
discourse xv, 95–6, 99, 191–6, 220
   discursive formation   195, 200, 206
   discursive techniques   193–4, 206
   ethnocentric   201–5
   hierarchy of discourses   66
   institutionalised   95–6
   medical   195–6, 220
   phallocentric   200, 205, 210–11,
      214–6
Doane, Mary Ann   217, 221
documentary film   43–4, 46, 49, 188
   anthropological   111, 189, 201–2

Donald, James 184
Donnellan, Philip 177
Douglas, Michael 221
drag 149, 206, 211
Dreyfus, Hubert 217
Duel In The Sun 92, 215–6
Dyer, Richard 123, 125, 127, 142–4,
    185–8, 191, 197, 199, 210, 217,
    219–20

Eagleton, Terry 161, 184, 220
Eastenders 135
Eastwood, Clint 121
Eisenstein, Sergei 37, 218
Elle 9, 79
Ellis, John 58, 64–5, 80, 92, 127–8,
    130–1, 218
Elton, Arthur 44, 47
Emergency Ward 10 98
empiricism 70, 91–2, 95, 97, 113,
    162, 164, 167
Engels, Frederick 160
Englishness 28, 171, 175, 179
Enlightenment 168, 176
epic film 210
ethnography 191, 196, 201, 207, 217
Everage, Dame Edna 147–9
Ewen, Stuart 133–4, 140, 142–4,
    149–50

Face To Face 145–6
Fairclough, Norman 150
Faith, Adam 145
Falklands War 18
femininity 3–5, 90, 140, 148
    cult of 155
    mythology of 5
feminism 10, 57, 140, 154, 158, 181
Ferguson, Margorie 155
fetishism 199, 204
    of commodities 162–3
Feuer, Jane 80, 91
film noir 12, 91–2, 199
1st On Video 106, 109–10, 120, 122
Fiske, John 27, 51
Ford, Harrison 105–6, 109, 120–2,
    124, 126, 129
Ford, John xiii
Forrester, Phyllis 139–141, 144
Forsyth, Bruce 59
Foucault, Michel 192–6, 220, 217
Frank, Lisa 221
Freeman, Robert 145

Freud, Sigmund 142
Fromm, Erich 133
Frost, David 59
Frye, Northrop 93
Fryer, John 22, 64
Fugitive, The 105–6, 109, 120, 219

Gable, Clark 121
Gaines, Jane 119
Gamman, Lorraine 217
gangster films 91–3, 123
Garbo, Greta 141–2
Garfield, John 197, 200
Garland, Judy 127–9
genre xvi, 85–99, 120–2, 125, 127,
    129, 149, 165–6, 192, 200, 202,
    215–6
    genericity 108–9, 117
    genre film 93–4
    hybrid genres 92, 108
    sub-genres 89–90, 98, 215
Geraghty, Christine 219
Giddens, Anthony x
Gieben, Bram 184
Gilda 197
Gillette advert 75–6
Gilroy, Paul 176–181, 187
glamour 12, 56, 114–19, 139–141
Glasgow University Media Group 18,
    218
Gledhill, Christine 128–9, 132, 150
Goddard, Peter 104
Goldberg, Whoopi 124
Goldblum, Jeff 73, 79
Goldie, Grace Wyndham 145
Goldman, Robert 78
Goons, The 148
Gordon's Gin advert 13–15, 17, 29,
    32, 78
Graham Billy, 33–8, 48
Gramsci, Antonio 160, 164, 181
grand dichotomy 169, 176, 190, 202
Grant, Cary 92
Grant, Linda 203
Greer, Germaine 148
Grice, H.P. 84
Grierson, John 47
Guardian, The 99, 203, 220

Hall, Stuart 27, 161, 163–4, 184
Hall-Duncan, Nancy 113
Hamilton, Linda 109, 211
Hancock, Tony 141, 145

Hancock's Half Hour   102–4, 135, 137
Harding, Gilbert   145
Hart, David   104, 135
Hartley, John   27
Hauer, Rutger   73
Hayworth, Rita   119, 197
Healey, Denis   64
Heath, Stephen   26, 51, 66–70
Hebdige, Dick   35, 180, 219–20
hegemony   156, 164, 171, 174, 176
Henriques, Pauline   220
Hepburn, Audrey   141
Herdsmen Of The Sun   205–6
Herzog, Charlotte   119
Herzog, Werner   205–6
Heston, Charlton   147–8
High Anxiety   92
Highway Code   15
Higson, Andrew   46, 52, 191
Hiley, Michael   117
Hitachi advert   109–111
Hitchcock, Alfred xiii, 69
Hobson, Dorothy   218–9
Hood, Stuart   52
Hollywood   12–13, 65, 67–70, 91–2, 105–7, 109, 119, 121–2, 125, 137, 196–200, 202, 210, 215–6
  and genre   91–2
  and glamour   13
Holsten Pils adverts   79
Horst P.Horst   115–6
Horton D. and Wohl R.   59, 104
Housing Problems   44–7, 49, 191
Hussain, Athar   217, 221
hyperbole   9, 12
Humphries, Barry   147
Humphreys, John   19, 64

icon(ic)   126–7, 131, 141, 154, 199, 210, 214, 219
iconography   91, 94–5, 112, 116, 165–7
idealism   91, 93–5, 113, 127
ideal-types   93–5, 112
identification   51, 55–7, 74–6, 113, 199
ideology   56, 70, 154–83, 186–7, 191–2, 220
  dominant   154–7, 160–1, 176, 180–1
  of individualism   157, 160
Independent, The   99

Independent Television (ITV)   62, 98, 134, 144, 174
  news (ITN)   137, 145
Interflora   5
intertextuality   12, 117, 121
interpellation   56, 59, 61–2, 66–8, 70, 78, 139, 162–3, 179–80, 187
interviews   45–7, 145–6, 193–4

Jhally, Sut   72, 76, 219
Jordan, Glenn and Weedon, Chris   176–7, 183
Julien, Isaac   187

Kamen, Nick   214
Kaplan, E. Ann   80
Kleenex advert   3, 28
Kline, Stephen   72
King, Martin Luther   145
Kosloff, Sarah   41–2, 51
Krutnik, Frank   219
Kuhn, Annette   219
Kumar, Krishnan   25

Langer, John   126, 145–6, 149
Lapsley, Robert   218
Larrain, Jorge   184
Leboff, Gary   98
Leiss, William   72, 80
Letterman, David   147
Leone, Serge   210
Levi   501s advertising   78, 214–5, 219
Levinson, Stephen   84
Lippmann, Walter   186–7
Lloyd, Fran   221
Lovely To Look At   119
Lux advert   10, 29, 32

McArthur Colin   167, 169
MacCabe, Colin   66
McCroskey, James   30–32
McKenzie, John   184
McLuhan, Marshall x
MacUre, John   98
Madonna   124, 211–12
Make Up Your Mind   137
Mandela, Nelson xi
Marshment, Margaret   216
Marx, Karl   160–5, 167, 192
masculinity   71, 74–7, 90, 109, 123–6, 128, 159, 199, 200–11, 212–6
  'new man'   75–7, 125, 214

Maskouri, Nana   148
masquerade   201, 205, 211, 215–6,
   221, 217
Masterman, Len   27, 218
Meet Jeanne Heal   135
melodrama   91–2, 129, 146, 149
Mercer, Kobena   187
metaphor xiii, xiv, 6, 26, 30, 37, 125,
   199
metonomy   13, 167
Metro-Goldwyn-Mayer   92
Metz, Christian   66
Mildred Pierce   92
Miles, Robert   184
Mills and Boon   85–90, 92
Mitchell, Andrew   189
Mitchell, Denis   177
Mitchelmore, Cliff   135
mode of address xv, 53, 57, 70–9, 104,
   130, 173
   direct address   41, 56–65, 71–3, 139
   'voice of God'   57, 74, 218
Modleski, Tania   80, 86–7, 89–90, 219
Monaco, James   218
Monkhouse, Bob   39–43, 55, 131,
   139, 146, 149
Monkey Business   143–4
Monroe, Marilyn   116, 126, 141–4,
   153, 196–7, 199
montage   29, 35–37, 47, 51, 55, 75–6,
   109, 173–4, 177, 212
Montgomery, Martin   61–2
Monty Python's Flying Circus   148–9
Moore, Demi   221
Moore, Patrick   130
Moore, Suzanne   99
Moores, Shaun x
Morley, David   24
Morse, Margaret   80
Mort, Frank   212, 219
Morton, Andrew   220
Mosquito Coast   122
Mulvey, Laura   198, 210–11, 215–6
MTV   108
musicals   91
mythology   3, 7, 9–10, 12–13, 17,
   25–6, 55–6, 62, 112, 119, 141,
   154, 165, 166

narrative xiii, 29, 38, 49, 51, 55, 85,
   93, 109, 197, 204, 210
   narrative functions   87–9
   oral narrative   39–43, 65, 186

Nationwide   24
national lottery   218
naturalisation   7, 13, 24, 26, 119, 216
Neale, Steve   90, 92, 95–6, 99–100,
   112, 119, 210, 219
news   17–26, 43, 62, 64–5, 102, 137
   Nine o'Clock News   18–25
   TV News interviews   22–3, 64, 145
Newton, Helmut   114–6
Niagara p144
Nielson, Brigitte   124
Nightmail   44, 49–51, 69
Norman, Barry   96

Odyssey   189
Oedipus complex   89, 199
Oklahoma!   92
Orwell, George   47
O'Sullivan, Tim x, xvii, 218–9

Page, Patti   137–9
Palmer, Jerry   51, 93, 119
Panorama   137
paradigm(atic)   28, 35, 76
para-social interaction   59, 62, 64,
   104, 130
Parkinson, Michael   145
Paterson, Richard   99, 102, 104
Pearce, Gary   221
Peckinpah, Sam   210
personality   59–60, 117, 126–140,
   144–50
   media personalities xvi, 64, 130
   'picture' personalities   122
   TV personalities   73, 104, 130–1,
      145–6
perspective   67, 166
Peugeot Car advertising   216–7
Philips, Deborah   86, 90, 92
Phillips, William   100
photography:
   mythology of   112
   fashion   112–9, 140
   glamour   197–200
   landscape   166
   pin-up   142
   male pin-up   123–4, 210–11
   star portrait   119
Photoplay   119, 122
Pickles, Wilfred   130
Pierce, Charles S.   126, 219
Pilkington, Edward   220
Pines, Jim   220

Pitt, Brad　215
Planet Hollywood　124
Plato　93
Playboy　142, 144
point of View　69, 74, 76, 197–200, 210, 214–5
polysemy　9, 23, 25, 29, 206
popular memory　98, 104, 119, 121, 173, 175
pornography　116–7, 200
Porter, Vincent　52
Postman Always Rings Twice, The　197–8, 221
Power and the Passion, The　83–91
Predictor advert　9–10, 12, 29–32
preferred reading　10, 17, 22–5, 27, 62, 84, 156
Presley, Elvis　214
Pretty Polly advert, 119
Prince Buster　180
Propp, Vladimir　39, 88–89
Psycho　69
psychoanalysis　70, 89–90, 199–200, 210
punk　35

Rabinow, Paul　217
racism　176–86
radio　58–62, 72, 102, 135
Radio Times　96–105, 135
Radway, Janice　87–90, 94
Raiders Of The Lost Ark　106
realism　14–15, 44, 66–8, 112, 162
representation xv, 155
rhetoric　6, 13, 30, 32, 69–70, 201–2
　'of authenticity'　127–8
Rhys-Jones, Griff　79
romance　159
　as mythology　5, 7, 9–10
　as genre　85–90, 94
　gothic　89–90
　Harlequin　89
Romanticism　168–9, 189
Ross, Jonathan　147
Rutherford, Jonathan　184, 212, 219
Ryall, Tom　93–4

Sarup, Madan　217
Saussure, F de　6, 15–17, 28, 186, 219
Scannell, Paddy　60, 171–2, 174, 219
Shakespeare, William　93
Scargill, Arthur　18–26, 43, 64
Schatz, Thomas　105–8

scheduling　58, 99–100, 102–4, 130
Schwarz, Bill　184
Schwartz, Tony　76
Schwarzenegger, Arnold　109, 124
Schwichtenberg, Cathy　221
Screen　66, 70, 187, 217
Sellers, Robert　219
semiology xv, 6, 16, 26, 77, 84, 95, 155, 191–2, 196
Seven Year Itch, The　144, 196
Sheltering Sky, The　135
Shields, Rob　170, 221
signification　16, 188
signifying practice　188, 190–2
signs　5–6, 16–19, 28, 35–9, 76–7, 186, 219
　arbitrary nature of　15–17
　motivated　15, 35, 126
　signifier/signified　5–6, 9, 15–17, 29
Small, Millie　180
Smiley Culture　180–1
Smith, Adam　167
Smith, Julian　114
Smith, Marcelle d'Argy　154, 158–9
Smith, Paul　221
soap opera　97
Some Like It Hot　92
Soviet Film　35, 38, 70, 218
Spall, Timothy　134
Spartacus　210
Specialist, The　134
spectacle　108–9, 197, 202–5, 207–9
Stacey, Jackie　217
Stallone, Sylvester　122–9, 131, 134, 209, 211
　as Rambo　122–6, 134, 209
　as Rocky　122–5, 134, 207, 210
Stam, Robert　80
Stars xv, 119–134
　stardom　12–13, 121–2, 125, 142, 150
　star image　154
　star persona　122, 128–9, 141–2
Star Wars　108, 121
stereotypes　43, 65, 129, 140, 185–91
Storey, John　27, 184
story/discourse　41, 65
Straayer, Chris　211
Streetcar Named Desire, A　214
Strinati, Dominic　184, 219
Strike　37
structuralism　38–9
Sullivan, Michael　25, 64

Sun, The 98, 124–5, 174–5
*Sunday Night At The London
    Palladium* 137
Susman, Walter 150
Sutcliffe, T? 99
Swayze, Patrick 124
syntagm(atic) 28, 35, 37, 39, 44, 47,
    51, 53, 55

Take That 212
Talk shows 145–9
Tango and Cash 124
Tasker, Yvonne 108–9, 119, 122,
    211, 221
tautology 32
Taylor, Elizabeth 130
Tebbit, Norman 64, 176, 220
television 58–9, 64–5, 106, 111
    and genre 97–105
Terminator 2 109, 211
Thelma and Louise 215–6
This Is Your Life 102, 137
Thompson, John 184
Thompson, Kristin 218–9
Time magazine 142
Todorov, T 93, 95
Tonight 102–4, 137
Tolson, Andrew 80
Tomlinson, Alan 150
Tomlinson, John 184
Trivial Pursuit xi
Tully, Susan 135
Turner, Lana 150, 197–9, 201, 221
Turton, David 216
TV Quick 97, 135
TV Times 134–140, 220
Twiggy 116

typification 187–9

Valentino, Rudolph 150
video 106–8, 111, 202, 207, 212
Vogue 114–16

Wagg, Stephen 184, 219
Walkerdine, Valerie 207–9
Warhol, Andy 142
Warner Bros 92, 106, 219
Washes Whiter 71–8
Watt, Harry 49
Weaver, Sigourney 109
westerns 91–4, 108, 111, 123, 210,
    215
Westlake, Michael 218
What's On TV 97, 135
What The Papers Say 137
Williams, Raymond 91, 93, 97,
    126–7, 129
Williamson, Judith xvii, 16, 27, 57, 218
Willis, Bruce 108, 124
Willis, Sharon 216
Wilson, Elizabeth 155
Winfrey, Oprah 130, 135
Winship, Janice 154–60, 163–5, 181,
    192, 221
Witness 106, 122
Wogan, Terry 39, 130–1, 145–6
Womack, Peter 167–9
Woman's Own 156
Woodhead, Leslie 202–3
Woollacott, Janet 119
Wordsworth, William 168
Wright, Basil 49

Young Guns 108, 210